WORLDLY THEOLOGIANS

The Persistence of Religion in Nineteenth Century American Thought

Michael D. Clark

UNIVERSITY
PRESS OF
AMERICA

Library of Congress Catalog Card Number: 80-5840

PREFACE

I am of course indebted to many people for the opportunity and the means to accomplish this study--more than I can properly thank here.

My parents, Louis Dorsey Clark and Helen Gambrill Clark, nurtured my earliest interests in history and in ideas. Professor Frank W. Klingberg sparked my particular fascination with Henry Adams and others of that remarkable generation while I was a graduate student at the University of North Carolina, and Professor Elisha P. Douglass served as my advisor for a doctoral dissertation from which parts of the present work have been adapted.

Of my colleagues in the Department of History at the University of New Orleans, I should like to single out for mention Jerah Johnson, an ever patient and helpful Chairman, and the late George Windell, who contributed a critical reading of my manuscript, and who provided a splendid example of what a scholar and teacher should be. Students can be more helpful to their professors than they realize, and I thank those at U.N.O. with whom I exchanged ideas on the subjects of this book.

My wife, Mary Dugan Clark, had the arduous task of preparing the final copy of this book for publication. She did so while pursuing her own career as Instructor of English at the University of New Orleans, and without faltering in her constant devotion to husband and children. This book is dedicated to her.

M. D. C.

New Orleans, Louisiana
April, 1981

iii

TABLE OF CONTENTS

INTRODUCTION

This is a study of the movement of religious into secular ideas, and in particular of the traces left in nineteenth century American thought by the providential understanding of the universe. As subjects through whom to pursue this theme, I have chosen George Bancroft, John Fiske, Josiah Royce, William James, and Brooks and Henry Adams. It may be presumptuous to select such figures, all of whom have been studied from many different angles, but I doubt that any others would serve the purpose as well. None of them, of course, were theologians in the ordinary sense of the term; not all of them could even be described as religious believers. Yet in all, in disparate ways but through the common medium of New England ancestry, the burden or treasure of the Christian tradition was heavy. They all felt compelled to come to terms with it in their formal thought. They were in a certain sense theologians of the world, who found in otherwise secular ideas the vehicles of explicit or implicit religious expression. It is not too much to say, for example, that evolution <u>was</u> the theology of John Fiske, or that history was a religious discipline for George Bancroft, with democracy and progress as its theological terms. Idealistic and Pluralistic philosophy, and even the Second Law of Thermodynamics, could similarly serve. Henry Adams best caught the spirit of the enterprise when he described himself as a mixture of Thomas Aquinas and Lord Kelvin--a diluted mixture, he qualified modestly. In one way or another, the subjects of this book all sought to locate the sacred in the profane.

This was a project to which the nineteenth century penchant for universal systems of thought gave free play. Such titles as Fiske's Outlines of Cosmic Philosophy and Royce's The World and the Individual, even James's A Pluralistic Universe, well illustrate the macrocosmic scale of so much formal thinking in the period punctuated by the seemingly macrocosmic catastrophe of World War I. The "cosmos" was more, of course, than an enormous quantity of physical matter; it meant the universe understood as an orderly and harmonious system. It carried generally also the connotation of belief in a universe hospitable to human values. This was, however, a conception being called increasingly into question. James attacked the presumptive monism of the system, and the Adamses in their imperious exasperation turned it inside-out to produce an anti-cosmos of chaos. Yet both James and the Adamses continued to think on the cosmic scale. And only the latter, of the subjects of this study, really glimpsed the spectre of "Nonbeing," as described in its distinctively double twentieth century aspect by Paul Tillich: "The one type is the anxiety of annihilating narrowness, of the impossibility of escape and the horror of being trapped. The other is the anxiety of annihilating openness, of infinite, formless space into which one falls without a place to fall upon." Both, Tillich emphasized, are faces of the same reality.[1]

For most, it remained natural into the late nineteenth century to think of humanity swimming like fish in the hospitable waters of the universe, or at least, as in the terms offered by James, as potential recruits in a moral struggle of universal import. It is symbolically appropriate, and perhaps not entirely coincidental, that until late in the century belief was general in the physical medium of the "luminiferous ether" binding the cosmos together. The Michelson-Morley experiments, apparently disproving the ether theory, imputed a stark dissociation to the component parts of the universe that made all seem alien to all in a new way. According to the old Puritan formula, the godly man was in the world but not of it. But if not belonging ultimately to this world, the Puritan had regarded himself as "of" the cosmos, as the whole creation and plan of Providence. In contrast, it can be said of twentieth century man that he is disposed to regard himself as of the world but not of the cosmos. If the universe is "absurd," or at least not providentially bounded, there indeed is no cosmos in the traditional sense. For some in the nineteenth century it was possible to think of oneself as being an alien neither to world nor cosmos. But there was a precarious balance between the smug satisfaction with things as they were to which such universal acceptance easily led, and the despair which followed as a natural consequence of any gross disillusionment with them.

The nineteenth century offered to American thinkers an intellectual climate particularly conducive to new combinations of religious and secular speculation. The Protestant, and particularly the Calvinist, tradition, was in the throes of a spectacular disintegration. Away from the conventional and orthodox center flew new religious sects such as the Mormon or Christian Scientist, in which aspects of orthodox belief were heightened or transformed; the religio-philosophical school of transcendentalism; religion one-sidedly of the mind, as in Unitarianism, or of the heart, as in the later Revival; and finally, of present concern, the theologies of the world offered by certain philosophers and historians. But orthodox habits of thought remained strong, even in these last developments. The pietistic belief in the access to universal truth of the individual remained central; whether the term be couched in literal religious terms or translated into secular

3

and rationalist ones, William G. McLoughlin points out, America has been a nation of pietists. (Even American pragmatism, McLoughlin notes, has had a "pietist-perfectionist tone.")[2] Individual, society, and cosmos, it may be added, comprise a triad which is necessarily involved in any attempt to understand human life, but the members of it may bear widely varying weights. The twentieth century has tended to truncate cosmos, except as a function of astronomy, or of other of the physical sciences. Society is now invested with much of the authority that cosmos used to have; the axis between society and the individual becomes the strongest. In the American intellectual world of the nineteenth century, still Protestant as well as liberal in its basic assumptions, the major axis was between the individual and the cosmos. Society, when not actually denigrated, was apt to be accepted as little more than a convenience, or in the form of nationalism become bloated with cosmic purpose. With the important exception of Josiah Royce, the subjects of this study reserved their first concern for the individual in the cosmos, and there was much of the pietist even in Royce.

If God was accessible to the individual, He was nonetheless sovereign, and the divine omnipotence emphasized in the Protestant tradition cast a long shadow over later American thought. The problem of unity and multiplicity, so central a concern of Henry Adams, was no less important to Fiske, Royce, and James. The old-fashioned providential scheme had seemed to reconcile the one and the many. Although the obvious principle of unity, even the Protestant God represented also the plenitude and diversity of life, whether schematized in "a great chain of being," or by the later religious adherents of Charles Darwin in a branching tree of biological evolution. Although the problem might, as Henry Adams thought, be insoluble in strict logic, to the everyday understanding God had meant neither rigid monism nor chaos, but a oneness-in-diversity of life.

4

Protestantism contained also a libertarian principle; even in its strictest Calvinist form it taught that the individual was not ultimately dependent on any human authority. The covenant of grace was a transaction directly between God and the individual, without intermediaries. Perhaps this exclusive relationship was, as Bancroft and Fiske believed, an historically powerful solvent of traditional political authority. In any event the libertarian element was heightened in America, both because organized religion associated itself closely with the movement for independence, and even with later democratic movements, and because American Protestant theology by the nineteenth century was shifting decisively in the direction of free-will. Yet the Calvinist God was not so easily tamed, and in the widespread belief in the preordained expansion of freedom, articulated in different ways by George Bancroft and John Fiske, liberty and necessity coiled like a Protestant Yin and Yang.

Protestantism in America proved remarkably adaptable, moreover, to the major strains of rationalist and scientific thought, however much Deism and Darwinism might be decried from particular pulpits. The ecclesiastical embrace of democracy, and even more the churches' heavy involvement in the anti-slavery and other reform movements, show the practical impact of the Enlightenment shibboleths: reason, progress, and the goodness (or potential goodness) of man; at the same time they show organized religion's ability to absorb them. That much of the religious zeal for reform was fueled by the post-millenarian expectation that social progress would prepare the way for Christ's reign on earth does not greatly vitiate the point; the means chosen of attaining the millennium were as significant as the end in view. On a more rarified intellectual plane, it was possible to combine Providence, democracy, and science into an apparently coherent and comprehensive understanding of the world--a veritable Protestant-democratic cosmology, or as Brooks Adams called it, the "democratic dogma."

Science was the most dangerous element in the formula, posing always the positivist temptation of reducing all to its own terms, as well as the more insidious possibility that those who trusted it would be carried beyond the bounds of the providential scheme. But science seemed to offer too a broader canvas on which to paint the the glory of God, or, to vary the metaphor, under which to sail the "all-navigable sea"[3] of the knowable cosmos. The theory of evolution by natural selection posed a notorious challenge to organized religion, but many thinkers both within and without the folds of orthodoxy made an enormous moral and intellectual investment in it as a new revelation of the plan of Providence. In particular, the Darwinian theory offered a reprieve for the faltering idea of progress which popular philosophers like Fiske were quick to seize upon, but it also helped for a time to salvage the cosmos itself in its harmonious and rational character by opening up a vast new time dimension within which all apparent disparities, all seeming chaos, might be reconciled. The vistas that unfolded to the evolutionary vision, once undreamt of stretches of biological, geological, and finally astronomical time, were furthermore sufficiently awesome to suggest a mighty purpose at work in the universe, virtually to demand, indeed, the acknowledgement in this aggrandized setting of an old cosmic teleology.

Yet this drastic expansion of the subjective environment--extended in space as well as time, with interstellar distances being estimated in the thousands of light-years by the end of the century--threatened to lose the human imagination in the vast dimensions of the universe. The work of much nineteenth century thought was to find a philosophical container for this exploded cosmos. This was, on the whole, still believed possible. But the efforts to encompass this universe stretched philosophy to the breaking point. When it was couched in theistic terms, God Himself became hopelessly

diffused in the endless reaches of time and space.
(The eternity and infinity traditionally attributed to Him seemed, paradoxically, far more accessible when set like a jewel in the frame of
six thousand years and a comparatively modest
geocentric, or even heliocentric, universe.)
Against the abstract and bloodless quality of the
more ambitious cosmologies, William James and
others were finally driven to rebel--as much to
salvage old providential verities as to discard
them.

The theme of this book is the persistence
of the religious impulse among those who sought
intellectually to come to terms with the modern
universe, and the forms of thought to which this
impulse contributed. The figures treated im-
parted at the least a religious dimension to
their ideas of progress, evolution, community,
the strenuous world of striving, and even to
that of an anti-cosmos of determined chaos. At
the most, they made of such largely mundane material their own theologies. These efforts represented both the disparate attenuations of a
religious tradition and the kindling of new
lines of thought which at their best illuminated
both nineteenth and twentieth century thought.
For all their differences, these figures had
this in common: a moment in intellectual history when the American sense of the providential
cosmos encountered its own farthest reaches and
bounds.

Footnotes

1. Paul Tillich, The Courage to Be (New Haven: Yale University Press, 1952), pp. 62- 63.

2. William G. Mc Loughlin, "Pietism and the American Character," American Quarterly, XVII (Summer, 1965), 164, 185-186.

3. The phrase is Ralph Barton Perry's, applied to William James's conception of the universe. See below, Chapter IV.

CHAPTER I

GEORGE BANCROFT: THE CELESTIAL POEM

It has seldom been denied that the Calvinist
religious tradition of New England left an indel-
ible mark on American life, but the nature and
process of the imprint have continued to be in-
tricate problems. The "Protestant Ethic," Puritan righteousness and self-righteousness, the
sense of mission generated by successful establishment of the "Zion in the Wilderness"--all
such terms offer partial solutions, as well as a
susceptibility to glibness and caricature.

There has been particular interest in the
political issue of Puritanism. It seems well-es-
tablished that Puritan society in America, however intolerant and authoritarian in the seventeenth century, contained elements which permitted it to evolve in a democratic direction, and
to contribute to the liberties commonly associated with democracy. The congregational organization of the New England churches was potentially democratic in character, providing in its departure from the hierarchical structure of more
traditional ecclesiastical systems a model of
local deliberation and self-determination. The
sense of society as held together by covenants,
which the seventeenth century "federal theology"

9

fostered, fitted well with the notion of government as a compact, invoked to such advantage by later American Whigs. The largely middle class composition of church membership, the encouragement which Puritan values extended to achievement in worldly vocations, and Puritan hospitality to education and scientific inquiry, can also be plausibly associated with the emergence of a liberal and democratic society.

The Calvinist theological determinism, remarkably persistent despite the hedging of the seventeenth century federal theology and the later erosion of the doctrine of predestination, is more difficult to relate to a modern libertarian spirit. Allowing for all the subtleties of theological and political thought, how does a tradition which includes the proposition that men are born predestined to eternal bliss or torment comport with the presumption that men are born with the inalienable right of liberty?

The most obvious answer is that Calvinism was a theological relic which was indeed incompatible with the American idea of freedom, and which for this reason gave way to free-will doctrines, most urgently during the Second Awakening of the early nineteenth century. Yet in an earlier period, Alan Heimert argues, the Calvinism of the Great Awakening, with its evangelical enthusiasm and millenarian optimism, had a greater affinity with revolutionary and democratic politics than did a theological liberalism which remained wedded to the rationalism of an elite minority.[1]

Of course the final answer to this apparent contradiction is that there is no necessary relation between religious and political beliefs. They can coexist in separate compartments of one's life, as one may accept hierarchical or even congregational authority in a church of the sort that one would reject in the state. In the realm of ideas, one's beliefs about proper political policy need not reflect other planes of one's philosophy. The willingness of many post-Calvinist Americans, fully committed to political liberties, to accept more modern versions of determinism--social Darwinian or behaviorist, for examples--demonstrates that metaphysical free-will and political freedom are not inseparable intellectual companions.

It is as rash to conclude that there is no relation between theological and political conceptions of liberty, however, as it is to conclude that they have a constant relation. They may have circumstantial and contingent relationships. It may be that the Puritans' prostration before the omnipotent sovereignty of God made them all the more resistant to worldly authority without the proper spiritual credentials. Yet to a later generation there might seem to be a natural correlation between the freedom of the individual to vote Whig or Democratic, his presumptive freedom in the laissez faire dispensation to choose wealth or penury, and his ultimate liberty to select God or Satan as his master.

i.

One way in which such disparate religious and political elements could be brought together, and not only brought together but woven into a system of which it was difficult to pick out the separate strands, is shown by the life and thought of George Bancroft. Perhaps more clearly than anyone else of his generation, in particular, Bancroft illuminates the continuity between the Calvinist and the democratic strains in American life. As the author of the monumental History of the United States he supposed that his task was one simply of describing objectively the unfolding of the providential plan of history. That his merits were not those of objectivity requires little emphasis today; he seems however to have felt the need to find coherence in a national experience which must encompass Predestinarian theology as well as libertarian

11

politics. That the coherence was there to be found, he never doubted. His confidence in it is exemplified by his comment on a pivotal American patriot:

> The approach of military rule in 1768 convinced Samuel Adams of the necessity of American Independence. From this moment, he struggled for it deliberately and unremittingly as became one who delighted in the stern creed of Calvin, which, wherever it has prevailed, in Geneva, Holland, Scotland, Puritan England, New England, has spread intelligence, severity of morals, love of freedom, and courage. He gave himself to his glorious work, as devotedly as though he had in his keeping the liberties of mankind, and was a chosen instrument for fulfilling what had been decreed by the Divine counsels from all eternity.[2]

Bancroft's personal background incorporated the disparate elements which he attributed to Samuel Adams. Theologically, his heritage was ambiguous. His grandfather, Samuel Bancroft, was described by George as having been "known as a strict Calvinist, and a thorough supporter of Jonathan Edwards"; indeed, he had been a dissenting member of the council that dismissed Edwards from his pulpit in Northampton, Massachusetts. "So my father," George Bancroft recounted, "was trained in his boyhood in the straitest school of orthodoxy; but 'the throes of his own youthful mind' as he used to say revolted against the dogmas of predestination and election." Bancroft added that his father's theology "was a logical consequence of the reaction against the severities of our Puritan fathers, such as all now censure. He was thoroughly a protestant and a congregationalist."[3]

Aaron Bancroft's rebellion against Calvinist rigors was more thorough than his son's comment indicates. He became a central figure in a group of liberal ministers in Worcester County, Massachusetts, and finally participated in 1825 in the organization of the American Unitarian Association. He was honorary president of the association from its founding until 1836.[4] Aaron emphasized a rational approach to religion. "He considered reason," his son wrote, "as a primary and universal revelation of God to men of all nations and all ages; he was sure of the necessary harmony between reason and true religion; and he did not scruple to reject whatever was plainly in contradiction with it."[5] Most radical was Aaron's insistence on the primacy of individual conscience, to the point that he opposed fixed religious doctrines. "He believed it impossible for one generation to prescribe opinions for another," according to his eulogist and successor as pastor in Worcester, "and looked upon all creeds and confessions of faith, wherever and by whomever imposed, as obstacles to the soul's freedom, as a snare to the conscience. . . . He believed them inconsistent with the spirit of Protestantism; for, this he regarded as a declaration of religious liberty."[6]

Aaron Bancroft explained his opposition to creeds in a sermon on "The Nature and Worth of Christian Liberty," delivered in 1816. Creeds, he thought, were simply the most effective method of perpetuating errors. They made men either tyrants or slaves in religion; they "shackle the human mind in its honest inquiries after Christian verities. . . ." Bancroft wished to show, rather, the "unalienable nature and inestimable worth of Christian liberty," which he referred to as "the holy thing which may not be touched by the unhallowed hand of man."

> The foundation of Christian
> liberty is laid in the constitu-
> tion of man. . . . Through all the
> moral administrations of Heaven,

13

> appeals are made to the under-
> standing and free agency of man;
> and God accepts only those ser-
> vices which proceed from the mind
> and the heart of the individual who
> performs them. As Christians, we
> derive our liberty immediately from
> the Author of our religion.[7]

This very Protestant sense of "Christian
liberty" could have been expressed as easily by
the son as the father. But the larger relation
of George Bancroft to this religious genealogy
has been a matter of some dispute. Russel B. Nye
in 1939 viewed Bancroft's religion as a further
stage in the evolution of his family from Calvinism to liberalism. Nye thought that Bancroft,
who had early been at the German "fountainhead"
of transcendentalism, deserved reconsideration
as "a pioneer New England transcendentalist, par-
alleling in his development and reaching more or
less independently through his own education and
speculation most of the broad conclusions of
transcendentalist philosophy." Bancroft's idea
of God seemed to Nye close to Emerson's "Over-
soul," and he felt that "Both Emerson and Bancroft express the same distinction from the Calvinistic concept of a capricious and fickle
Providence." However, Nye acknowledged that
Bancroft was more of a determinist than Emerson,
assuming as he did that men could not depart
from the divine plan. Indeed, "Bancroft, to
achieve consistency with his idea of progress,
must necessarily have accepted the lack of human
free will."[8] More recently, Nye has concluded
that Bancroft's creed "borrowed both from the
liberal Calvinism of his family environment and
nineteenth-century transcendental philosophy."
Bancroft, he pointed out, could not accept the
Calvinist view of man as depraved; this was precluded by the character of his belief in prog--
gress, and in the faculty in men for "discerning
the counsels of God." Yet Nye acknowledged in
Bancroft's History of the United States something
of the "powerful and sovereign Calvinist

14

God. . . ."9

Despite these qualifications, Nye has been criticized for overemphasizing the degree to which Bancroft rejected Puritan ways of thinking. David W. Noble, for example, characterized Bancroft as a rebel against the Enlightenment rather than against Calvinism. Noting the extent of the New Englander's debt to the theologies of Calvin and Edwards, Noble found a basic commitment to a predestinarian God. "Bancroft," he pointed out, "was absolute in his defense of the individual's freedom from restraint by worldly institutions. He was also absolute in his defense of God's power to shape the destiny of the individual." Indeed, in this view, men were to be free from institutional restrictions in order that they might be more perfectly obedient to the will of God. Noble further pointed out that the German thinkers who influenced Bancroft converged in their critical stance toward the Enlightenment with the philosophical idealism of Jonathan Edwards.10 Bancroft's "transcendentalism," then, reflected more the Calvinist bias of his mind than the influence of liberal rationalism.

On balance, George Bancroft seems the heir of both his father and his grandfather. It helps to make a distinction between Bancroft the individual believer, and Bancroft the historian. In his personal theology, he was not a Calvinist in the direct and literal way of Samuel Bancroft; he never endorsed the view that individual salvation is predestined. Yet the God who rules his history does have some of the lineaments of the omnipotent Calvinist God, and as an historian he located in the Calvinist tradition the ark both of true religion and of political liberty. Neither as private believer nor as historian was he hostile to liberal or rationalist ideas in themselves; his own thought in one aspect was strongly liberal and rational itself. He did emphatically reject the Enlightenment in its irreligious character; reason divorced from God was for him sterile and futile.

As I shall try to show, however, it is to
Bancroft's history that one must look to find his
theology--in the radical sense that history was
his theology. Although his personal belief in
God was certainly strong and sincere, with nothing in it to contradict his professional work, he
seemed apart from his character as an historian
to have no great need clearly to define his
creed. He was strongly influenced in his youth
by Jonathan Edwards, and often then spoke in the
tones of an orthodox and even conservative Protestant. Yet as a graduate student he expressed
the approving belief that liberal Christianity
would establish itself in Germany, while rejecting the hope that "Unitarianism will soon become
the language of the German world" as "too grand a
thought." He added that he could endorse the
theological representation of God in the Trinity
as he had sometimes heard it explained in Germany, wherein God's "strict unity is not in the
least infringed upon, nor the strict humanity of
Christ in any way doubted."[11] Later in his life
he rejected Unitarianism altogether. (Mark De-
Wolfe Howe noted that by 1854 his views could not
be reconciled with that doctrine.) Cleaving ultimately to Trinitarianism, he rejected membership in the Unitarian Club of Boston in 1888,
noting that "I was brought up a Congregationalist, and am not willing at this time of life to
adopt any other name."[12]

Such distinctions bore little on Bancroft's
history, but the mark of his religious background
is conspicuous in his more general attitudes and
assumptions. Something even of the harsher side
of Calvinism remained, for example, and certainly
much of its uncompromising moralism. While not
sharing in the Calvinist sense of the total depravity of man, Bancroft was by no means oblivious to the insight which inhered in the doctrine
of original sin. "So desperately wicked is the
heart of man," he exclaimed of the Salem witch-
craft trials, that witnesses could knowingly deceive and ministers misjudge from vanity and love

of power.[13] Be sure, he wrote Edward Everett in 1834,

> that very young persons are often
> very corrupt; that all the noble
> qualities are usually the growth of
> time & reflection; & that early life
> is full of the frivolities & the pet-
> ulance & the thoughtless criminality,
> which years of manhood repudiate.
> Boys are not saints; and the Calvin-
> ists are more than half right in in-
> sisting on the strong natural pro-
> pensity to evil indulgence.[14]

Overt pessimism about human nature was an occasional and secondary note, however. Bancroft is properly associated with the more optimistic transcendentalist strains of thought which broadened his metaphysical vision. During his years of graduate study in Germany he became well acquainted with the idealist and romantic elements of nineteenth century transcendentalism. But he took Germany on his own terms. Although he returned to New England with some continental mannerisms and eventually became a strong Germanophile, the youthful Bancroft reacted with an amusing priggishness to the "vulgarity" of his German professors and the profanity of German women. He reported himself "rejoiced" to find a young companion with "a great deal of moral principle for an European," who frowned on illicit sex and "had a glimmering perception, a twilight notion 'of the high mystery' of chastity. . . ." More important, he was "displeased & disgusted with Göttingen because I found there a want of religious sentiment, an absence of moral feeling." In the long run these negative impressions were more than offset by his admiration for men like Friedrich Schleiermacher, and by his discovery of the "tendency . . . towards the purest & most ideal virtue" in German philosophic speculations. But the evidence is strong that he adhered to his early resolve that "I study

17

Christianity as a Christian, & have no fear of
the result."15

As a Christian, it is undeniable that Bancroft learned enormously from German culture.
His professor at Göttingen, Arnold H. L. Heeren,
probably taught him more than anyone else about
historical method.16 An indirect Hegelian influence has been noticed in his work, although
Bancroft found Hegel "unintelligible" when he
heard him lecture in Berlin, and denigrated as
"nonsense" that which he could make out.17 This
example of graduate student intolerance is unusual in his lifelong response to German
philosophy, however. His History of the United
States pays tribute to it explicitly as well as
implicitly. He was careful to note that "the
truest and best representatives of German intelligence" welcomed American independence in 1776,
and that their ideas justified it. "Lessing
contemplated the education of his race as carried
forward by one continued revelation of truth, the
thoughts of God, present in man, creating harmony
and unity, and leading toward higher culture,"
was a characteristic comment.18

Bancroft recognized the fundamental importance of Immanuel Kant, and the influence of the
critical philosophy has been noted in the American's work. But Kant served to reinforce rather
than to challenge Protestant and democratic pre-
dispositions. Thus Bancroft's "conscience," as
one critic notes, "was the 'voice within,' the
categorical imperative of Kant and the 'inward
monitor' of Christianity."19 While a student in
Germany, Bancroft grasped the significance of
the philosopher, and defended him from charges
that he had undermined Christianity. Kant, he
thought, had effected a revolution in philosophy
comparable to that of Copernicus in astronomy.
Whereas Locke, for instance, had represented "the
external world as certain, & the mind as a fixed
substance, tabula rasa," for Kant "the whole Universe is in motion & the mind is in motion with
it." Bancroft then characterized Kant's system

18

as "transcendentalism, for the mind does, as it were, pass beyond the regions of matter & external things."[20]

Kant was later invoked in the History of the United States as the prophet of true religious and political principles. Bancroft characterized him as "the man who, alone among Germans, can with Leibnitz take a place among the wise by the side of Plato and Aristotle, [and who] reformed philosophy as Luther had reformed the church, on the principle of the self-activity of the individual mind. . . . His method was, mind in its freedom, guided and encouraged, moderated and restrained, by the knowledge of its powers."[21] The substitution of Luther for Copernicus as counterpart to Kant was not accidental; Bancroft had already placed the philosopher in this context:

> Out of Calvinistic Protestantism rose in that day four great teachers of four great nationalities, America, Great Britain, Germany, and France. Edwards, Reid, Kant and Rousseau were all imbued with religiosity, and all except the last, who spoiled his doctrine by dreamy indolence, were expositors of the active powers of man. All these in political science, Kant most exactly of all, were the counterpart of America, which was conducting a revolution of the highest principles of freedom with such circumspection that it seemed to be only a war against innovation.[22]

The French departure from the religious sources of "free thought," Bancroft added, had led to a far more vengeful revolution.

Despite Bancroft's sense of his significance, Kant influenced him less directly than did Johann Gottfried von Herder and Friedrich

19

Schleiermacher. The historian was well and favorably acquainted with the work of both Herder
and Schleiermacher, commenting on it not only
in the History but in his essays on German literature. The two Germans developed lines of
thought which often paralleled or complemented
each other, and together they reinforced Bancroft's transcendentally tinged Christianity.
"To Bancroft," Nye points out, "Herder was especially important because of his belief that
the instruments of the mind by which men discovered their relationship to God were the
property of every man--that 'the elevated feelings' which testify to God's existence, as he
put it, 'obtained in all humanity.'"[23] Herder's
idea of God as working through humanity, not
only on the individual level but on that of the
Volk, and of the species as a whole, was congenial to Bancroft, as was the precept that it
was the function of the individual existence to
act by the laws of the highest Existence. Herder
shared with Johann Georg Hamann the formulation
of the romantic concept of "history and nature as
the twin commentaries on the divine Logos,"[24]
which well accorded with Bancroft's understanding
of history as the revelation of God's will.

Herder died while Bancroft was a small
child in Massachusetts, but the American saw
Schleiermacher personally during his student
days, "how often & with how much profit," he remarked upon at the time. "I honour Schleiermacher
above all the German scholars, with whom it has
been my lot to become acquainted," he wrote in
1820. The theologian showed a course between
orthodoxy and rationalism that appealed to Bancroft, and at a time when the world of German religious thought seemed to be "moving & totter-
ing," he was gratified that "Schleiermacher has
remained a Christian, true to the moral principles of Plato & Jesus."[25] He studied educational
theory with Schleiermacher, and was evidently
much influenced in this area as well as with
respect to religious thought. It has been

pointed out that the student adopted a solution
to the problem of evil which was in accord with
that of his professor. "Since man had a dual
nature the presence of moral evil had to be related to how his nature worked. Reason was not
corrupted. Nor was nature corrupted. Nevertheless, when reason and nature acted jointly, as
they necessarily must in dualistic man, moral
error sometimes resulted."[26]

Seen in larger perspective, Schleiermacher
had a sense of the cosmos which resembled Bancroft's and was undoubtedly a source of it. The
German's idea of the universe was of the world
viewed in its totality, or as unity in plurality, a universe which "includes all being in a
harmonious way, organized with a perfection which
justifies describing it as a work of art." His
theological empiricism, describing the religious
experience in terms of sense perception, fitted
well with the Edwardsian doctrines which Bancroft adapted. The historian could easily have
agreed that "religion is interpretation, the
seeing of an event as a part or manifestation of
the whole, the perception of its meaning or
significance or unique purpose in the plan and
order of the whole." Particularly congenial must
have been Schleiermacher's view of history as
"the greatest object of religion, the most convenient show-place where the acts of the universe
can be contemplated." This show-place revealed a
progressively unfolding drama. "Fate in history
is moving toward the elimination of the dead and
the inert, the supremacy of life, the organized
and the rational," as Richard B. Brandt interprets Schleiermacher. "History is, for him, the
process by means of which the active reason in
human individuals 'moralizes,' viz., organizes
rationally or in accord with the 'intent' of the
universe everything with which it is confronted."[27] So it was for Bancroft.

Transcendentalism with its sources in German
philosophy and theology seems in all to have extended Bancroft's basic Protestant vision rather

than to have fundamentally altered it. John W. Rathbun concludes sensibly that "for a time, when transcendentalist fever was running high, he projected Transcendentalism into the sort of <u>Weltan-schauung</u> of Emerson and Thoreau. He borrowed from both Calvinism and mid-nineteenth century Transcendentalism."[28] It might be added that for one not more concerned with fine theological distinctions than was Bancroft, the two elements easily converged. "You call yourself a Unitarian," he wrote to Ralph Waldo Emerson in 1856,

> Fie! Fie! you are none of it
> though it may be that you confine
> your worship to the Holy Ghost. No-
> body is more convinced than you that
> the Divine dwells in everything;
> your faith in this primal truth is
> as fixed as that of Duns Scotus him-
> self, who when his adversaries
> thought to daunt him, by asking
> him if God dwelt in the stones,
> bravely answered yes.[29]

Such twentieth century commentators as George Santayana and Perry Miller have viewed Calvinism and transcendentalism as different phases of the same tradition.[30] Bancroft's life and thought make a good argument in support of this interpretation. In Miller's interpretation, which is the more applicable to the present case, the common thread between Edwards and Emerson was their insistence upon direct individual experience of God. This was for Bancroft the root principle of religion, which reduced to secondary significance even such major theological questions as that of the Trinity. At the same time, transcendentalism was a mediating principle which helped to reconcile Calvinism with democracy. In extending the grace once vouchsafed only the Elect to the commonality of men, it provided a universal providential principle which was essential to Bancroft's scheme of history.

It was the first self-imposed task of George Bancroft the historian to render the Calvinist tradition as the source of American freedom. The theocracy of John Calvin himself, even the intolerance of the American Puritans were, he was sure, involved in the modern epochal liberation of the human spirit. There was, as he saw further, an even greater paradox: the doctrine of predestination, of divine omnipotence and human impotence, was the charter of this liberation.

Protestantism was most radical in the social atomism which it implied; Martin Luther, Bancroft observed, had "lifted each human being out of the castes of the middle age, to endow him with individuality. . . ." In a fundamental sense, it seemed to the historian, "the principle of justification by faith alone solved every problem. It is freedom against authority; self-activity against superstitious trust in other men. . . . It was censured as fatalism, while in truth it is the strongest possible summons to self-activity. The principle can never be surrendered so long as the connection between man and eternal truth shall endure." Yet "Luther's was still a Catholic religion: it sought to instruct all, to confirm all, to sanctify all. . . . Calvinism was revolutionary; wherever it came, it created division. . . ."[31] But this was a division between the spiritually Elect and non-Elect, not between social orders. Before heaven the Puritan consequently "prostrated himself in the dust"; yet he had to respect himself and others whom God had redeemed. Puritanism therefore could be said to have had "two cardinal principles: Faith in the absolute sovereignty of God, whose will is perfect right; and the Equality of all who believe that his will is to be done."[32] The doctrine of Election, in thus reducing all mundane distinctions to insignificance, was an unprecedentedly powerful weapon against social inequality and arbitrary authority, and Bancroft explained its liberating effect partly in this way:

> Against the authority of the church of the middle ages Calvin arrayed the authority of the Bible; the time was come to connect religion and philosophy, and show the harmony between faith and reason. Against the feudal aristocracy, the plebian reformer summoned the spotless nobility of the elect, foreordained from the beginning of the world; but New England, which had no hereditary caste to beat down, ceased to make predestination its ruling idea. . . .[33]

"He that will not honor the memory and respect the influence of Calvin," Bancroft thought, "knows but little of the origin of American liberty."[34]

The connection thus traced was in a sense adventitious, but there was a more essential affinity between predestination and individual liberty:

> God is the absolute sovereign, doing according to his will in the armies of heaven and among the inhabitants on earth. Scorning the thought of free agency as breaking the universe into countless fragments, the greatest number in New England held that every volition, even of the humblest of the people, is obedient to the fixed decrees of Providence, and participates in eternity.
> Yet, while the common mind of New England was inspired by the great thought of the sole sovereignty

of God, it did not lose personality and human freedom in pantheistic fatalism. Like Augustine,
who made war both on Manicheans
and Pelagians; like the Stoics,
whose morals it most nearly
adopted--it asserted by just dia-
lectics, or, as some would say, by
a sublime inconsistency, the power
of the individual will. In every
action it beheld the union of the
motive and volition. The action,
it saw, was according to the strongest motive; and it knew that what
proves the strongest motive depends
on the character of the will. The
Calvinist of New England, who longed
to be "morally good and excellent,"
had, therefore, no other object of
moral effort than to make "the will
truly lovely and right."[35]

Bancroft views Calvinism here as a theology of
movement, or "action." Each individual, as a
spiritual atom, moves according to his will. But
this will is not free, in the sense of being un-
determined; were this the case the universe would
be a chaos of detached wills; it would, as Bancroft says, be broken into "countless fragments."
But neither are men so many particles of iron,
passively to be moved as in a magnetic field.
Such "pantheistic fatalism" is unthinkable as a
creed of action, or of freedom. Hence the precarious joining, by what Bancroft is driven to
admit may be a "sublime inconsistency," of divine
omnipotence and individual will. The will gov-
erns the spiritual atom, determining its motives;
all depends, therefore, on the "character of the
will." "Action, therefore, as flowing from an
energetic, right, and lovely will, was the ideal
of New England."[36]

Bancroft had been indelibly impressed in his
youth by Jonathan Edwards' essay on the Freedom
of the Will, and he followed here the tenor of

its argument. Edwards had attempted to demonstrate that nothing happens without a cause and that the human will necessarily acts on its strongest motive. To suppose otherwise, with the "Arminian" champions of free will, was tantamount to supposing that the will acted indifferently and haphazardly (i.e. without motive). "For contingence is blind, and does not pick and choose for a particular sort of events," Edwards argued. "Nothing has no choice."[37] Such blind contingence is actually an enslavement to accident or chance, and has nothing to do with moral choice; a moral action could be only that determined by a good motive. Motives operate by destroying freedom in the Arminian sense; they bring the will "into subjection to the power of something extrinsic, which operates upon it, sways and determines it, previous to its own determination."[38]

Edwards was attempting not to destroy the notion of freedom of the will, however, but to redefine it. He did so by distinguishing between the natural inability to act and the moral inability to do so. It made no real sense, he thought, to speak of a man as unfree in any given situation, unless he lacked the natural ability to do what he would.[39]

> But one thing more I would observe concerning what is vulgarly called liberty; namely that power and opportunity for one to do and conduct as he will, or according to his choice, is all that is meant by it; without taking into the meaning of the word, anything of the cause or original of that choice; or at all considering how the person came to have such a volition; whether it was caused by some external motive, or internal habitual bias; whether it was determined by some internal antecedent volition, or whether it happened without a

26

cause; whether it was necessarily
connected with something foregoing,
or not connected. Let the person
come by his volition of choice how
he will, yet, if he is able, and
there is nothing in the way to hinder his pursuing and executing his
will, the man is fully and perfectly
free, according to the primary and
common notion of freedom.[40]

Bancroft was not greatly interested in the
intricacies of the theological maze, but he could
see sufficiently with the Calvinist vision to
discern the juncture of freedom and necessity,
and the interconnectedness of the two became basic to his own thought. "Election implies faith,
and faith freedom."[41] The aphorism appeared in
the context of a discussion of the antinomians,
whose excesses Bancroft rejected, but he did not
deny the principle. He not only accepted, but
made a cardinal part of his philosophy, the
ancient Christian belief that one is truly liberated only by the grace of God, predestined or
not. At the same time, Bancroft ascribed a
transforming role to Jonathan Edwards which presaged the broader transforming role in world history of the United States. Edwards, in this
view, had completed a shift of emphasis in American Calvinism from the harsher aspects of predestination, used as a battering ram against
the worldly hierarchies of Europe, to a more
benevolent conception of grace as love. Secondly, Edwards strongly had affirmed the tradition
within Calvinism which accorded final validity
to individual revelation and judgment; the faith
now more than ever was one of private religious
truth. With little menace in New England of
prelacy or aristocracy, it was thus permitted Edwards to give "Calvinism its political euthana-
sia, by declaring virtue to consist in universal
Love."[42] The theologian bequeathed to the historian, finally, a large and radiant vision of
God as "Being in general," His glory including
"the glory and the perfecting of the universe";

and of the whole human race as one "complex person" or moral whole to be redeemed. Liberation and redemption were one. "Nor can any outward authority rule the mind;" as Bancroft interpreted Edwards; "the revelations of God, being emanations from the infinite fountain of knowledge, have a certainty and reality; they accord with reason and common sense; and give direct, intuitive, and all conquering evidence of their divinity."[43]

Jonathan Edwards, consequently, could be a prophet of liberty. At a stage of history in which the ancient social hierarchies and structures of authority were breaking down, especially in the United States of the nineteenth century-- dynamic, expansive, relatively atomistic--Bancroft saw the Protestant principle as not only the concomitant, but as the very condition of individual freedom. For what else was to keep this welter of liberated, mobile social atoms from becoming a chaos, precluding both a decently ordered society and the chance of progress to which the American experiment was so fully committed? Neither practically nor metaphysically was chaos compatible with liberty. The Protestant idea, rejecting the sacramental theory of salvation, obviating the essential mediation of the church and its priests, made salvation a direct transaction between God and the individual. By a natural extension, Calvinists, Quakers, and other progeny of the Reformation placed intense emphasis on the access of the individual heart to God. This provided for Bancroft the ordering principle, and the principle of freedom.

Bancroft did not view this as merely a matter of balancing freedom and order; he identified the two. This was possible because they were for him religious conceptions which transcended their mundane categories and were united in a ruling Providence. Individual choice offered the great blessing of conformity to God's will, as opposed to the curse of deviation from it. The believer

28

in God, Bancroft wrote, properly "seeks to bring his own will into harmony with the divine will. Piety studies the law, obeys the law, and through perfect obedience becomes perfectly free. For liberty is the daughter of necessity."[44] We are led back to a specifically Calvinistic--and indeed, Augustinian--concept of liberty. "As for free will," Bancroft wrote to Ralph Waldo Emerson in 1860, "I hold with Augustine, that true liberty consists in being under an inward irresistible necessity of doing right: that the woman who deliberates is lost; that freedom of choice is already apostacy."[45] This did not contradict Bancroft's view of the scope of individual freedom in history, for he had learned from Jonathan Edwards that freedom, in the only sensible meaning of the term, meant the unimpeded ability to do what one had a will to do. The historian needed to inquire no further into the freedom of the will. But in the movement of history as well as in the individual soul--and this was the principle that joined history to the individual conscience--it was the service of God which was perfect freedom. This was the freedom toward which, in Bancroft's vision of progress, humanity inexorably tended.

With good reason, liberty has been called "Bancroft's major terms of analysis. . . . Liberty and slavery played out their long dialectic in Bancroft's historical essays as the cities of God and Man had done in the masterwork of St. Augustine."[46] In the conventional categories of individual and social freedom, Bancroft was a reasonably consistent champion of liberty. Liberty meant the civil liberties guaranteed by the Constitution, freedom of inquiry, and freedom of movement, geographical and social (horizontal and vertical mobility, as it would later be called). As a Jacksonian Democrat, he espoused a generally laissez faire economic philosophy, and adhered to the doctrine of local freedom known in the United States as "state rights." He was no abolitionist, but always regarded slavery as an evil which

the progress of American freedom would inevitably
eliminate, and he welcomed the expiration of the
institution in the Civil War.

Active freedom, Bancroft believed, was "a
necessary condition of intelligent existence.
Liberty had its foundation in human nature, and,
he was sure, "the impulse of free spirits is felt
in every state of society and in spite of all
constraints." Yet liberty remained for Bancroft
inherently a religious concept, and bound to an
absolute; it was "the daughter of God, and dwells
in unchanging tranquility beside his throne. . .
."[47] He was highly critical of those men of the
eighteenth century who had

> thrown off the importunate fear
> of an overruling Providence, and
> would no longer know of anything
> more god-like than themselves.
> They refused to look for anything
> better; the belief in the divine
> reason was derided like the cow-
> ering at spectres and hobgoblins;
> and the worship of humanity became
> the prevailing idolatry. Art was
> commissioned to gratify taste;
> morality had for its office to in-
> crease pleasure; forgetting that
> the highest liberty consists in
> being forced by right reason to
> choose the best, men cherished
> sensualism as a system, and self-
> indulgence was the law of courts
> and aristocracies. . . .[48]

This uncompromisingly positive sense of
freedom, as consisting in obedience to the voice
of God, is particularly difficult to appreciate
today. In the realm of formal thought, twentieth
century man is apt to conceive of freedom in the
negative terms of indeterminacy, absence of restraint, or the subjective, "existential" reality
of making choices. In politics the notion of

30

positive freedom is sometimes invoked to connote
the policy of active governmental intervention in
social and economic life to promote a greater
range of practical choices for individuals. But
both these philosophical and political sets of
ideas have ultimately to do with the absence or
removal of determining factors which preclude
genuine choice. Yet we fail to understand Bancroft if we insist on viewing him in this light,
dismissing his religious rhetoric as an accident
of his time and place. He was not concerned
merely that unnecessary barriers to individual
development and self-expression be removed. If
the religious element in his thought could be
subtracted, such a formula of personal liberty
would be substantially what was left. But it
cannot be subtracted. To be free, for Bancroft,
was not merely to be released from worldly
shackles; equally, it was to act according to
a divinely furnished gyroscope of reason--to
"live in the light," in the Quaker terms which
the historian notably admired.

It was this positive vision of freedom which
made plausible the conjunction of liberty and
order. Bancroft was able not only to refute the
conservative Old World association of liberalism
with anarchy, but to turn the tables. The in-
equalities and restrictions of traditional society, he insisted,did not make for order in the
deepest sense. In the mid-eighteenth century,
he wrote, "anarchy lay at the heart of the institutions of Europe; the germ of political life
was struggling for its development in the people
of America. While doubt was preparing the work
of destruction in the Old World, faith in truth
and the formative power of order were controlling
and organizing the free and expanding energies of
the New."[49] It was true that Roman Catholicism
had represented an order and unity that Protestantism had broken, but this fragmentation merely
presaged a truer order. "Society would be organized again; but not till after the recognition
of the rights of the individual. Unity would
once more be restored, but not through the canon

31

and the feudal law; for the new Catholic element was the people."[50] Unity and freedom were unequivocally one:

> The subtle and irresistible movement of mind, silently but thoroughly correcting opinion and changing society, brings liberty both to the soul and to the world. . . . Every fallacy that man discards is an emancipation; every superstition that is thrown by is a redeeming from captivity. The tendency towards universality implies necessarily a tendency towards freedom, alike of thought and in action.[51]

iii.

The formula of evolving and liberating universality served as the basis of a conception of man and the world which it is hardly exaggerated to call a cosmology--at least in its sweep. Protestant and democratic in its assumptions, it was an American version of the ancient western vision of a cosmos in which prolific variety was harmonized in an eternal order, in which, as Bancroft put it, "all creation is a manifestation of the Almighty; not the result of caprice, but the glorious display of his perfection. . . ." Above all, the universe was a rational moral system, "and immutable laws of moral existence must pervade all time and all space, all ages and all worlds."[52] Science provided no note of dissonance; the modern thinker of Bancroft's day could still greet the advance of scientific knowledge as verifying and expanding the religious sense of divine order. Such an advance contributed indeed to a sense of the cosmos more sublime than any that had been possible earlier. Bancroft's thought cannot be fully appreciated except in terms of this vision:

32

From immeasurable distances in
the material universe the observer
of the stars brings back word, that
the physical forces which rule our
neighborhood maintain an all-pervading energy; and the records im-
bedded in the rocks, teaching how
countless myriads of seasons have
watched the sun go forth daily from
his chamber, and the earth turn on its
axis, and the sea ebb and flow, demonstrate that the same physical forces
have exerted their power without
change for unnumbered periods of by-
gone years. The twin sciences of the
stars and of the earth establish the
cosmical unity of the material universe in all that we can know of time
and space. But the conception of the
perfect order and unity of creation
does not unfold itself in its beauty
and grandeur, so long as the guiding
presence of intelligence is not apprehended. From the depth of man's
consciousness, which envelopes sub-
limer truths than the firmament over
his head can reveal to his senses,
rises the idea of right; and history,
testing that idea by observation,
traces the vestiges of moral law
through the practice of the nations
in every age, proves experimentally
the reality of justice, and confirms
by induction the intuitions of
reason.[53]

The intelligence governing the universe,
then, is accessible to human beings. This simply
states in more general terms the Protestant emphasis on the individual's direct access to God,
or as Bancroft phrased it, "our good [Protes-
tant] doctrine of the direct communion of the
individual with the divine. . . ."[54] It was this
capacity of coming into connection with the

33

infinite" that was the distinguishing mark of mankind, and which made possible freedom, democracy, and progress. This assumption was the heart of the system, which without it was only lifeless abstraction, as Bancroft believed that much Enlightenment philosophy had been in denying it.[55]

Access to infinity was neither a completely rational nor a completely nonrational phenomenon; "the intuitions of reason" was an apt phrase with which to describe it. In a youthful sermon, on the "Reasonableness of Glorying in the Gospel," Bancroft expounded on the theme that Christianity was a rational as well as a revealed religion. "Reason hails its appearance, as the presence of her kindest ally and firmest supporter." Christian doctrines invited rational scrutiny and elevated the understanding. But, Bancroft emphasized,

> it is false and fatal to esteem Christianity as a religion of reason alone. The heart is the true sanctuary of the gospel. The new covenant is an affectionate one; and its first commandment does but enjoin the love of God: that sacred, fervent and habitual love, which may purify every exercise of the affections, lend beauty and innocence to every resolution and desire, and imbue the whole soul with gentleness, humility and devotion.[56]

For Bancroft in 1823, the heart of the matter was that Christians "maintain a faith, which connects our natures with God, and our hopes with another world, while it prompts us to active virtue in this."[57] The historian maintained as the basis of his philosophy a conception of religious truth as the spiritually animating principle

34

within each heart. This was entirely compatible
with the Edwardsian position on the freedom of
the will: individual freedom was the freedom to
act according to the character and the habit of
the soul.

Bancroft called the divine principle in man
"reason," but it was not to any cold and detached
faculty of ratiocination that he referred. Reason, rather, was the perception of the excellence
of God and his creation, much as the concept of
grace had been for Jonathan Edwards. He was
sure that

> we have functions which connect us
> with heaven, as well as organs which
> set us in relation with earth. We
> have not merely the senses opening
> to us the external world, but an in-
> ternal sense, which places us in con-
> nexion with the world of intelligence
> and the decrees of God.
> *   *   *
> Reason exists within every breast.
> I mean not that faculty which deduces
> inferences from the experience of the
> senses, but that higher faculty, which
> from the infinite treasures of its own
> consciousness, originates truth, and
> assents to it by the force of intuitive
> evidence; that faculty which raises us
> beyond the control of time and space,
> and gives us faith in things eternal
> and invisible.[58]

This faculty of "reason" liberated men from the
fetters of human authority and tradition even as
the attainment of grace liberated Calvinists from
sin. This is why Bancroft viewed Luther's principle of justification by faith alone as so
broadly and deeply revolutionary, a principle "to
overturn every tyranny, to enfranchise, convert,
and save the world." Although scornful of those
who had carried "the great truth of justification

by faith to Antinomian absurdities," he was impressed that the seventeenth century antinomians, as the most radical of Calvinists, had "asserted absolute freedom of mind."[59] But for the historian, who did not espouse predestination in its exclusive character, each man was of the Elect and carried the liberating germ of reason. He need only heed it.

So essential was this principle of "reason" that it served as the crucial distinction between systems that might otherwise have seemed compatibly liberal. Bancroft devoted a significant section of his History of the United States to a comparison of the ideas of John Locke and William Penn. The author immensely admired the Quakers, who in his estimation had brought to their fullness the ideas of "intellectual freedom, the supremacy of mind, universal enfranchisement," relying more completely than any people theretofore on "the light of universal reason; the voice of universal conscience. . . ." Despite his American associations, Locke's philosophy seemed far inferior:

> . . .Locke kindled the torch of liberty at the fires of tradition; Penn at the living light in the soul. Locke sought truth through the senses and the outward world; Penn looked inward to the divine revelations in every mind. Locke compared the soul to a sheet of white paper, just as Hobbes had compared it to a slate, on which time and chance might scrawl their experience; to Penn, the soul was an organ which of itself instinctively breathes divine harmonies, like those musical instruments which are so curiously and perfectly framed, that, when once set in motion, they of themselves give forth all the melodies designed by the artist that made them. . . . The system of Locke lends itself to contending

factions of the most opposite interests
and purposes; the doctrine of Fox and
Penn, being but the common creed of
humanity, forbids division, and insures
the highest moral unity. . . .

No wonder that Locke as an American lawgiver had
constructed such an aristocratic system for the
colony of Carolina, while Penn projected his
"'free colony for all mankind'";[60] no wonder too
that Bancroft should refer in a letter to Ralph
Waldo Emerson to "the opposite systems of Locke
& George Fox."[61]

It is apparent then that Bancroft's political philosophy rested on his thoroughly religious
conviction of the wisdom of the people. He believed that democracy lay at the heart of the
Protestant revolution; "the voice of the majority
was the voice of God; and the issue of Puritanism," he was convinced, "was therefore popular
sovereignty."[62] Accepting quite literally this
concept of majority will, Bancroft viewed democracy as inherently a religious institution. It
was "ETERNAL JUSTICE, RULING THROUGH THE PEOPLE";
it rested on "the strongest possible foundation;--
on the law of God in the soul of man." In sum,
"democracy knows nothing, recognizes nothing, as
a perpetuity, but the law of God."[63] Whiggery,
by contrast, regarded society as established by
contract, with liberty the result of a bargain
between government and governed; Toryism idolized
power, and provided for liberty only as a boon.
Only democracy was derived from God: "the tory
looks out for himself; the whig for his clan;
democracy takes thought for the many. The tory
adheres to the party of Moloch; the whig still
woships at the shrine of Mammon; democracy is
practical Christianity."[64]

Bancroft's conception of political truth,
as he himself acknowledged, was a direct adaptation of the Christian, and specifically Edwardsian, concept of grace. Citing an argument made

37

by Jonathan Edwards in 1734, Bancroft postulated

> an instinct of liberty; a natural per-
> ception of the loveliness and beauty
> of freedom. . . . I speak no new doc-
> trine. I do but repeat what was known
> to our fathers; I do but echo the words
> that were pronounced in Old Hampshire,
> one hundred and two years ago. The
> gift of feeling moral truth, of which
> political science is a branch, was
> rightly declared by our fathers, "to
> be from God. Nothing the creature re-
> ceives is so much a participation of
> the Deity: it is a kind of emanation
> of God's beauty, and is related to God
> as light is to the sun. It is not a
> thing that belongs to reason; it de-
> pends on the SENSE OF THE HEART. . . ."
> It was because our fathers freed them-
> selves from prejudice and selfish
> passion, and making themselves like
> little children, listened calmly to the
> voice within, that the book of politi-
> cal wisdom was thrown wide open to
> their gaze; that they gave their af-
> fections to democratic liberty as
> naturally and as firmly as they adored
> their Creator or loved their off-
> spring.[65]

As democracy was practical Christianity, so the
spirit of true religion was the animating principle of both religious and civil liberty, and
Bancroft noted that "the people of the United
States, where civil and religious liberty are
most fully developed, is the most religious
people on earth."[66]

The Christian and democratic system which
Bancroft described was not of course static; it
was progressively realized in the fullness of
time. The historian did not accept the theory of

38

biological evolution when it became an acute issue late in his life, and could not therefore make of it the powerful historical engine that John Fiske and others did. Yet while rejecting the notion that one species grew from another, his own thinking was in important ways in tune with the evolutionary mentality. Regarding "the strong resemblances exhibited in structure" in nature, he was content in 1858 to regard these "as evidence of the connection & harmonious analogy of all her works." But he had a less old-fashioned sense of life proliferating from a few "original forces," being "more than willing to believe, that nature tried her hand a million times over at any plant or animal, before she gave it a certificate of being worth repeating & preserving; that a countless variety of effort preceeded the lily or the robin, rather than that the robin or the lily came into existence by the transmutation of some inferior form."[67] One may infer that the transmutation of species posed too great a threat to the immanence of divine action which was central to Bancroft's thought. He was nevertheless impressed with the work of geology in revealing "the majestic march of creative power, from the organism of the zoophyte entombed in the lowest depths of Siluria, through all the rising gradations of animal life, up to its sublimest result in Godlike man."[68]

Although not deeply moved by the beginning of modern theories of biological evolution, Bancroft evinced strongly the romantic sense of the "organic" growth of institutions in history. He believed that historical change was gradual and without essential breach in continuity. A radical democrat in his belief in the divine sources of popular wisdom, he could nevertheless denigrate abrupt social change in tones reminiscent of Edmund Burke. With respect to the English Civil War, he noted that "nations change their institutions but slowly: to attempt to pass abruptly from feudalism and monarchy to democratic equality, was the thought of enthusiasts, who

understood neither the history, the character,
nor the condition of the country. It was like
laying out into entirely different new streets,a
city that was already crowded with massive
structures,resting on firm foundations."[69] The
American Revolution, on the other hand, had successfully maintained historical continuity.
"America," the historian suggested, "neither
separated abruptly from the past, nor adhered to
its decaying forms. The principles that gave
life to the new institutions pervaded history
like a prophecy. . . ."[70]

There is a tension in Bancroft's history
between this sense of continuity and the very
American notion of making a fresh start. If the
American Patriots built upon the past, at the
same time it appears that "American history
knows but one avenue to success in American leg-
islation--freedom from ancient prejudice. The
truly great lawgivers in our colonies first became as little children."[71] But the tension is
not necessarily a contradiction. There is at
work always a process of interpreting the past,
of translating it into the more pure and exalted
terms which Providence progressively vouchsafes
to a receptive people. The past is sifted. Thus,
for example,

> . . .Democracy is not destructive; she
> makes no war on the past; she plans no
> overthrow of the present. On the con-
> trary, she garners up and bears along
> with her all the truths that past gen-
> erations have discovered; she will not
> let go one single idea, not one prin-
> ciple, not one truth. She has an hon-
> est lineage; she is, under God's prov-
> idence, the lawful offspring of ad-
> vancing humanity, and she claims as her
> rightful inheritance the glorious in-
> ventions, the rich discoveries of the
> past. But Democracy does not, like the
> Egyptians, embalm the dead; she does

not bear along with her decayed institutions, errors that have inflicted on
themselves their own death blow.[72]

In this sifting process, the conventional categories of opinion all play their parts. History,
Bancroft suggested, is "ever a rope of three
strands"; conservatives try to keep things as
they are, radicals to bring society into conformity with eternal standards, and a middle group
attempts to mediate and "reconcile" the other
two. "Without all the three, the fates could not
spin their thread."[73]

For Bancroft, the future existed potentially
and incipiently in the past. The spirit of liberty, he thought, was as old as creation, though
it had to be brought to fruition through the long
course of time.[74] The Patriots at Lexington
"fulfilled their duty not from an accidental impulse of the moment; their action was the ripened
fruit of Providence and of time. The light that
led them on was combined of rays from the whole
history of the race," from the Hebrews and classical sages, from Christ Himself, Paul and Augustine, the Saxon immigrants to England, Calvin and
the Massachusetts Puritans. "The present," in
Bancroft's summary view, "is always the lineal
descendent of the past. A new form of political
life never appears but as a growth out of its
antecedents. In civil affairs, as much as in
husbandry, seedtime goes before the harvest, and
the harvest may be seen in the seed, the seed in
the harvest."[75]

This conception made for an historical determinism which clearly owed much to Bancroft's
religious background, modified and elaborated
certainly by German idealist strains of thought.
Although predestination no longer meant literally
for the historian the preordained salvation or
damnation of the individual, the deterministic
counterpoint to the liberating element in Protestantism was not lost. Translated to the plane

41

of history, the Calvinist vision of divine sovereignty suggested that not necessarily individuals,
but rather masses of men were predestined. Bancroft made it clear that he was a strict historical determinist, and his determinism if anything
became more pronounced with the years. This did
not mean that, as in some modern schemes of determinism, the individual was reduced to a ci-
pher. Heeding the voice of reason or not, the
individual might move with history or futilely
obstruct it, achieving or rejecting a sort of
historical grace. And history from time to time
cast up leaders who heard its voice with extraordinary clarity, a special Elect. George Washington, Bancroft noted, had been surveying in the
woods while the Treaty of Aix-la-Chapelle was
being negotiated.

> And yet God had elected, not Kaunitz
> nor Newcastle, not a monarch of the
> house of Hapsburg nor of Hanover, but
> the Virginia stripling, to give an im-
> pulse to human affairs; and, as far as
> events can depend on an individual, had
> placed the rights and the destinies of
> countless millions in the keeping of
> the widow's son.[76]

God, Bancroft emphasized repeatedly, rules
absolutely in the affairs of men, and God is visible in history. The historian was sure that
"nothing is by chance. . . . The deeds of time
are governed, as well as judged, by the decrees of
eternity. The caprice of fleeting existences
bends to the immovable omnipotence, which plants
its foot on all the centuries and has neither
change of purpose nor repose."[77] Not "blind destiny" but a "favoring Providence. . .has con-
ducted the country to its present happiness and
glory." The authors of the Constitution, evidently like Adam Smith's economic competitors,
"seemed to be led by an invisible hand" to play
their preordained roles.[78] Bancroft quite
properly acknowledged in this connection the

tutelage of Jonathan Edwards, to whom he attributed, in 1739, the first conception of the office of "universal history." Edwards' history, although "still cramped and perverted by theological forms not derived from observation," was he thought nobler than that of Vico or Bossuet, because "it embraced in its outline the whole 'work of redemption'--the history of the influence of all moral truth in the gradual regeneration of humanity. The New England divine, in his quiet association with the innocence and simplicity of rural life, knew that, in every succession of revolutions, the cause of civilization and moral reform is advanced."[79]   The New England historian knew this too.

Bancroft was thus unequivocal that the human race was locked into a cosmic order, obedient necessarily to the historical plan of God. The very perfection of God demanded it, and one could not cavil at its determinism:

> I know that there is a pride which
> calls this fatalism, and which rebels
> at the thought that the Father of life
> should control what he has made. There
> are those who must needs assert for
> their individual selves the constant
> possession of that power which the
> great English poet represents the bad
> angels to have lost heaven for once
> attempting to usurp. . . . Unsatisfied
> with having been created in his image,
> they assume the liberty to counteract
> his will. They do not perceive that
> cosmical order depends on the univer-
> sality and absolute certainty of law;
> that for that end, events in their
> course are not merely as fixed as Ara-
> rat and the Andes, but follow laws
> that are much older than Andes or Ara-
> rat, that are as old as those which up-
> heaved the mountains. The glory of God
> is not contingent on man's good will,
> but all existence subserves his pur-

poses. The system of the universe is
as a celestial poem, whose beauty is
from all eternity, and must not be
marred by human interpolations.[80]

America, of course, had a special role in
the providential drama; in the vanguard of the
long march of history, it was at once the most
liberated and the most truly orderly of nations.
This country was "the chief heir of the reformation in its purest form," and like the New England Puritans, Americans in general could well
regard themselves as a new chosen people. The
United States, Bancroft declared on the Fourth
of July, 1826, was "a light to the world, an
example to those who would be free, already the
benefactress of humanity, the tutelary angel of
liberty." Bancroft did not hold that Americans
were detached from, or superior to, other peoples, but only that their nation held the
"noblest rank" in the great work of "regen-
erating the world."[81]

America was chosen partly for the political
and social qualities which her fresh environment
could nourish, but Bancroft's major theme was
that of religious pilgrimage. "Nothing," he
wrote in his History, "came from Europe but a
free people."

> The people, separating itself from
> all other elements of previous
> civilization; the people, self-con-
> fiding and industrious; the people,
> wise by all traditions that favored
> its culture and happiness--alone
> broke away from European influence,
> and in the New World laid the
> foundations of our republic. Like
> Moses, as they said of themselves, they
> had escaped from Egyptian bondage to
> the wilderness, that God might there
> give them the pattern of the taber-
> nacle. Like the favored evangelist,

44

> the exiles, in their western Patmos,
> listened to the angel that dictated
> the new gospel of freedom. Over-
> whelmed in Europe, popular liberty,
> like the fabled fountain of the
> sacred Arethusa, gushed forth pro-
> fusely in remoter fields.[82]

There is some suggestion that by the middle of
the nineteenth century, Bancroft had become sufficiently disillusioned with the prospects of
American democracy to fear that the nation was
declining from grace. But at most this only
dimmed the central vision, in which he contemplated the profound convergence of national and
cosmic purposes, and "the faith of the American
people in the moral government of the world,"
springing from "the deep sentiment of harmony
between their own active patriotism and the infinite love which founded all things and the
infinite justice which carries all things forward in continuous progression." Spurred the
more to "self-relying dilligence" by their
consciousness of this harmony, Bancroft had
written, Americans "had the confidence and joy
of fellow-workers with 'the divine ordering' for
the highest welfare of mankind."[83]

Clearly that progress of which America was
so great an avatar was for Bancroft a conception
inseparable from religious faith. The assumptions and uses of the modern idea of progress
have been many, but Bancroft rejected secular
interpretations, such as that of positivism,
which impressed him merely as "an afterbirth
of the materialism of the last century." The
atheist was simply cut off from the source of
all truth.

> The atheist denies the life of life,
> which is the source of liberty. Pro-
> claiming himself a mere finite thing
> of to-day, he rejects all connection
> with the infinite. Pretending to

45

search for truth, he abjures the spirit of truth. Were it possible that the world of mankind could become without God, that greatest death, the death of the race would ensue. It is because man cannot separate himself from his inward experience and his yearning after the infinite, that he is capable of progress; that he can receive a religion whose history is the triumph of right over evil, whose symbol is the resurrection.[84]

Progress was to Bancroft an empirical reality, manifest in organized religion, morality, and increase of knowledge. In a retrospect of the 1880's, he had no difficulty in citing steam power and the telegraph among its material evidences. But progress was above all a metaphysical and theological necessity, stemming from a "fundamental desire of perfection" at work in the universe, and guiding history. "Each people that has disappeared, every institution that has passed away, has been a step in the ladder by which humanity ascends toward the perfecting of its nature."[85]

In 1838 Bancroft set forth his views in an article entitled "On the Progress of Civilization, or Reasons Why the Natural Association of Men of Letters is with the Democracy," with the object of illustrating "the capacity of the human race for progress, and the evidence of its reality." The principle of progress was the faculty of reason in every man. "There is nothing in books," Bancroft thought, "which had not first, and has not still its life within us. Religion itself is a dead letter, wherever its truths are not renewed in the soul. And here unchangeable truth asserts its prerogative."[86] Truth, always existing in potentiality, must in the nature of things grow as the conscious property of men, because truth is one and eternal; error is fragmentary and transient:

> Truth is one. It never contradicts
> itself. One truth cannot contradict
> another truth. Hence truth is a bond
> of union. Men agree in sustaining it.
> The common mind asserts and reveres
> it. But error not only contradicts
> truth, but may contradict itself. . . .
> Truth is therefore of necessity an
> element of harmony; error as neces-
> sarily an element of discord. Thus
> there can be no judgment but a right
> one. Men cannot agree in an absurdity;
> neither can they agree in a false-
> hood.[87]

The public mind, Bancroft supposed, could
not entertain "unmixed error." Where error had
been "cherished by the masses," the difficulty
lay in the complexity of the ideas involved; error was entwined with truth. But over the long
course enduring truth must be winnowed from
transient error; thus every sect that has ever
gained a popular following has ultimately added
to the common store of truth, which "emerges in
her brightness from the contradictions of individual opinions; she raises herself in majestic
serenity above the conflict of sects; she ac-
knowledges as her nearest image the general
voice of mankind; the expression of universal
reason; the concurrent testimony of the race."[88]
Progress is effected, then, through the infusion
of universal principles into the common mind. As
truth is never lost, the "irresistible tendency
of the human race is to advancement. Absolute
power has never succeeded in suppressing a single
truth. . . . The tendency of the species is upward, irresistibly upward. The individual is
often lost; Providence never disowns the race.
. . . Humanity has always been on the advance;
its soul has always been gaining maturity and
power."[89]

47

Bancroft gave a more fully elaborated version of his concept of progress in an address in 1854, entitled "The Necessity, the Reality, and the Promise of the Progress of the Human Race." This later statement has appeared drastically less optimistic to one critic, who notes that it showed a weakening faith in man as a reasonable being, with God now acting largely outside of man's consciousness. But although his confidence in progress did become somewhat muted, as Russel B. Nye notes, he never relinquished his conviction of the reality and the historical necessity of progress.[90]

In 1854, Bancroft stressed again the constancy of human nature. Denying that progress rested on any sort of biological evolution, he insisted that

> No science has been reached, no thought generated, no truth discovered, which has not from all time existed potentially in every human mind. The belief in the progress of the race does not, therefore, spring from the supposed possibility of his acquiring new faculties, or coming into the possession of a new nature.

Rather, truth is immortal: "the progress of man consists in this, that he himself arrives at the perception of truth. The Divine mind, which is its source, left it to be discovered, appropriated and developed by finite creatures." The movement of the collective mind of humanity is always toward the better, as it must progressively compare "ideal truth and partial error."[91]

In what did progress consist? Raised to the highest level of meaning, progress for Bancroft was the increasing knowledge of God. History was noble because God was visible in it, and through the historical process God became increasingly visible:

> For the regeneration of the
> world, it was requisite that the
> Divine Being should enter into the
> abodes and the hearts of men, and
> dwell there; that a belief in him
> should be received, which should
> include all truth respecting his
> essence; that he should be known
> not only as an abstract and abso-
> lute cause, but as the infinite
> fountain of moral excellence and
> beauty; not a distant Providence
> of boundless power and uncertain
> or inactive will, but as God
> present in the flesh; not as an
> absolute lawgiver, holding the
> material world and all intelligent
> existence in the chains of neces-
> sity, but as a creative spirit,
> indwelling in man, his fellow-
> worker and guide.[92]

God was (as later for Josiah Royce) a principle
of community; his relationship with man constituted the unity of the human race. "If," as
Bancroft had earlier remarked, "it be the duty
of the individual to strive after a perfection
like the perfection of God, how much more ought
a nation to be the image of Deity."[93] Progress
meant the advancement of the race toward unity,
which was at the same time an advancement toward freedom.

There is an apparent paradox in this scheme
of history. Bancroft was a determinist, believing history to represent the unfolding will of
divine providence. Yet a predetermined plan of
progress seems logically incompatible with the
increasing freedom which was the very object of
progress. Bancroft suggested a partial solution
to this problem with the maxim that individuals
are free in the course of history, while the

masses of people are not. "Nothing appears more
self-determined than the volitions of each individual;" he wrote in his History of the United
States, "and nothing is more certain than that
Providence will overrule them for good. The
finite will of man, free in its individuality,
is in the aggregate subordinate to general
laws."[94] Shorn of the providential element,
the approach would be perfectly compatible with
modern uses of statistics: the mass statistical-
ly predictable, the individual not.

    Bancroft's purpose was not to build history
upon statistics, however; it was to define a human condition of expanding freedom. Seen in this
light, the difficulty remains, as it would seem
that a more generous notion of human freedom than
Bancroft's would include some margin of freedom
whereby the individual might affect the course of
humanity. For the individual to be precluded
this possibility is itself a severe limitation
on his freedom, for no sharp distinction can
really be drawn between the freedom of the individual and that of the mass. Personal freedom
for Bancroft, then, is on one level superficial
and transitory, a moment of futile self-satis-
faction without wider impact.[95] The only thing
indeed which saves it from frivolity is the religious alchemy which renders liberty as obedience to the plan of Providence, proclaiming that
in God's service lies perfect freedom. Lacking
this mystical bond between his will and that of
the ruler of the universe, the individual would
find himself trapped in a machine of history
oblivious to his wishes.

    This emerges clearly from Bancroft's his-
tory, which at once tremendously magnifies the
individual and reduces him to insignificance.
Bancroft had a transcendentalist sense of the
individual's access to the universe, which indeed
merely universalized his Edwardsian understanding
of grace as the perception of the excellence of
God in his manifold creation. Such access gave

50

the individual tremendous moral stature. Yet at
the same time, the individual did not really
matter on the plane of great social movements,
any more than he matters in any other deterministic scheme of history. "Individuals are but
shadows," Bancroft remarked in 1835, "too often
engrossed by the pursuit of shadows; the race is
immortal. . . ." "The individual is often lost;
Providence never disowns the race." His imagery
was similar in 1854: "the life of an individual
is but a breath; it comes forth like a flower,
and flees like a shadow." And still later, with
reference to America, Bancroft availed himself
of a recurrent image: "In this happy abode of
universal freedom, individual men, even the best
of them, compared to the people, are but as drops
that glisten for a moment in the light, before
they fall into the mighty and undecaying ocean."[96]

iv.

As the ocean furnished a metaphor of individual transience, it also provided Bancroft
with his most powerful representation of popular
power and freedom--freedom expressed as movement:

> As the sea is made up of drops, Ameri-
> can society is composed of separate,
> free, and constantly moving atoms, ever
> in reciprocal action, advancing, reced-
> ing, crossing, struggling against each
> other and with each other; so that the
> institutions and laws of the country
> rise out of the masses of individual
> thought, which, like the waters of the
> ocean, are rolling evermore.[97]

The image, recalling on the one hand the
Emersonian Over-Soul of which each droplet of humanity forms a part, and suggesting on the other
the grimier competition of laissez faire, con-
tains ambiguities which seem to dog the idea of

51

193956

freedom in America. To a less sanguine and more modern temper than Bancroft's is here, the atomic-oceanic metaphor represents not so much a free society as a chaos of haphazard motion and meaningless collision. The problem is compounded by Bancroft's facile equation of a sea composed of drops with a society composed of atoms. The metaphors are not true equivalents, and are in one way opposites: drops lose their individual existence in the ocean, while atoms, viewed as islands in a void, have only individual existence. The confused figure suggests the nominalist-realist controversy which Henry Adams was to find still the axis of philosophy; which is real, the individual or the universal? Bancroft might more consistently have depicted American society as a gas, the darting "atoms" of which contrive to fill every available void, as the Democratic apostles of Manifest Destiny, with whom Bancroft allied himself, believed that the North American continent would be filled. But the confusion is rooted in the nature of American society itself, as it could be perceived in the nineteenth century. Where lay its real meaning: in the frenetic running and darting of its millions of social atoms, or in the current that, it was assumed, drove them ultimately in its own direction?

The first stage of Bancroft's solution to this riddle lay, as we have seen, in a simple dualism: free in their individuality, men are "in the aggregate subject to general laws." Up to a point, this formula satisfied the historian's search for continuity between the ancestral world of the New England Puritans and his own far different world of Jacksonian democracy and liberal capitalism; it appeared to demonstrate that providence and liberty were compatible terms. But of itself, the formula also left them isolated categories; the individual freedom which it postulated bore no subjective relation to the determination of the mass.

52

Bancroft did not, of course, leave it at that. He relied further on the Protestant assumption of the individual's direct access, without need of intermediaries, to divine truth. Romantic and transcendentalist notions helped to enlarge the rather exclusive and narrow Calvinist formulation of this idea, but did not essentially alter it. The individual who listened to the divine voice of "reason" within himself was free not merely as an untethered social atom but free in God's service, an infinitely more exalted liberty.

This was for Bancroft the key both to history and to democracy as history's goal. In certain respects, Bancroft projected a particularly Calvinist brand of Protestantism on history. It would be simplistic to say that the old Calvinist doctrine of predestination, upon which Bancroft never insisted for the individual, was merely writ large upon the movements of masses of men. But certainly in Bancroft's history, there was much of the omnipotent God of John Calvin, before whom men were mere shadows of sentient existence, and yet morally called to account, as Bancroft called to account the figures who walked his pages. With the historian, of course, the Calvinist legacy took on a lighter, more optimistic cast, a change which Bancroft himself associated with Jonathan Edwards. But Calvinism, particularly in the form of American Puritanism, was not the unremittingly gloomy creed of popular misconceptions, and contained at its most eloquent a dazzlingly brilliant vision of the beauty of God, all the brighter against the vivid blackness of Satan and all his works. In scarcely more muted tones, Bancroft's History preserved the light on the shadows, as good struggled against evil, the forces of progress against those of reaction. To the most spiritual understanding, Bancroft perhaps offered no more exalted a cosmic prospect than did the old orthodoxy. Yet to the ordinary understanding his story of the resistless progress toward the

attainment of freedom in the knowledge of God
constituted the optimistic transformation of a
Calvinism confronted with secular progress--a
dissolution of Puritan salt in the oceanic mobility of American society. And basic to this
pilgrimage was the individual's access to universal, divine truth. It was basic as well to
democracy: the authority of God manifest in
human "reason" minimized the need for mundane
authority. Divine sovereignty could not tolerate, indeed, the encroachment of the merely
political.

History and democracy were actually terms
of theology for George Bancroft, encompassing in
the dimensions of time and of politics the knowledge of God and His relation to the world. We
fail adequately to understand Bancroft's work if
we suppose that he merely decorated with piety
his historical and political opinions. Intended
in his youth for the ministry, he never was sufficiently interested in theology in the usual
sense as even to define his personal views with
any precision, leaving later historians to sort
out the Unitarian, Trinitarian, and Transcendentalist influences in his thought. Only in the
historical progress of the human race, and in
the providential ordering of free energies which
American democracy offered as the last proof of
this progress, could God be truly understood.
Theology had to enter the world.

The resulting construct was a fragile one,
because more weight was placed on the iron Protestant axis between individual and infinite than
it could readily bear. Bancroft made too little
provision for the intermediate aggregations of
people. He did suggest that communities, like
individuals, might attain the freedom which is
the willing service of God. God, as universal
love, was the very principle of community, and
it was possible for institutions built in the
light of reason to conform to the divine lineaments; the nation, wrote Bancroft, is properly

54

the image of the Deity. The nation which most closely approached this ideal was of course the United States. No more than the Visible Church of the Puritans was the nation beyond the defilement of the unregenerate, but in principle it was the political representation of God. Yet this identification of the nation with divine purpose attributed to it a universality which overpowered and absorbed its identity as a particular community. Without the weighty social and institutional support that can exist only on a plane between God and the individual, the tension between personal liberty and providential necessity threatened always to become too great.

Intellectually, then, all depended upon God's direct access to individual understanding. But Bancroft posed what by any standards is a real and practical question: is libertarian democracy possible without the sort of common vision expressed by his conception of "reason"? Or does liberty without such a common vision tend fatally toward anarchy or toward some arbitrary political or intellectual sway? What was a system of ordered freedom for Bancroft could only appear as one of determined chaos for Henry Adams, born a generation later, and the difference was God. Held together at its religious core, Bancroft's vision was one of irresistibly expanding freedom in the plan of Providence; deprived of this religious core, it disintegrated to a chaos, the components of which obeyed equally irresistible forces inaccessible to the human soul and insensible to human needs.

Footnotes

1. Alan Heimert, Religion and the American Mind from the Great Awakening to the Revolution (Cambridge: Harvard University Press, 1966), passim. Ralph Henry Gabriel is among those who have noted the correlation between the stress on the free individual in the "romantic, democratic faith," and the doctrine of political liberty. Conversely, Gabriel found Calvinist determinism incompatible with "the democratic theory of manmade progress," and attributed its decline to this. The Course of American Democratic Thought, second edition (New York: Ronald Press, 1956), pp. 34, 38. But Bancroft, as this essay attempts to show, found Calvinist and democratic elements eminently compatible.

2. George Bancroft, History of the United States, from the Discovery of the American Continent, 10 volumes (Boston: Little, Brown, and Company, 1834-1875), VI, 192. (Hereinafter cited as Bancroft, History.)

3. Massachusetts Historical Society, George Bancroft Papers, Bancroft to William B. Sprague, January 28, 1862. (Hereinafter cited as MHS); Samuel A. Eliot, ed. Heralds of a Liberal Faith, 4 volumes (Boston: American Unitarian Association, 1910), II, 20. (Hereinafter cited as Eliot, Liberal Faith.)

4. Eliot, Liberal Faith, II, 24-25; Russel B. Nye, George Bancroft: Brahmin Rebel (New York: Alfred A. Knopf, 1944), p. 11. (Hereinafter cited as Nye, Brahmin Rebel.)

5. MHS, Bancroft to William B. Sprague, January 28, 1862.

6. Alonzo Hill, A Discourse on the Life and Character of the Rev. Aaron Bancroft, D. D. Senior Pastor of the Second Congregational Society

56

in Worcester, Delivered at His Interment, August 22, 1839 (Worcester, T. W. & J. Butterfield, 1839), p. 12.

7. Aaron Bancroft, The Nature and Worth of Christian Liberty, Illustrated in a Sermon Delivered Before the Second Congregational Church and Society, on the Twenty-Third Day of June, 1816. With an Appendix, Containing Strictures on the Attempt to Establish Consociation in Massachusetts (Worcester: William Manning, 1816), pp. 21-22, 4.

8. Russel B. Nye, "The Religion of George Bancroft," The Journal of Religion, XIX (July, 1939), 222, 230, 226-228.

9. Russel B. Nye, George Bancroft (New York: Washington Square Press, 1964), p. 128. (Hereinafter cited as Nye, Bancroft.) Nye's Brahmin Rebel was closer to his 1939 article in interpretation. In it, he remarked that after Bancroft set sail from New England for graduate study, "in spirit he never returned to it" (p. 32).

10. David W. Noble, Historians Against History: the Frontier Thesis and the National Covenant in American Historical Writing Since 1830 (Minneapolis: University of Minnesota Press, 1965), pp. 19, 22. Noble believes that Bancroft "prepared the philosophical foundations for assuring his generation that it was out of history, that it had achieved permanent harmony as a chosen people protected by a covenant with God from the perils that pursued the rest of mankind." (p. 22). I think that this provocative thesis underestimates both the degree to which Bancroft understood history as a continuing process, and the extent to which he associated the American mission with the progress of humanity at large. Others who have criticized Nye's interpretation include Richard G. Vitzhum, who

asserted that Bancroft's basic beliefs were always essentially Edwardsian, and that his philosophy of history was deeply tinged with Edwardsian
theology. "Theme and Method in Bancroft's History of the United States," New England Quarterly, XLI (September, 1968), 365. (Hereinafter
cited as Vitzhum, "Theme and Method"); and C.
Carroll Hollis, "Brownson on George Bancroft,"
South Atlantic Quarterly, XLIV (January, 1950),
52. (Hereinafter cited as Hollis, "Brownson.")

11. MHS, Bancroft to Andrews Norton, December 25, 1820.

12. Mark Antony DeWolfe Howe, ed., The Life
and Letters of George Bancroft, 2 volumes (New
York: Charles Scribner's Sons, 1908), II, 310,
Bancroft to S. Austin Allibone, August 29, 1887.
(Hereinafter cited as Howe, Life and Letters.)
In 1854, Bancroft enthusiastically acknowledged
the "truth of the triune God." "The Necessity,
the Reality, and the Promise of the Progress of
the Human Race," Literary and Historical Miscellanies (New York: Harper & Brothers, 1855),
p. 504. (Hereinafter cited as Bancroft, Miscellanies.) Bancroft can never be said to have embraced Unitarianism. Near the end of his life,
he is reported to have said that "he had little
sympathy for the Unitarianism of his day, for
its theology no, for its spiritualism yes." He
attended a Congregationalist church in Boston,
rented a Unitarian pew in Washington, but rarely
occupied it. Shortly before he died he cited
Christ as the Redeemer of men, and insisted emphatically to a Unitarian minister on one occa-
sion that he was a Congregationalist. Samuel
Swett Greene, "George Bancroft," Proceedings of
the American Antiquarian Society (April 29, 18-
91), pp. 18-19; Nye, Bancroft, p. 127; John W.
Rathbun, "George Bancroft on Man and History, "
Transactions of the Wisconsin Academy of Sciences, Arts and Letters, XLIII (1954), 61-62.
(Hereinafter cited as Rathbun, "George Bancroft.") With respect to the theology in

Bancroft's history, Vitzhum notes that the New Englander shared with Puritan writers the notion that writing history was an act of worship. "Theme and Method," 367.

13. Bancroft, History, III, 76.

14. MHS, Bancroft to Edward Everett, July 11, 1834.

15. Ibid., Bancroft to Andrews Norton, February 7, 1820 and June 1, 1820; Diary, December 3, 1820; Bancroft to Levi Frisbie, April 13, 1821; Bancroft to Norton, May 1, 1819. Vitzhum notes that Bancroft clung tightly to the New England religious tradition while he was in Germany. "Theme and Method," 368.

16. Nye, Brahmin Rebel, p. 98.

17. Rathbun, "George Bancroft," 54; MHS, Bancroft to Edward Everett, December 3, 1820; Bancroft to Levi Frisbie, April 13, 1821.

18. Bancroft, History, X, 92-93, 89.

19. Rathbun, "George Bancroft," 63.

20. MHS, Bancroft to Levi Frisbie, April 13, 1821.

21. Bancroft, History, X, 87.

22. Ibid., IX, 502.

23. Nye, Bancroft, p. 112.

24. Robert T. Clark, Jr., Herder: His Life and Thought (Berkeley: University of California Press, 1955), pp. 274, 346, 417.

25. MHS, Bancroft to Edward Everett, December 28, 1820; Bancroft to Andrews Norton, November 5, 1820 and December 25, 1820; Diary, Decem-

ber 3, 1820.

26. Rathbun, "George Bancroft," 64.

27. Richard B. Brandt, The Philosophy of Schleiermacher: the Development of His Theory of Scientific and Religious Knowledge (New York: Greenwood Press, 1968), pp. 81-82, 98, 129, 253. (Hereinafter cited as Brandt, Philosophy of Schleiermacher.)

28. Rathbun, "George Bancroft," 61-62.

29. MHS, Bancroft to Ralph Waldo Emerson, August 11, 1856.

30. George Santayana, "The Genteel Tradition in American Philosophy," Winds of Doctrine: Studies in Contemporary Opinion (London: J. M. Dent & Sons, 1913), pp. 186-215; Perry Miller, "From Edwards to Emerson," Errand into the Wilderness (Cambridge: Harvard University Press, 1964), pp. 184-203.

31. George Bancroft, History of the United States of America from the Discovery of the Continent, 6 volumes. The Author's Last Revision (New York: D. Appleton and Company, 1883), II, 403-404. (Hereinafter cited as Bancroft, History, ALR); Bancroft, History, X, 74-75.

32. Bancroft, History, ALR, I, 317-318.

33. Ibid., II, 405.

34. Bancroft, "Calvin the Reformer," Miscellanies, p. 406.

35. Bancroft, History, ALR, II, 407.

36. Ibid.

37. Jonathan Edwards, Freedom of the Will. Edited by Paul Ramsey (New Haven: Yale University

press, 1957), p. 184.

38. *Ibid.*, p. 328.

39. *Ibid.*, pp. 457-464, Jonathan Edwards to John Erskine, July 25, 1757.

40. *Ibid.*, p. 164.

41. Bancroft, *History*, II, 463.

42. *Ibid.*, II, 462-463.

43. *Ibid.*, IV, 155-157.

44. Howe, *Life and Letters*, II, 114-115, Bancroft to George Ripley, September 12, 1857.

45. MHS, Bancroft to Ralph Waldo Emerson, December 27, 1860.

46. R. W. B. Lewis, *The American Adam: Innocence, Tragedy and Tradition in the Nineteenth Century* (Chicago: University of Chicago Press, 1955), p. 176. (Hereinafter cited as Lewis, *American Adam*.)

47. Bancroft, *History*, ALR, I, 611; George Bancroft, *An Oration Delivered on the Fourth of July, 1826, at Northampton, Mass.* (Northampton: T. Watson Shepard, 1826), pp. 4, 22. (Hereinafter cited as Bancroft, *Oration at Northampton*.)

48. Bancroft, *History*, ALR, IV, 372.

49. Bancroft, *History*, IV, 182.

50. *Ibid.*, V, 5.

51. Bancroft, "The Necessity, the Reality, and the Promise of the Progress of the Human Race," *Miscellanies*, p. 515.

52. *Ibid.*, p. 489.

53. Bancroft, *History*, VIII, 117.

54. Howe, *Life and Letters*, II, 228, Bancroft to C. C. Perkins, June 12, 1869.

55. Bancroft, "The Necessity, the Reality, and the Promise of the Progress of the Human Race," *Miscellanies*, p. 510; Bancroft, *History*, IV, 372-373.

56. G[eorge] B[ancroft], *Reasonableness of Glorying in the Gospel* (1823), p. 254.

57. *Ibid*., p. 255.

58. Bancroft, "The Office of the People in Art, Government, and Religion," *Miscellanies*, p. 409.

59. Bancroft, *History*, ALR, I, 613; III, 328; Bancroft, *History*, II, 463.

60. Bancroft, *History*, II, 372, 342.

61. MHS, Bancroft to Ralph Waldo Emerson, May 13, 1837. "And yet," he mused, "it is so absurd to prefer a shoemaker's apprentice to the prefect of Oxford & the friend of Shaftesbury!"

62. Bancroft, *History*, I, 462.

63. George Bancroft, *Address at Hartford, Before the Delegates to the Young Men of Connecticut, on the Evening of February 18, 1840* (pamphlet, n. d.), pp. 4, 6-7. (Hereinafter cited as Bancroft, *Address at Hartford*). "Democracy, I have said, is reason ruling through the people. It therefore never can begin an offensive war; and, if it could pervade the civilized world, there would be an end of all wars" (*ibid*., p. 9).

64. George Bancroft, *An Oration Delivered Before the Democracy of Springfield and Neighbor-*

ing Towns, July 4, 1836 (Springfield, Mass.: George and Charles Merriam, 1836), pp. 4-6, 10-11. (Hereinafter cited as Bancroft, Springfield Oration.) Fred Somkin calls attention to the theme of altruism in Bancroft's thought; "Obvious self-interest," he notes, "was the blackest sin in Bancroft's catalogue of vices. . . ." Indeed, Somkin finds the "most striking characteristic of the History "its quality as a multi-volume sermon against 'selfishness.'" The favorable reception of Bancroft's work, in this view, "showed that a society straining to snap the last barriers against unrestrained economic competition felt a strong need to re-emphasize its genetic and spiritual congruity with a past believed to be based on the highest of altruistic motives." Unquiet Eagle: Memory and Desire in the Idea of American Freedom, 1815-1860 (Ithaca: Cornell University Press, 1967), pp. 199-201.

65. Bancroft, Springfield Oration, p. 18.

66. Ibid., p. 20.

67. MHS, Bancroft to Ralph Waldo Emerson, July 15, 1858. It was the next year, of course, that Darwin's Origin of Species was published. In a letter to Mrs. Bancroft in 1860, Bancroft expressed "pleasure in a London Quarterly review in refutation of Darwin: 'the faith in ideas is exactly what I approve of; and I believe "preventing grace" precedes the formation of every living thing; as well as of every regeneration of a soul, or any event in history.'" Howe, Life and Letters, II, 115.

68. Bancroft, "The Necessity, the Reality, and the Promise of the Progress of the Human Race," Miscellanies, p. 498.

69. Bancroft, History, II, 17.

70. Ibid., IX, 283.

71. _Ibid._, II, 145.

72. Bancroft, _Address at Hartford_, p. 10.

73. Bancroft, "The Necessity, the Reality, and the Promise of the Progress of the Human Race," _Miscellanies_, pp. 486-487.

74. MHS, Bancroft to Edward Everett, July 27, 1826.

75. Bancroft, _History_, IV, 156-157; V, 199.

76. Bancroft, _History_, ALR, II, 313.

77. Bancroft, "The Necessity, the Reality, and the Promise of the Progress of the Human Race," _Miscellanies_, p. 492; George Bancroft, _Memorial Address on the Life and Character of Abraham Lincoln, Delivered, at the Request of Both Houses of the Congress of America, Before Them, in the House of Representatives at Washington, on the 12th of February, 1866_ (Washington: Government Printing Office, 1866), p. 3. "Of the four historians [whom David Levin characterizes as "romantic," Bancroft, William Prescott, John Lothrop Motley, and Francis Parkman] , only the transcendentalist Bancroft," Levin finds, "expressed a personal view of piety which emphasizes the sovereignty of God." _History as a Romantic Art: Bancroft, Prescott, Motley, and Parkman_ (Stanford: Stanford University Press, 1959), p. 97.

78. Bancroft, _History_, ALR, I, 3; VI, 277.

79. _Ibid._, II, 269.

80. Bancroft, "The Necessity, the Reality, and the Promise of the Progress of the Human Race," _Miscellanies_, p. 490.

81. Bancroft, _History_, ALR, VI, 444; Bancroft, _Oration at Northampton_, p. 25; Bancroft,

"The Necessity, the Reality and the Promise of the Progress of the Human Race," Miscellanies, p. 507. Rathbun notes that Bancroft's "idea of organicism led to the concept of national character. The Edwardsian element and the notion of national character are essential to his thought, both acting as mediating links between his views of human nature and his philosophy of history." "George Bancroft," 73.

82. Bancroft, History, ALR, I, 609.

83. Bancroft, History, X, 150-151.

84. Bancroft, "The Necessity, the Reality, and the Promise of the Progress of the Human Race," Miscellanies, p. 506.

85. Bancroft, History, ALR, II, 324-325; VI, 5-7. R. W. B. Lewis suggests that "there is a sense in which his notion about history was a response to this feeling of instability--in himself, in the world. For Bancroft turned to history as the body of knowledge which could make sense out of an experience characterized by incessant change. . . .history became for Bancroft a myth which revealed the purpose behind the change: an explanation of the very essence of the New World." American Adam, p. 162.

86. George Bancroft, "On the Progress of Civilization, or Reasons Why the Natural Association of Men of Letters Is with the Democracy," The Boston Quarterly Review, I (October, 1838), 390-391. (Hereinafter cited as Bancroft, "Progress of Civilization.") The article was based on Bancroft's 1835 oration, "The Office of the People in Art, Government, and Religion," Miscellanies, pp. 408-435.

87. Bancroft, "Progress of Civilization," 395-396.

88. Ibid., 396-397.

89. _Ibid._, 404-406.

90. Benjamin Walter Heineman, Jr. I believe
somewhat overestimates Bancroft's disillusionment
in the 1850's. "The Historical Mind of George
Bancroft" (Unpublished Thesis Presented to the
Department of History in Partial Fulfillment of
the Requirements for the Degree with Honors of
Bachelor of Arts, Harvard University, 1965),
pp. 57-75, 83-86, and _passim_. Nye notes that
Bancroft "did, as time passed and his own experience widened, temper his enthusiasm for the popular judgment without disturbing his conviction of
its infallibility." The 1854 address was the
last statement of its kind, Nye adds, and Bancroft pruned some of the paeans to progress from
the later revisions of his history. _Bancroft_,
pp. 185, 127. C. Carroll Hollis characterizes
Bancroft's 1854 position as more realistic than
that of the 1830's. Hollis points out that in
1854, Bancroft assigned a more positive role to
Christianity in the progress of society. "Brownson," 48-49, 52.

91. Bancroft, _Miscellanies_, pp. 483-486.

92. _Ibid._, pp. 502-503.

93. _Ibid._, pp. 505-507; Bancroft, "The Office of the People in Art, Government and Religion," _ibid._, p. 422.

94. Bancroft, _History_, ALR, II, 269-270.

95. Cf. Nye: "Men have, he believed, free
will at a surface, transitory level of action,
none at the deeper, permanent level." _Bancroft_,
p. 120. Similarly, Schleiermacher seems to say
"that while, from the point of view of action,
what is done is determined without constraint by
the acting self, from the point of religion from
which the self too must be considered in its
place in the system of nature, the self which
determines its actions freely must be regarded

as itself a consequence of the nature which brought it forth. From the point of view of the whole system, only the world as a whole is ultimately what it is because of its own nature." Bancroft, _Philosophy of Schleiermacher_, p. 135.

96. Bancroft, "The Office of the People in Art, Government, and Religion," _Miscellanies_, pp. 424, 434; Bancroft, "The Necessity, the Reality, and the Promise of the Progress of the Human Race," _ibid._, p. 485; George Bancroft, _Joseph Reed: a Historical Essay_ (New York: W. J. Middleton, 1867), p. 59. Nye mentions that Bancroft was somewhat suspicious of reformers: "Whittier, Garrison, and the others saw the sufferings of the individual and attempted to find a specific, immediately applicable remedy for his plight. Bancroft thought in larger terms of the race, of mankind in the aggregate. . . . History had shown him that the fate of the individual was merged in the fate of the race, that evil and injustice were temporary, and that the inevitable flow of events brought a remedy, in time, for the economic and social evils against which the reformers fought." _Brahmin Rebel_, p. 139.

97. Bancroft, _History_, ALR, VI, 443.

CHAPTER II

JOHN FISKE: COSMIC DARWINIST

Of all significant American thinkers, it
would be difficult to find one who more comfortably belonged to the nineteenth century than John
Fiske. Born in 1842, a generation and a half
after George Bancroft, he regarded his senior
colleague as hopelessly old-fashioned,yet maintained those essentials of Bancroft's historical
vision which could still seem fresh and enlight-
ened to a modern-minded late Victorian. Coming
into the world the same year as William James
and four years after Henry Adams, Fiske had little of the prophetic quality of the former two,
but he was the most representative figure among
them. Intellectually, Fiske belonged to an earlier period than they. His ideas "did not develop
after the 1880's," according to his biographer,[1]
while the most impressive achievements of both
Adams and James came after 1890. Fiske, captured
permanently by the grand philosophical system of
Herbert Spencer, does not offer any original
vision, but in his character both as an intellectual and as a popularizer, he brilliantly adapted
that system to American attitudes, and particularly to American religious attitudes. A phil-

osophic hippopotamus," as Vernon Louis Parrington called him, "warming the chill waters of
Spencerian science with his prodigious bulk,"[2]
Fiske performed a function which was more important in its nineteenth century context than it
may appear today. As the leading American evolutionary philosopher of his time, he indeed
exerted "great influence. . .on the shaping of
the modern mind."[3]

Like Bancroft, Fiske came from a Calvinist
background (theologically more immediate in
Fiske's case), and like Bancroft he accorded a
central historical role to the Protestant Reformation and its heirs. Yet like Bancroft too,
Fiske satisfied his religious impulses in fields
beyond the doctrine of any church. If Bancroft
made a theology of history and its product in
American democracy, Fiske did the same with the
larger vision of cosmic progress afforded by
evolutionary thought.

i.

John Fiske was brought up in an orthodox
Protestant family where "the doctrines of Calvin
and Jonathan Edwards were still taught and emphasized." There was not, as in Bancroft's case, a
father who had rebelled against orthodoxy; this
was left for Fiske himself. He evidently accepted his family's faith quite earnestly until his
late boyhood, undergoing the experience of conversion at fourteen. "I was brought up in the
most repulsive form of Calvinism in which I remained until I was sixteen years of age," he remarked to Spencer in 1864. "My skepticism, ex-
cited in 1858 by geological speculations, was
confirmed in the following year by the work of
Mr. Buckle."[4] Despite his later rediscovery
of the strengths of the Calvinist tradition,
Fiske wholeheartedly abandoned it as religious
doctrine, going so far, in the first flush of

apostaey, as to characterize John Calvin as "a
sort of incarnation of the Devil he talks about."
As an evolutionist he emphatically rejected the
principle of salvation by faith alone; "God," he
thought, "never meant that in this fair but
treacherous world in which he has placed us we
should earn our salvation without steadfast
labour."[5]

Fiske's ultimate resolution of his personal
religious questioning had in it strong elements
of idealism and transcendentalism, akin to those
in Bancroft. Unlike Bancroft, Fiske began his
career after the transcendentalist movement had
passed its years of great vitality, but the
younger man recognized and appreciated its historical significance. The Unitarians, he noted,
had transiently held an untenable position between orthodoxy and freethinking,

> when the ground began to be cut from
> under it by the transcendentalists,
> whose native temperaments, not wanting
> in kinship with that of Edwards, were
> stimulated by a brief contact with
> Kantian and post-Kantian speculation
> in Germany. In Emerson's poetic soul
> the result was a seminal influence
> upon high thinking, in America and in
> the Old World, the power of which we
> cannot but feel, but which it is as
> yet too soon to estimate. . . . When
> German criticism, with the other
> weapons in the powerful hands of Theo-
> dore Parker, freed us from the spectre
> of bibliolatry, it might be said that
> the promise of the Protestant Reforma-
> tion was at length fulfilled. . . .
> On every side, the last quarter of the
> nineteenth century has been preeminent-
> ly the age of the decomposition of
> orthodoxies.[6]

Like Herbert Spencer,Fiske found in Emerson a

thinker in harmony with himself in certain important respects; indeed, H. Burnell Pannill suggests, when from 1860 on "Fiske spoke of 'religion' he referred primarily to this liberal, transcendentalist tradition."[7] Although Emerson in his old age did not embrace the evolutionary doctrine espoused by Spencer and Fiske, the latter discerned a foreshadowing of it in his work, "not only as the divine method of creation, but also as a key to the right understanding of the phenomena of the cosmic universe, including organic life with conscious man as its crowning feature."[8]

More fundamentally, Fiske recognized Emerson's idea of God as similar to his own; perhaps it is not too much to say, with Russel B. Nye, that Fiske's concept of "Omnipresent Energy" was essentially the same as Emerson's "Oversoul." In this view, "Fiske's Cosmic Theism represented Transcendentalism plus science, a blend of the religious-philosophical thought of Emerson with the cosmic science of Darwin and Spencer, the religion of New England as it appeared from the laboratory in the later nineteenth century."[9] This "Cosmic Theism" shared with transcendentalism not strictly a pantheism but a panentheism, the notion of an immanent God not identifiable with the physical universe, but acting in that universe at every point. It was this kind of religion, as has been noted, which could most easily be reconciled with modern scientific understanding.[10] Precluding miracle, it unified physical phenomena through a highly idealistic scheme of uniformly acting divine law. Yet God was not removed from His creation, as in Deistic conceptions, but directly manifest in it. Thus transcendentalism provided a medium by means of which Fiske could interpret science and religion to each other, as it had served Bancroft as a medium for the mutual interpretation of religion and democracy. Indeed, this transitional, interpretative quality in the transcendentalist movement may have been its most lasting significance.

Behind transcendentalism, as its most vital American source, was the Calvinist tradition extending through Jonathan Edwards, and if Fiske removed himself farther from Puritan theology than did Bancroft, he scarcely less bore the marks of his New England background. The two were particularly at one in the strongly Protestant bias of their history, and in their identification of Protestantism with history's liberating forces. Fiske acknowledged the services rendered to civilization by the Roman Catholic Church during most of the Middle Ages, but "after the close of the thirteenth century," it seemed to him, "the whole power of the Church was finally thrown into the scale against the liberties of the people. . . ."[11] Six centuries later, the historian looked forward to the time when "barbarous sacerdotalism and despotic privilege shall have vanished from the face of the earth, and the principles of Protestantism, rightly understood, and of English self-government, shall have become forever the undisputed possession of all mankind."[12] He understood modern history as the struggle between the "Roman" idea of authority, hierarchy, and ritual, and the "English" idea which combined religious individualism with the love of self-government. "From this fortunate alliance of religious and political forces," it seemed to him, "has come all the noble and fruitful work of the last two centuries in which men of English speech have been labouring for the political regeneration of mankind." During a crucial period the English idea had been entrusted to the Puritans, and Fiske found that "among the significant events which prophesied the final triumph of the English over the Roman idea, perhaps the most significant--the one which marks most incisively the dawning of a new era-- was the migration of English Puritans across the Atlantic Ocean, to repeat in a new environment and on a far grander scale the work which their forefathers had wrought in Britain." He added that "it was to this unwonted alliance of intense religious enthusiasm with the instinct of

73

self-government and the spirit of personal independence that the preservation of English free-
don was due."[13] The climactic struggle between
the Roman and the English ideas, however, was the
French and Indian (or Seven Years) War, a conflict which had extraordinary significance for
Fiske. Of the defeat of France in 1763 he noted
that

> It was proclaimed on that day that the
> institutions of the Roman Empire, how-
> ever useful in their time, were at last
> outgrown and superseded, and that the
> guidance of the world was henceforth to
> be, not in the hands of imperial bu-
> reaus or papal conclaves, but in the
> hands of the representatives of honest
> labour and the preachers of righteous-
> ness, unhampered by ritual or dogma.[14]

Fiske found in the Protestant Reformation
much the same philosophical significance as had
Bancroft. The Protestant struggle, he believed,
was one against the assumption of corporate responsibility for "opinion and ceremonial," and on
behalf of individual responsibility. In general,
he thought, "the most energetic Protestants have
been found on the side of absolute freedom in
politics, which always means absolute freedom in
religion sooner or later." In sum, he concluded,
"the Protestantism of Luther is significant mainly as a revolt against primeval notions of the
relations of the individual to the community,
which have long since survived their usefulness."[15]

As with Bancroft, too, John Calvin had a
pivotal historical significance for Fiske; not-
withstanding Fiske's personal distaste for the
Reformer, he felt that "it would be hard to over-
rate the debt which mankind owe to Calvin. The
spiritual father of Coligny, of William the Silent, and of Cromwell must occupy a foremost rank
among the champions of modern democracy. . . .
Calvinism left the individual man alone in the

presence of his God." It brought to the individual, Fiske argued, the sense that "his soul was. . .of infinite value, and the possession of it was the subject of an everlasting struggle between the powers of heaven and the powers of hell." With eternity in the balance, "all distinctions of rank and fortune vanished. . . ." Calvin, then, made men feel, "as it had perhaps never been felt before, the dignity and importance of the individual human soul." In the long run he taught men to fight for freedom. At the same time, Fiske found in Calvinism much that was in striking harmony with modern scientific thought. For example, as he elsewhere noted, "the principle of natural selection is in one respect intensely Calvinistic; it elects the one and damns the ninety and nine."[16]

It was remarkable that the onetime rebel against Protestant orthodoxy should stand finally with such respect for the Calvinist religious vision. If a seventeenth century Calvinist could return to life, Fiske speculated, "he might well say that the God which Mr. Mill offers us, shorn of the attribute of omnipotence, is no God at all. . . . Nay, more, the Calvinist would declare that if we really understood the universe of which humanity is a part, we should find scientific justification for that supreme and victorious faith which cries, 'Though he slay me, yet will I trust in him!' The man who has acquired such faith as this is the true freeman of the universe. . .the man whom nothing can enslave, and whose guerdon is the serene happiness that can never be taken away." In their emphasis on the omnipotence of God, Fiske found the Calvinists to be "much more nearly in accord with our modern knowledge than are Plato and Mill." The progress of modern science, he believed, led

irresistibly to what some German philosophers call monism, but I prefer to call it monotheism. In getting rid of the Devil and regard-

ing the universe as the multiform
manifestation of a single all-pervading Deity, we become for the first
time pure and uncompromising monothe-
ists,--believers in the ever-living,
unchangeable, and all-wise Heavenly
Father, in whom we may declare our
trust without the faintest trace of
mental reservation.[17]

"No loftier ideal has ever been conceived than
that of the Puritan who would fain have made of
the world a City of God": this was John Fiske's
ultimate judgment of Calvinism.[18]

Fiske shared with Bancroft not only the
sense of the liberating function of Calvinism,
but also the concomitant sense of New England's
special role in history. Fiske acknowledged that
American Puritanism was not peculiar to New England,[19] but it was New Englanders who had borne
the Ark of the Covenant:

In all history there has been no
other instance of colonization so
exclusively effected by picked and
chosen men. The colonists knew this,
and were proud of it, as well they
might be. It was the simple truth
that was spoken by William Stoughton
when he said, in his election sermon
of 1688: "God sifted a whole nation,
that he might send choice grain into
the wilderness."[20]

England itself owed much to Puritanism, but as
for the United States, Fiske thought, "what is
noblest in our history to-day, and of happiest
augury for our social and political future, is
the impress left upon the character of our people
by the heroic men who came to New England early
in the seventeenth century."[21]

Above all, the Puritans demonstrated the

76

close connection between Protestantism and liberty:

> . . .when under Elizabeth's successors the great decisive struggle between despotism and liberty was inaugurated, we find all the tremendous force of this newly awakened religious enthusiasm coöperating with the English love of self-government and carrying it under Cromwell to victory. From this fortunate alliance of religious and political forces has come all the noble and fruitful work of the last two centuries in which men of English speech have been labouring for the political regeneration of mankind.[22]

Fiske maintained that there were two main sources of liberal thought. The first was the secular spirit of Galileo, often useful, but tending to "deaden" into the worldliness of a Franklin. The other was "the intense devotion to spiritual ideals which, in spite of all inherited encumbrances of bigotry and superstition, never casts off its allegiance as the final arbiter." This spirit could commit many errors,

> but its drift is toward light and stimulus and exaltation of life as typified in an Emerson. In the darkest days of New England Puritanism the paramount allegiance to reason was never lost sight of; and out of this fact came the triumph of free thinking, although no such result was ever intended.[23]

Massachusetts, therefore, originally the most bigoted colony, became in time the principal American source of free thought. "Hence we find in the New England of to-day a deep religious sense combined with singular flexibility of mind and freedom of thought."[24]

Fiske acknowledged that the Puritans had not
intended to establish religious liberty, yet
their Protestant principle that "religious opinion must be consonant with reason, and that religious truth must be brought home to each individual by rational argument," had fostered an intelligence both conservative and flexible in
which at least limited theological debate could
take place.

> The inevitable result was the liberal
> and enlightened Protestantism which is
> characteristic of the best American
> society at the present day, and which
> is continually growing more liberal as
> it grows more enlightened--a Protestant-
> ism which, in the natural course of de-
> velopment, is coming to realize the
> noble ideal of Roger Williams, but from
> the very thought of which such men as
> Winthrop and Cotton and Endicott would
> have shrunk with dismay.

Only an intensely religious spirit, Fiske
believed, could have accomplished emancipation on
this scale. "The passion for liberty as felt by
a Jefferson or an Adams, abstracted and generalized from the love of particular liberties, was
something scarcely intelligible to the seventeenth century. . . . But the spirit in which
the Hebrew prophet rebuked and humbled an idola-
trous king was a spirit they could comprehend."
It was, then, to the alliance of religious freedom with the "Englishman's love of self-government" that modern freedom owed its existence.[25]

Like Bancroft, Fiske much admired Jonathan
Edwards. The theologian seemed to him "a man who
was one of the wonders of the world, probably the
greatest intelligence that the western hemisphere
has yet seen," and he did not hesitate to rank
him withAugustine, Aquinas, and Calvin. Fiske
regarded him as a prime example of the tendency
in the English Protestant tradition to combine
faith and reason, but he found also an indis-

pensable mystical element in Edwards' thought. "Such mysticism," he supposed, "may be found in minds of medium capacity, but in minds of the highest type I believe it is rarely absent. A mind which has plunged deeply into the secrets of nature without exhibiting such a vein of mysticism is, I believe, a mind sterilized and cut off in one direction from access to the truth."[26]

Fiske agreed further with Bancroft that Edwards had worked a subtle but crucial transformation of Puritan theology:

> As Calvinism enhanced the value of the individual soul by representing it as the subject of a mighty struggle between the powers of heaven and those of hell, so Edwards, while setting forth this notion in all its grimness, gave it a touch of infinite tragedy and pathos through the power with which he conceived the situation of the soul whose salvation trembled in the balance. The distinction between the converted and the unconverted became in his hands more vitally important than the older distinction between the elect and the non-elect. . . . It was due to Edwards that the prime question with every anxious mind was not so much, Am I one of the Elect? as this other question, Have I surrendered my heart to Christ?

This new point of view, he thought, had "worked a vivifying change in the religious consciousness of New England," as manifested in subsequent revivals. The Great Awakening, of which Edwards was a leader, had heightened and deepened the religious life of New England, touching with intense emotion a faith vitiated by "dry logical formulas." As Bancroft had found in Edwards the paramount lesson of universal love, so Fiske concluded that "in producing the tenderness of soul in which the

nineteenth century so far surpassed the eighteenth, a considerable share must be assigned to
the preaching and self-searchings, the prayers
and tears, the jubilation and praise, of the
Great Awakening."[27]

Fiske noted that Edwards had been important in a negative way too, in prompting a reaction in the direction of Arminianism, and
leading ultimately into the channels of Unitarianism and transcendentalism. "In seventeenth-
century Puritanism, therefore, in spite of its
rigid narrowness, there were latent the speculations of an Edwards, the further conclusions
to which some of them were pushed, the reaction
against them, the keen edge of the critical faculty in New England, and much of the free thinking of a later age.'" While Deism had had a
significant degree of appeal, "the dominant influence in New England down to the rise of the
transcendental movement," Fiske believed, "was
that which could be traced back to Edwards." He
perceived that the transcendentalists themselves,
although influenced by German thought,were "not
wanting in kinship with that of Edwards. . . ."[28]
Fiske provided here a glimpse of his own intellectual genealogy.

That the two American historians, Bancroft
and Fiske, should understand the lineaments of
the national history in similar terms, and according to the dominant prejudices of their
countrymen, is not surprising, and does not
prove any fundamental congruence of philosophy.
Yet in many ways, Fiske's understanding of the
universe was similar to Bancroft's. Both took
an essentially Edwardsian position on the question of the freedom of the will, and both regarded the growth of the individual freedom to act
upon the dictates of the will (regarded by Fiske
as a process rather than an entity) as an essential part of progress. Both viewed progress as
the inevitable consequence of the working out of
natural laws, and conceived of the end as in some

sense Christ's reign on earth. Both regarded
this universal progress from a Protestant standpoint, reflecting at important points a common
New England Calvinist background. In both there
was the paradoxical idea of the predestined expansion of freedom.

Yet there is a break as significant as the
continuity between Bancroft and Fiske. The most
obvious difference is the central importance for
the latter of Darwinian and Spencerian evolution,
so dramatically a departure from the Biblical
creationism assumed by Bancroft. On one plane it
might seem that evolution merely provided the
younger man with a more spacious and apparently
more scientific canvas on which to paint the same
romantic-progressive picture of history. But as
religious thinkers the two performed crucially
different functions. Bancroft in interpreting
Calvinism to democracy sought above all to maintain the Protestant assumption of the direct
access of the individual to God. For Fiske this
was no longer a question of central importance.
He undertook the task, at once grander and more
modest, of interpreting to theism the cosmos un-
veiled by nineteenth century physics and biology.

ii.

It was no accident that Fiske entitled his
major work Outlines of Cosmic Philosophy (1874).
He intended his work to be truly cosmic in scope,
defining not only the individual's place in society, but also his place in the universe. If
Fiske's debt to the theory of biological evolution must yield a label, "Social Darwinist" is
less appropriate than "Cosmic Darwinist." His
own choice of terms was deliberate. While he was
willing to admit that earlier philosophies had
also been "cosmic," in attempting to provide
some explanation of the universe, he believed
that never before his own age had "the business

81

of philosophy, regarded as a theory of the universe, been undertaken with so clear and distinct a conception of its true scope and limitations."[29]

Fiske premised "Cosmos" as the "antithetical correlative" of "Chaos." "It denotes the entire phenomenal universe; it connotes the orderly uniformity of nature, and the negation of miracle or extraneous disturbance of any kind."[30] In fact, though, the concept of cosmos carried far more emotional freight. The nineteenth century was in passage from the ancient sense of the universe as man's proper home to the modern feeling that the universe is alien or indifferent to man. The progress of the physical sciences had opened up prospects which could inspire a religious awe even as they chilled with their immensity those who contemplated them. Fiske readily acknowledged that

> the grandest conceptions of Dante and Milton are dwarfed in comparison with the truths which science discloses. But it seems to me that we may go farther than this, and say that we have here reached something deeper than poetry. In the sense of illimitable vastness with which we are oppressed and saddened as we strive to follow out in thought the eternal metamorphosis, we may recognize the modern phase of the feeling which led the ancient to fall upon his knees and adore--after his own crude, symbolic fashion--the invisible Power whereof the infinite web of phenomena is but the visible garment.[31]

Fiske never entirely reconciled his realization that most of the universe was inaccessible to human understanding with his insistence on universal purpose. At best, like the Calvinists, he made a virtue of the mystery of the Absolute; that which was beyond understanding was a fit

82

subject for worship. "Hegel," he thought, "was rash with all the metaphysician's rashness when he said that Humanity is the most perfect type of existence in the universe. Our knowledge of the Cosmos has been aptly compared by Carlyle to the knowledge which a minnow in its native creek has of the outlying ocean."[32] Furthermore, Fiske's insistence on the teleology of the evolutionary process was not an unsophisticated attempt to inscribe human purposes on the universe, nor did it, as eventually qualified, seek to lock the universe into a single evolutionary sequence. Fiske took cognizance particularly of Chauncey Wright's criticism of the Spencerian school of thought. Wright, as he noted, was suspicious of any sort of teleology; "he was inclined to doubt or deny any ultimate coherency among cosmical events. . ."

> From his peculiar point of view, it seemed more appropriate to look upon phenomena as drifting and eddying about in an utterly blind and irrational manner, though now and then evolving, as if by accident, temporary combinations which have to us a rational appearance. "Cosmical weather" was the tersely allusive phrase with which he was wont to describe this purposeless play of events, as if to liken the formation and dissipation of worlds to the capricious changes of the wind.

Wright's objection, he thought, applied only to a popular conception of evolution--as "a presumptuous attempt to go back to the beginning of the universe and give some account of its total past career in terms of progress." One could still take the nebular hypothesis, according to which the solar system was supposed to have evolved out of a "mass of vaporous or nebulous matter," and see in the process it described "a kind of progress judged with reference to human ends." Yet this process need not be regarded as universal or

83

eternal, Fiske pointed out; "it is most explicitly regarded as local and temporary." Throughout
the universe, presumably, similar processes were
going on, but at various stages of "youth, maturity, or decline." In every case, the process of
evolution would eventually come to an end, and
the matter of the extinct system be dissipated.
Indeed, it was "just this endlessly irregular al-
ternation of progress and retrogression, of epochs
of life with epochs of decay, which the doctrine
of evolution asserts as one of its leading theorems," Fiske pointed out. "In no department of
Nature, whether in the heavens or on the earth,
in the constitution of organic life or in the
career of human society, does the doctrine of
evolution assert progress as necessary, universal, and perpetual, but always as a contingent,
local, and temporary phenomenon." Although an
intelligence sufficiently vast could no doubt
discern a "dramatic tendency" in the whole (whether or not toward humanly appreciable ends), Fiske
was obliged to admit that Wright's notion of cosmical weather comported with actual human ignorance:

> As the wind bloweth where it listeth,
> but we know not whence it came, nor
> whither it goes, so in the local con-
> siderations and rarefactions of cos-
> mical matter which make up the giant
> careers of stellar systems we can de-
> tect neither source nor direction. Not
> only is there no reference to any end
> which humanity can recognize as good
> or evil, but there is not the slightest
> indication of dramatic progress toward
> any denouement whatever. There is
> simply the never-ending onward rush of
> events, as undiscriminating, as ruth-
> less, as irresistible, as the current
> of Niagara or the blast of the tropical
> hurricane.[33]

Such concessions to the immensity and unknowability of the universe, although rather twentieth century in tone, seem in the context of Fiske's work as a whole argumentative and reluctant. They did not much affect the import of his message. "The events of the universe are not the work of chance," he elsewhere insisted, "neither are they the outcome of blind necessity." True, other evolutionary processes might be at work in other parts of the cosmos, but in the corner that directly concerned man, one could see "all things working together toward the evolution of the highest spiritual attributes of Man. . . ."[34] He took issue with Thomas Huxley's position that natural process had no relation to moral ends. Rather, asked Fiske, "does not the cosmic process exist purely for the sake of moral ends?" The answer was emphatic:

> Our historical survey of the genesis of Humanity seems to show very forcibly that a society of Human souls living in conformity to a perfect Moral Law is the end toward which, ever since the time when our solar system was a patch of nebulous vapour, the cosmic process has been aiming.[35]

The subjects of this study did not necessarily insist on literally universal purpose; like William James, indeed, they might explicitly reject it. What they did expect, in man's part of the universe, was, as Fiske put it, "a discernible dramatic tendency"--this much even James could have endorsed--and generally too "a clearly marked progress of events toward a mighty goal."[36] The theme of cosmic drama is a recurrent one; we are reminded of Carl Becker's assertion that it is the consciousness of it that separates the Enlightenment from our own century. The generation of Fiske and James was present at the fading of the drama, but Fiske in his enthusiasm for the prospects opened by science, and especially by Darwinism, mistook its last glow for a new illumination of cosmic purpose. It seemed to him as the nineteenth century drew to a close that

As the startling disclosures of the
past century become assimilated in our
moral structure, we see that man is
now justified in feeling himself as
never before a part of nature, that
the universe is no inhospitable, wander-
ing place, but his own home; that the
mighty sweep of its events from age to
age are but the working out of a cosmic
drama in which his part is the leading one; and that all is an endless
manifestation of one all-pervading Power, Protean in its myriad phases, yet
essentially similar to the conscious
soul within us.[37]

The paradox was that the more western man came
to regard himself as a part of nature, the less
at home he felt in it.

Fiske represents a point of balance, at
which the sense of cosmic hospitality was not yet
overcome by alienation, and at which the hubris of
human progress was tempered by an awareness that
human purpose was far from coextensive with the
universe. For present sensibilities, the hubris
was insufficiently tempered, and Fiske seems consequently smug and sentimental. He was of too
sanguine a temperament to see the fragility of
his system, as precarious in its hope as the
Thomistic system symbolized as the Gothic cathedral by Henry Adams a generation after Fiske's
major work. Fiske was far from being the most
brilliant articulator of a Zeitgeist, but his
"cosmic philosophy" amounted to a dangerously
balanced cathedral of nineteenth century confidence and fear. Had he possessed a more ironic
temperament, he might have been struck by the
curiosity of a situation in which man attained
godlike knowledge and powers even as the quality
of godliness became unknowable to him:

While in the study of the stellar
universe we contemplate the process
of evolution on a scale so vast that

86

reason and imagination are alike baf-
fled in the effort to trace out its
real significance, and we are overpowered by the sense of the infinity
that surrounds us; on the other hand,
in the study of the moral sense we
contemplate the last and noblest product of evolution which we can ever
know,--the attribute latest to be unfolded in the development of psychical
life, and by the possession of which
we have indeed become as gods, knowing
the good and the evil. The theorems
of ethics present to us the process of
evolution in its extremes of extension
and of intension respectively. For although upon other worlds far out in
space there may be modes of existence
immeasurably transcending Humanity, yet
these must remain unknowable by us.
And while this possibility should be
allowed its due weight in restraining
us from the vain endeavour to formulate
the infinite and eternal Sustainer of
the universe in terms of our own human
nature, as if the highest symbols intelligible to us were in reality the
highest symbols, nevertheless it can
in no way influence or modify our
science. To us the development of the
noblest of human attributes must ever
remain the last term in the stupendous
series of cosmic changes, of which the
development of planetary systems is the
first term.[38]

Fiske was not a man to remain long comfort-
able on what William James called the "perilous
edge" of life, where intellectual safety ends.
His proper function was that of an interpreter;
interpreting science and religion to each other,
he attempted the transmutation of traditional
anthropomorphic theism into a cosmic theism. But
if this seems now an unadventurous project, it

was not without its risks--the fact that the
"cosmic" system has since collapsed is proof of
this--nor was it an ignoble one. Like William
James, Henry Adams, and other perceptive members
of his generation, Fiske glimpsed the limitations
both of religious orthodoxy and of science in its
positivistic pretensions. If his solution seems
less interesting than theirs, it is partly because he attempted the larger task of preserving
their essential elements in a unified system.
His failure was consequently magnified.

Fiske's rejection of positivism, despite his
sense of science as the source and standard of
truth, stemmed from his idealistic and religious
temperament. Although admiring Auguste Comte for
"introducing the objective method into depart-
ments of research where previously metaphysical
interpretation had reigned supreme and unques-
tioned," Fiske came to regard the great positivist as "a mighty though fallen thinker," "a great
mind utterly shattered and ruined."[39] The "fatal
defect" in Comte, he thought, was his "total
omission of moral feeling as a factor in social
evolution." And if the positivist's apparent
amorality ran counter to the American grain, so
equally did his lack of a vision of freedom; it
seemed to Fiske that "Comte's ideal state of society is a state in which the units of the community possess no more individual freedom than
the cells which make up the tissues of a verte-
brate animal"--virtually a spiritual despotism,
and one which would reverse the course of social
development toward greater freedom. Above all,
Fiske distinguished between positivism and his
own "Cosmic Philosophy" from a religious point of
view, emphasizing that

> with reference to the fundamental
> truths of Christianity, and like-
> wise with reference to the time-
> honoured institutions which are
> woven into the fabric of modern
> society, our Cosmic Philosophy is

eminently conservative,--owning no fellowship either with the radical Infi-
delity of the eighteenth century or
with the world-mending schemes of Positivism.[40]

Were the world "peopled with automata," Fiske
thought, "then materialism perhaps would afford
a satisfactory explanation of the world. But the
moment the first trace of conscious intelligence
is introduced, we have a set of phenomena which
materialism can in no wise account for." The
gulf between mind and matter yawned as wide as in
the time of Descartes.[41]

Of all those with whom in his youth Fiske
associated a positivistic point of view, Herbert
Spencer most seized upon his imagination. Indeed, it was Fiske's misfortune as a thinker that
he never escaped the gravitational attraction of
the English "synthetic" philosopher. Spencer
"showed that same amazing power of thought and
that same inconceivable amount of learning which
he shows in whatever he undertakes to write
about," Fiske reported in 1863. "I felt a sense
of awe after closing the book, as if I had been
holding communion with Omniscience: and this I
never have felt when reading any one else."[42]
It was a judgment that Fiske never revised. Ten
years later, he was of the opinion that only
Aristotle, Berkeley, and Kant could be compared
with Spencer for insight into mental processes.[43]
In his Cosmic Philosophy he did not shrink from
comparing the Synthesist's "unique power of
psychological analysis" with the highest mathematical genius:

As in grandeur of conception and
relative thoroughness of elaboration,
so also in the vastness of its con-
sequences--in the extent of the revolution which it is destined to effect
in men's modes of thinking, and in
their views of the universe--Mr.

> Spencer's discovery is on a par with
> Newton's. Indeed, by the time this
> treatise is concluded, we may perhaps
> see reasons for regarding it as, in
> the latter respect, the superior of
> the two.[44]

What Fiske most admired in Spencerian philosophy was the universality with which its principles of evolution could be applied. There was
no subject unaffected by the doctrine, no area
that could escape the sweep of Spencer's thought.
The law of evolution, Fiske believed, was "the
first generalization concerning the concrete
universe as a whole which has been framed in
conscious conformity to the rigorous requirements
of the objective method, and which has therefore
served to realize the prophetic dream of Bacon, by
presenting Philosophy as an organism of which
the various sciences are members."[45] What was
Spencer's "sublime discovery," comparable to Newton's discovery of the law of gravitation? It was
that "the Universe is in a continuous process of
evolution from the homogenous to the heterogeneous.
. . ." Or, as Fiske stated the principle in the
Cosmic Philosophy:

> We are now prepared to show in-
> ductively that wherever, as in organic
> aggregates, the conditions permit, the
> integration of matter and concomitant
> dissipation of motion, which primarily
> constitutes Evolution, is attended by a
> continuous change from indefinite, in-
> coherent homogeneity to a definite, co-
> herent heterogeneity of structure and
> function, through successive differen-
> tiations and integrations.[46]

Spencer, in Fiske's view, had essentially completed the "unification of nature," which had
been the chief intellectual accomplishment of
the nineteenth century.[47]

90

Spencer and his American disciple attempted to close the gap between biological evolution and the evolution of society. Social progress, as Fiske understood it, consisted "primarily in the integration of small and simple communities into larger communities that are of higher and higher orders of composition; and in the more and more complete subordination of the psychical forces which tend to maintain isolation to the psychical forces which tend to maintain aggregation. In these respects the prime features of social progress are the prime features of evolution in general." In a highly abstract sense, then, the evolution of life and the evolution of society were identical processes subject to law. Indeed, the adequately trained sociologist should be able to predict in its basic outlines the future course of society as surely as the astronomer could the future position of the stars.[48]

There was, however, a crucial difference between biological and social evolution. "In organic development," Fiske explained, "the individual life of the parts is more and more submerged in the corporate life of the whole. In social development, corporate life is more and more subordinated to individual life. The highest social life is that in which the units have the greatest possible freedom."[49] He carefully avoided the simple determinism and amorality of a vulgar social Darwinism. The principle of the "survival of the fittest," he was aware, required important modifications when applied to human beings. From the human standpoint, indeed, nature's way seemed very wasteful and destructive of life; upon such a view, "the Cosmic Process appears in a high degree unintelligent, not to say immoral." Aware also of Thomas Huxley's distinction between natural and ethical process, Fiske did not think that Huxley had meant to suggest a real breach of continuity, both processes being parts of the general process of evolution. True, Fiske admitted, the "survival of the fittest" as such had no relation to moral ends. But,

91

he believed, there were other "agencies" at work in evolution besides that of natural selection, agencies which opened the door wide to moral purpose. "I think it can be shown," Fiske wrote in his late essay Through Nature to God, "that the principles of morality have their roots in the deepest foundations of the universe, that the cosmic process is ethical in the profoundest sense. . . ."[50]

On one point especially Fiske was emphatic; materialism was not sufficient to account for the phenomena of consciousness. Further, life itself progressed from the physical to the psychical. "It appears," he concluded, ". . . .that while in the vegetal world, and in the lower regions of the animal world, the life is purely or almost purely physico-chemical, it becomes more and more predominantly psychical as we ascend in the animal world, until at the summit it is mainly psychical." From the primitive stage of reflex action, life progressed to the reason and volition of its highest forms. Thus, "the glorious consummation toward which organic evolution is tending is the production of the highest and most perfect psychical life." Indeed, he believed, "the perfecting of Man consists mainly in the ever-increasing predominance of the life of the soul over the life of the body."[51]

This vision of human progression was essential to Fiske's thought. The Darwinian theory of evolution impressed itself on the popular mind largely as a challenge to religious orthodoxy, and it was the primary achievement of John Fiske to reconcile, probably more successfully than any other American of his day, evolution with a religious understanding of the universe. Evolution did not reduce man to insignificance or make existence meaningless. "The Darwinian theory, properly understood, replaces as much teleology as it destroys," he was confident. "From the first dawning of life we see all things working together toward one mighty goal, the evolution of

92

the most exalted spiritual qualities which characterize Humanity."[52]

The "theological question," Fiske thought, was left by the Darwinians where it was before. Evolution might provide an explanation for the "existence of highly complicated organisms"; yet the consistent theist could always postulate at every point of natural process "an immediate manifestation of the creative action of God." (Science itself, of course, could have recourse to no such explanation.)[53] Indeed, the evolutionary philosophy was virtually a system of theology for Fiske, in the same way that progress based on inspired reason was for Bancroft. Evolution, dressed as the Cosmic Philosophy, fixed man in the universe, in eternity, and in the sweep of universal processes in a new and, to a nineteenth century intellect, more plausible fashion. It related man anew to God. "Darwinism," Fiske concluded, "certainly displaced many time-honoured theological interpretations, but at this point it brought back ten times as much theology as it ever displaced."[54]

Fiske's outlook became not only increasingly religious and teleological, but increasingly and specifically Christian. Impressed in 1873 by the suggestion that Evolution required an Evolver, he expressed the opinion that the doctrine would soon be taken up by the orthodox.[55] In his own case, it could almost be said that orthodoxy was taken up by the evolutionist. While he never re-embraced the miraculous doctrines of Christianity, he obviously found shelter in the Cosmic Philosophy for other of its basic attributes. The universe clearly became the dwelling place of the Almighty:

> Thus while the Earth Spirit goes on, unhasting, yet unresting, weaving in the loom of Time the visible garment of God, we begin to see that even what look like failures and blemishes have been from the outset involved in

> the accomplishment of the all-wise and
> all-holy purpose, the perfecting of the
> spiritual Man in the likeness of his
> Heavenly Father.[56]

More directly, he looked forward to "a stage of
civilization. . .in which human sympathy shall be
all in all, and the spirit of Christ shall reign
supreme throughout the length and breadth of the
earth."[57] The one-time religious rebel discovered that the evolutionary philosophy taught finally the immanence of God,

> an ever present God,--not an absentee
> God who once manufactured a cosmic
> machine capable of running itself, ex-
> cept for a little jog or poke here and
> there in the shape of a special provi-
> dence. The doctrine makes God our
> constant refuge and support, and Nature
> his true revelation; and when all its
> religious implications shall have been
> set forth, it will be seen to be the
> most potent ally that Christianity has
> ever had in elevating mankind.[58]

In charting his course from "anthropomorphic" to "cosmic" theism, Fiske's approach was to
argue that this passage involved minimal change in
the substance of religious truth while working
radical change in its accidents. Indeed, he insisted, "in the progress from Anthropomorphism to
Cosmism the religious attitude remains unchanged
from the beginning to the end. And thus the apparent antagonism between Science and Religion,
which is the abiding terror of timid or superficial minds, and which the Positive Philosophy did
comparatively little to remove, is in the cosmic
Philosophy utterly and forever swept away."[59] In
this view the substitution of scientific for religious symbols worked no basic change in ethical
or religious values. "Far from rejecting as a
mythologic fiction the doctrine that sin is a
violation of God's decrees, entailing inevitable

94

punishment," for example, "science recognizes therein the anthropomorphic version of the truth that every failure in the system of adjustments in which life consists is followed inevitably by pain, in some one of its lower or higher forms."[60] Scientifically defined, sin was simply a "wilful violation of a law of nature," such as an action which tended to throw the individual out of balance with his environment.[61] Most important, though, was the supposition, reiterated by Fiske, that the evolutionary doctrine replaced, or more than replaced, any teleology that it destroyed. The new interpretation of religion maintained the cosmic drama intact.

This was intended as no mere palliative to religious sentiment. Fiske was convinced that evolution was the basis of a far greater theology than the traditional. He took pains to deny that his cosmic theism was tantamount to a hazy sort of pantheism. The deity was not the universe as pantheists believed; rather, he asserted, "while the universe is the manifestation of Deity, yet is Deity something more than the universe." Thus he expounded theism "in its most consistent and unqualified form." Cosmic theism, he argued, was the first truly to view God as an infinite being, unbound by human standards or conceptions. "Though as an act of lip homage anthropomorphism asserts the infinitude and omnipotence of God," he thought, "yet in reality it limits and localizes him."[62] Similarly, in adopting the Spencerian argument that moral beliefs were the product of evolution, he could argue that the immense length of time required to cultivate morality gave it a value proportionate to the effort. Right and wrong were thus rooted in the deepest foundations of the universe.[63]

Fiske sought to anchor his theism in both the knowability and the unknowability of God. In the case of anthropomorphic theism, every major scientific discovery was a threat to religion, because in advancing the sphere of naturalistic explanation, it correspondingly confined that of supernatural explanation. The cosmic theist, on the other hand, was able to see in the extension of knowledge only the confirmation of his faith. It was the tendency of modern science, he believed, to abolish the theological distinction between divine action and natural law. Indeed, he continued, "it is scientific inquiry, working quite independently of theology, which has led us to the conclusion that all the dynamic phenomena of Nature constitute but the multiform revelation of an Omnipresent Power that is not identifiable with Nature."[64] To understand these phenomena was, in one sense, to understand the "omnipresent Power" behind them.

In another way, however, Fiske's God was radically unknowable, and hence unassailable as the mere apotheosis of man. By the formula of his dualism, the deity was unknowable insofar as infinite and absolute, but knowable in the order of its phenomenal manifestations, and knowable as the eternal source of a moral law. This was a formulation well in keeping with standard Christain approaches to God. Fiske was particularly within the Protestant tradition in acknowledging, in his Outlines of Cosmic Philosophy, that the Absolute "is utterly and forever unknowable." But the existence of God was the supreme truth: "There exists a POWER to which no limit in time or space is conceivable of which all phenomena, as presented in consciousness, are manifestations, but which we can know only through these manifestations." Regarding God as "quasi-psychical" rather than "quasi-material," Fiske recognized that the Deity was not to be dissected by scientific inquiry:

> To us, therefore, as to the Israelite of old, the very name of Jehovah is that which is not to be spoken. Push our scientific research as far as we may, pursuing generalization until all phenomena, past, present, and future, are embraced within a single formula, we shall never fathom this ultimate

96

mystery, we shall be no nearer the
comprehension of this omnipresent
Energy. Here science must ever rev-
erently pause, acknowledging the presence of the mystery of mysteries.
Here religion must ever hold sway, re-
minding us that from birth until death
we are dependent on a Power to whose
eternal decrees we must submit, to
whose dispensations we must resign our-
selves, and upon whose constancy we may
implicitly rely.[65]

Yet whereas anthropomorphic theism, expecting of
God a quasi-human intervention in natural processes, depended on phenomena not yet scientifically explained, "the cosmic conception of Deity,
. . .being planted in the region of the Unknowable, which is coextensive with that of the Knowable, has no such precarious tenure, and all that
the progress of discovery can do is to enlarge
and strengthen it."[66]

Fiske saw clearly enough that an anthropomorphic God was unacceptable to a scientific
intelligence, and believed that the deanthropo-
morphizing process was a part of religious progress. Yet with all his intent to disown the anthropomorphic God, Fiske allowed a great deal of
anthropomorphism to remain in, or creep back into,his notion of the Absolute. Although the
grosser forms of anthropomorphism were properly
to be pursed, he remarked, "the notion of a kinship between God and man remains, and is rightly
felt to be essential to theism. Or, again, "take
away the ethical significance from our conceptions of the Unseen World and the quasi-human
God, and no element of significance remains. All
that was vital in theism is gone."[67] The comments reveal the dilemma of Fiske's theistic position, which was less easily soluble than he
would admit. The traditional anthropomorphic
God seemed scientifically no longer plausible,
while a denatured Absolute seemed hardly to matter.

Actually, of course, John Fiske's God was distinctly a Christian and even a Protestant God. His histories traced the progress of religious thought to its highest pre-cosmic theist expression under the aegis of Luther and Calvin. He acknowledged Christianity, "in the deepest sense," to be his religion, and predicted a stage of civilization in which Christ's spirit would reign supreme.[68] He went so far in the direction of orthodoxy as to entertain favorably the notion of personal immortality. "In the course of evolution," he remarked, "there is no more philosophical difficulty in man's acquiring immortal life than in his acquiring the erect posture and articulate speech." An essential part of the question, as he acknowledged, was "the craving, almost universally felt, for some theological solution to the problem of existence." The simple desire for immortality he thought was less strong than "the feeling which associates a future life" with such a teleology. While admitting that the problem carried one completely beyond the range of experience, Fiske—much like William James in this instance—thought it permissible to entertain a belief where the evidence was inaccessible.[69] Nothing more clearly indicates the import of his thought than this attempt to derive heaven from evolution.

iii

An essentially religious teleology more and more evidently formed the core of John Fiske's philosophy, a system of thought which in the tradition of Edwards and Bancroft taught the predetermination of the course of history, while making room for a larger sense of evolutionary heterogeneity. Like Edwards and Henry Adams, he mixed science with religion in the attempt to construct an intelligible cosmos, but remained far more bound to his time and place than either, despite his aspirations to universality. Lacking

the dark counterweights of hell or of chaos, his
thought was provincially optimistic; yet he merits respect for the spaciousness of vision within
which he attempted to reconcile the old antinomies of freedom and necessity, diversity and order, change and continuity.

Despite the modest evolution which his own
philosophy underwent over the years, Fiske remained consciously committed to a conception of
evolutionary progress that was fundamentally linear and deterministic. As an historian as well
as an evolutionist, he held that there could be
no compromise between law and blind chance. If
definite causation in history were denied, "all
conception of progress, as well as all conception
of order, is at an end. Thus the vast domain of
History. . .becomes an unruly Chaos. . . ." Re-
gardless of individuals, rather, he was persuaded
that history followed its predestined and upward
course:

> Now by far the most obvious and
> constant characteristic common to a
> vast number of social changes is that
> they are changes from a worse to a bet-
> ter state of things,--that they consti-
> tute phases of Progress. It is not as-
> serted that human history has in all
> times and places been the history of
> progress; it is not denied that at
> various times and in many places it has
> been the history of retrogression; but
> attention is called to the fact--made
> trite by long familiarity, yet none the
> less habitually misconceived--that
> progress has been on the whole the most
> constant and prominent feature of the
> history of a considerable and important
> portion of mankind.

Fiske's historical determinism was qualified, and
even at first glance contradicted, by the assertion that progress was neither necessary nor

universal. In particular, it seemed to him that
"the theological habit of viewing progressive-
ness as a divine gift to man, and the metaphysical habit of regarding it as a necessary attribute of humanity" were ". . .equally unsound
and equally fraught with error. . . . Far from
being necessary and universal, progress. has been
in eminent degree contingent and partial."[70] Yet
at bottom, Fiske's position seems hardly to have
differed from the providential and metaphysical
schemes which he thought too rigid. He remained
confident that a law of progress, adapted from
the Spencerian concept of progression from in-
definite, incoherent homogeneity to definite, coherent heterogeneity, was the proper law of history, and that social changes conformed to "fixed
and ascertainable laws."[71]

Like many other American thinkers, Fiske
felt obliged to wrestle with freedom as a philosophical question. A progressive and liberal
view of history, particularly one in the Anglo-
American political tradition, had somehow to be
reconciled with the rule of determined law. As
did Bancroft, Fiske identified progress with
the expansion of freedom. But what did Fiske
mean by "freedom"? On the abstruse but basic
question of the freedom of the will, he stood
comfortably within the Protestant tradition to
which Bancroft and Jonathan Edwards belonged.
He did not take the extreme determinist position
that free will was incompatible with the laws of
causation. As Philip Wiener points out, Fiske
did not deny the existence of uncaused and un-
conditioned free will, which he thought a meaningless concept, "but it was clear to Fiske that
the heart of the problem of free will is not the
imputing of necessity or fortuitousness to
events, but the pragmatic question of fixing
responsibility in moral and legal situations
relative to given psychological, social, and
political conditions." Individuality and law
were historically compatible for Fiske, Wiener
adds; an act of free will was "an individuation

100

of equally determined possibilities."[72]

Stripped of metaphysical jargon and restated
in precise scientific terms, Fiske thought, the
question of free will became easy. It was a myth,
he pointed out, that "the Will" was an entity
with desires and intentions of its own. "If instead of 'The Will' we look at the act of willing,--which is not an entity, but a dynamic process," he suggested, "--then it becomes absurd to
talk of this act as being either free or not free,
and we must seek for some other word than 'freedom' by which to designate its alleged want of
causal connection with preceding physical states."
Fiske agreed with Edwards that volition follows
the strongest motive; he agreed with him further
that "so long as circumstances allow volition to
follow the strongest motive, then we truly say
that we are free and responsible for our actions."[73]

> In point of fact a comet does
> "form its own future" in the same way
> that a man does. The state of a
> heavenly body at any given moment is
> a product, partly of the forces, molar
> and molecular, with which it was en-
> dowed at the preceding moment, and
> partly of the forces simultaneously
> exerted upon it by environing heavenly
> bodies. The case of human volition
> differs from this in nothing save the
> number and complexity, and consequent
> relative incalculableness, of the
> forces at work.[74]

The mind, Fiske was convinced, was impelled to
believe in the necessity and universality of
causation. However, he believed that the real
question was not whether the action of men could
be free, but whether causation was compatible
with freedom. Fiske's answer was that not only
were causation and liberty compatible, but that
"it is not causation, but the absence thereof,

which is as incompatible with liberty as it is with law." His argument was that the "causationist," believing that volition follows the strongest motive, could endeavor to strengthen certain motives and repress others, while on the theory that volitions are causeless, "all methods of self-discipline become of no avail. Causeless actions were robbed of their moral content, and a malefactor such as Philip II became merely a chance menace like the plague. Only if a villain's crimes were a necessary outgrowth of his character could moral value be attached. "Freedom of the Will," Fiske suggested, might better be called "lawlessness of volition," closer to fatalism than to liberty. Both fatalism and "free-will" ignored causation, he noted; "each is incompatible with personal freedom; the only difference between them being that the one sets up Chance, while the other sets up Destiny, as the arbiter of human affairs."[75]

On the social scale as well as on the individual, Fiske believed, it was necessary to assume causation. If causation were denied in history, pattern and progress would be at an end; history would be an "unruly chaos."[76] Here too, it appeared, the alternatives were Law and Chance, and Fiske scoffed at the idea that human life could be an exception to the universal sway of law. Organic existence had grown from nonorganic, following physical laws.

> Of this aggregate or organic existence, man, the most complex and perfect type, lives and moves and has his being in strict conformity to law. His periods of activity and repose are limited by planetary rotations. His achievements, physical and mental, are determined by the rate of his nutrition, and by the molecular structure and relative weight of the nervous matter contained in him. His very thoughts must chase each other along definite paths and contiguous channels marked out by the laws of

association. Throughout these various
phenomena, already generalized for us
by astronomers, geologists, biologists
and psychologists, we know that neither
at any time nor in any place is law
interfered with,--that yesterday, today and forever, the effect follows the
cause with inevitable and inexorable
certainty. And yet we are asked to believe that in one particular corner of
the universe, upon the surface of one
little planet, in a portion of the
organism of one particular creature,
there is one special phenomenon called
volition, in which the law of causation
ceases to operate, and everything goes
helter-skelter.[77]

To the contrary, no trace of hazard or incongru-
ity was there to be found in the universe.[78]

Fiske's conception of causation, like the
rest of his thought, took on an increasingly religious coloration. He came to the conclusion
that "the impetus of modern scientific thought
tends with overwhelming force towards the conception of a single First Cause, or Prime Mover,
perpetually manifested from moment to moment in
all the Protean changes that make up the universe." For this First Cause he preferred the
term "God" to Spencer's "Unknowable." He emphatically denied that determinism was tantamount to
materialism, citing Jonathan Edwards in ample
refutation of this notion. He himself, of course,
was no materialist. The decisive argument, for
him, was that "no mere collocation of material
atoms could ever have evolved the phenomena of
Consciousness."[79] As John Stephen Martin points
out, Fiske was essentially within the tradition
of idealism to which Jonathan Edwards and Ralph
Waldo Emerson belonged, although, unlike Edwards,
he did not consider the will to be an actual entity. In the modified idealism of Fiske's cosmology, Martin notes, "there is but one world,

103

phenomena, which can be known and which also includes our minds."[80]

This was a monism, however, which constituted a pluralizing process. Fiske's guiding Spencerian principle of evolution from incoherent homogeneity to coherent heterogeneity required him to champion diversity. "The great problem of civilization," he thought, "is how to secure sufficient uniformity of belief and action among men without going so far as to destroy variety of belief and action." Other things being equal, he added, the nation which most encouraged variety would achieve the highest civilization. This was true, for example, of local liberties and self-government. He was impressed by the English achievement of developing a complex civilization "without essentially departing from the primitive Aryan principle of government"--i.e. the principle of local self-government, as manifested notably in the town meeting of New England.[81] "How to insure peaceful concerted action throughout the Whole, without infringing upon local and individual freedom in the Parts,--this" he concluded, has ever been the chief aim of civilization, viewed on its political side," with the failure or success of nations judged according to this end.[82] But variety was no mere political technique; it was inherent in the central vision of his cosmic theism. "The consummate product of a world of evolution," Fiske suggested, "is the character that creates happiness, that is replete with dynamic possibilities of fresh life and activities in directions forever new. Such a character is the reflected image of God, and in it are contained the promise and potency of life everlasting."[83]

Heterogeneity thus defined freedom for Fiske, as the individual's obedience to divine revelation defined it for Bancroft. The principle was also well adapted to a sanguine version of moral progress, which in turn went hand-in-hand with a confident view of national destiny. Heterogeneity, he believed, was essential to moral growth, and the liberal Anglo-American political tradition seemed to him the fullest expression of coherent heterogeneity. In these respects, for Fiske as for many others, nineteenth century middle class optimism proved most seductive and misleading.

Progress to the cosmic theist meant above all moral progress, and in a particularly Christian sense. The fundamental characteristic of the process, Fiske stated in his <u>Cosmic Philosophy</u>, was "the <u>continuous weakening of selfishness and the continuous strengthening of sympathy</u>. Or--to use a more convenient and somewhat more accurate expression suggested by Comte--it is a gradual supplanting of <u>egoism</u> by <u>altruism</u>." Hostility, he believed, had been the normal state of primitive man, sympathetic and social feelings being then "confined chiefly to the conjugal relations." Yet in such minimal sympathies had been contained the germs of all social progress. At each successive stage in history, the altruistic feelings found a "wider scope for action," while egoism was correspondingly weakened. Above all, it appeared, "the spirit of Christianity, first rendered possible by Roman cosmopolitanism, has made,and is ever making, wider and deeper conquests as civilization advances."[84] Fiske installed the ethical process directly within the evolutionary or "cosmic" process. At bottom, he acknowledged, it was "all a process of the survival of the fittest. . . ." Yet moral sentiment was the natural result of the cosmic process and for the sake of survival, egoism had gradually to yield to altruism. And in practical terms, which seemed plausible enough in the late nineteenth century, moral progress meant the supplanting of the predatory and military phase of civilization by a peaceful and industrial phase, as men grew naturally less brutal and more humane.

Humanity progressed unevenly, of course.

105

Although contemptuous of George Bancroft's History of the United States ("Its grasp upon historical facts. . . .is feeble and its style soph-
omorical, while it abounds in vapid declama-
tion")[86] Fiske's version of history agreed with
Bancroft's in their view of the special American
mission in history. Fiske was by no means a
simple chauvinist, national or racial. "Through
the literature of all nations," he was aware,
"runs that same ludicrous assumption that our
people are better than other people, and from
this it is but a short step to the kindred assumption that the same national acts which are
wrongful in other people are meritorious in our-
selves."[87] He claimed to eschew the term "Anglo-
Saxon" as absurd and inaccurate, and commented
on "the fallaciousness of explaining all national
peculiarities by a cheap reference to 'blood' . .
. ."[88] Nevertheless, a people could play a special role in history, whatever the weakness of
racial categories, and Fiske believed that there
was such a role for the peoples commonly referred
to as Anglo-Saxon. Within a century, he predicted, "all the elements of military predominance on the earth, including that of simple nu-
merical superiority, will have been gathered into
the hands not merely of men of European descent
in general, but more specifically into the hands
of the offspring of the Teutonic tribes who con-
quered Britain in the fifth century." The very
laws of the universe seemed to be working for
these favored people.[89]

Still, Fiske's appreciation of American
democracy was more moderate and less mystical
than that of Bancroft, and his strictures on the
strident democratic sentiment in the United
States following the War of 1812 could have been
directed at the older historian: "There was," he
said, "a kind of democratic fanaticism in the air.
A kind of metaphysical entity called the People
(spelled with a capital) was set up for men to
worship. Its voice was the voice of God; and,
like the king, it could do no wrong. It had

106

lately been enthroned in America, and was going shortly to renovate the world. People began to forget all about the slow growth of our constitutional liberty through ages of struggle in England and Scotland."90 Bancroft had also recognized the evolutionary unfolding of American institutions, but there was in Bancroft's insistence upon the direct access of the individual to God an essentially radical principle, however moderate may have been his own political disposition. Fiske's understanding of historical evolution, lacking this sharply defined pietism, was basically more conservative.

It was in the nature of Fiske's Cosmic Philosophy that the progressive impulse was balanced and complemented by the conservative. As a thoughtful man of the nineteenth century, Fiske was aware of the modern acceleration of history, and noted the tremendous rate of scientific and technical progress in his own time. Being able to rationalize them within the evolutionary formula, he did not take the cataclysmic view of such developments that Henry Adams did. The more heterogeneous the organism became, he reasoned, the more heterogeneous its environment; the more heterogeneous its environment, the more heterogeneous the organism was required to become. This was to say that the more man increased in knowledge, the more complex he made his environment, and the more knowledgeable he must become, and so on indefinitely. It could be stated as a rule, then, that "the greater the amount of progress already made, the more rapidly must progress go on."91

But if evolution contained a built-in principle of accelerating progress, it also contained a stabilizing principle. For, "as civilization advances, the organized experience of past generations becomes to a greater and greater extent the all-important factor of progress. As Comte expresses it, in one of his profoundest aphorisms, the empire of the dead over the living increases from age to age." Thus the environment

107

of Americans, for instance, was determined to a far greater extent by the victory of the Greeks at Marathon and that of the Christians at Tours, by the Reformation and by scientific inquiry from Archimedes to Faraday, than it was by the direction of the Rocky Mountains or the course of the Gulf Stream.

This effect of the growing weight of the past simply reinforced the principle of continuity which was inherent in the idea of evolution. With this in mind, Fiske did not hesitate to face directly the question of whether "the critical temper of our Cosmic Philosophy tends toward the subversion or the conservation of that complex aggregate of beliefs and ordinances which make up the social order amid which we live." His answer, of course, was that the evolutionist views the historical process as one of slow growth rather than sudden conversion. He thus "owns no fellowship with Jacobins and Infidels, for he has learned that ingrained habits of thought and favourite theories of the world, being the products of circumstances, must be to a certain extent adapted to the circumstances amid which they exist. . . ." From this standpoint Fiske could attack in standard conservative fashion the eighteenth century and the French Revolution for attempting to break with the past (also criticizing, consistent with evolutionism, the reaction which followed it), and could condemn the Comtists for leaving God out of their system. Pure iconoclasm, he was sure, tended toward social dissolution.[93]

Fiske remarked virtually at the end of his Outline of Cosmic Philosophy "how truly conservative, in the best sense of the word, is the critical attitude of our philosophy."[94] It has been many times noted that the laissez faire and social Darwinist rationales to which Fiske's cosmic philosophy gave support were far removed from traditional Burkean conservatism with its emphasis on social cohesion and its sanction for political authority. On the other hand, evolutionism was eminently adaptable to the defense of existing economic and social arrangements. The assumption that progress was gradual but automatic sanctioned in a facile way both the optimistic Smithian vision of the advancement of society through the free market, and the complementary and pessimistic apprehension of Thomas Malthus and David Ricardo that the condition of most individuals could not be better than it was. Thus Fiske described the ideal state of society as that "in which the greatest possible fulness of life shall be ensured to each member of the community by the circumstance that in the long course of social equilibration the desires of each individual shall have become slowly moulded into harmony with the coexistent desires of neighboring individuals." This was necessarily a process realizable only in the indefinitely remote future, as he emphasized, and of course never absolutely realizable. It followed that the evolutionist would "look askance at the panaceas of radical world-menders, refusing to believe that the millennium can be coaxed or cheated into existence until men have learned, one and all, each for himself, to live rightly."95

Yet the Cosmic Philosophy was not simply a facade for the status quo. In his day the break with "anthropomorphic theism" was, in America, still a significant one. He might even have been suspected of obscuring its significance by his reiterated insistence that the cosmic philosophy preserved the true essentials of Christianity. Fiske referred in his Outlines of Cosmic Philosophy to the artifice which he characterized as "one of the chief agencies in forwarding social progress." This was the "legal fiction," that is, "the pretence that the novelty of belief or practice just inaugurated has its warrant in time-honoured precedent." Although noting that the device was more important in primitive societies, where suspicion of novelty

109

was particularly strong, he suggested also that it was "this disposition which leads the orthodox, after resisting some scientific heresy, until resistance is no longer possible, to discover all at once that the heresy was really taught by Suarez, or St. Augustine, or Moses."[96]

The legal fiction was thus an interpretative device, no less because it had in Fiske's definition the quality of "pretence." There is no evidence that he proposed his cosmic theism in such a spirit. Some of the temperamentally conservative may have been seduced into making concessions to heterodoxy by Fiske's obeisance to tradition, as a few of the more radical may have been tamed by the assurance that the world was on the path to the best of possible societies. For Fiske himself, to conserve and to innovate were simply complementary aspects of the evolutionary process. In a progressive society, he remarked, the cementing and the breaking of Walter Bagehot's "cake of custom" must go on simultaneously. Social progress transcended the tension between conserving and innovating; it was "a mighty process of equilibration or adjustment, in the course of which men's rules of action and emotional incentives to action become ever more and more perfectly fitted to the requirements arising from the circumstance of their aggregation into communities."[97]

iv

The equilibrating effect of evolutionary progress is a phenomenon which, obviously, the twentieth century has been unable to see demonstrated in its own historical experience, and Fiske is thus easily characterized as a naive Victorian optimist. It is difficult now to respond to the real spaciousness of his vision, or to appreciate, in particular, the generous intelligence with which he tried to reconcile science and religion. Attempting to translate

110

what he regarded as the eternal truths of Christianity into terms compatible with the scientific point of view, he offends the reductionist strain in modern thought--he seems less the evolutionist than one who simply wants to have it both ways. But that, of course, was the whole idea--the holistic idea--of "cosmic theism."

The religious aspect of Fiske's system was both large and attenuated. While the Protestant, liberal, and American biases of his historical writings make him appear in one perspective as simply George Bancroft with an evolutionary gloss, the cosmic scale with which he worked was considerably broader than that of his predecessor. The science upon which Fiske drew, after all, permitted him to describe man in a cosmos vastly more extended in time and space than the quaintly creationist-anthropomorphic system of Bancroft. The Spencerian law of progress which Fiske adopted--progression from incoherent homogeneity to coherent heterogeneity--was notoriously too big a "bag" to explain as much as it could contain, but it did permit him to entertain a notion of human freedom more satisfactory to the modern mind than Bancroft's equation of liberty with obedience to God. Freedom was for Fiske, within the bounds of his teleology, manifested in variety and diversity. Heterogeneity certainly is no adequate definition of freedom, but to an age which has learned to dread standardization, the association is a happy one.

At the same time, Fiske's Cosmic Philosophy pointed toward the disintegration of Bancroft's theology of freedom, finely balanced as it was between divine omnipotence and the sense of the individual as free agent. While it might be said that Fiske's vision of the cosmos, and of the workings of the laws of nature, were more sharply etched, his conception both of man and of God was less intense. Man was smaller in relation to the cosmic system; God was more diffuse. There was in Fiske nothing comparable to the inner light of reason, the sure bond which for

111

Bancroft tied the individual to divine truth.
Fiske's humanity did indeed march toward truth,
but not by way of intimate personal communion
with the Deity. And God Himself, deanthropo-
morphized, retained for the cosmic theist still
something of the character of Spencer's "Unknowable." He was more abstract than Bancroft's almost tribal American God, albeit the Anglo-
American world still represented the vanguard
of progress. (Unlike Bancroft, Fiske accorded
the British an equal role.) With the loss of
the sense of intimate connection between God and
man, the pressures inherent in Bancroft's system
reached the bursting point. If God is less sure
and less knowable, freedom--whether as mobility
or as heterogeneity--may not, after all, be compatible with a universal teleology; it may become, indeed, a chaos. Alternately, or perhaps
quite congruently, man without the liberating
quality of "reason" may turn out to lack any real
freedom; he may turn out to be the creature of
impersonal force in an impersonal universe.
John Fiske reflected, in his grand and desperate
scheme to hold the universe together, the acceleration of centrifugal intellectual forces which
had hardly fazed George Bancroft. Others of
Fiske's generation--William James and the Adamses, in particular--came to the shattering realization that the center would no longer hold.

Fiske failed, as we judge him today, for he
was unable to see this intimation in his own
work. It was this, more than the theistic quality of Fiske's system, which soon made it seem
antiquated. Theism was a legitimate idea to be
moved from an anthropomorphic to a "cosmic"
scheme, and he was frank in his intention to accomplish this. He embraced an uncompromising
monotheism, in which even evil was the necessary
creation of God--necessary, of course, for the
greater good.[98] The cosmic philosophy, he asserted, assigned to religion the place which it
had always occupied; "the existence of God--de-
nied by Atheism and ignored by Positivism--is

the fundamental postulate upon which Cosmism bases its synthesis of scientific truths." The antagonism between science and religion was therefore "utterly and forever swept away."99

It was in this sanguine expectation that Fiske developed his cosmic theism. As Bancroft had made history and democracy the major terms of his theology, so Fiske constructed a theology of evolution, understood on a cosmic scale. The transcendentalist sense of the immanence of God, as well as the science and social science of Charles Darwin and Herbert Spencer, were components of this theology, as historians have recognized. But the importance which Fiske himself accorded in his work to the historical role of Protestantism sould not be left out of account in gauging his own intellectual makeup. While he rejected the orthodox and particularly the Calvinist theology that was large in his personal background, he did not reject the purposefulness, the liberation from overbearing mundane authority, even the winnowing of the spiritually fit, that he found in that tradition. These elements he found to be eminently compatible both with Darwinian evolution and with his own temperament.

Applied to religion as well as to other aspects of life, evolution taught stability as much as it did change, by showing change to be orderly and according to law. For many who viewed it in this way, perhaps, the peril of modern life was not change, but discontinuity-- the break with the past. Change had come to mean progress, and as such was imbued with too great a moral investment easily to disavow. Yet progress itself was measured by moral absolutes forged in the past. The appeal of Fiske's cosmic philosophy was to join innovation to continuity, progress to unchanging absolutes. The evolutionary doctrine served as a vehicle for the interpretation of the past to the future, and of the future to the past. As applied to Fiske's

113

interpretation of Christianity, it was meant to conserve to the fullest extent the essence of traditional values, while effecting radical change in their accidental and ephemeral accretions.

This was a solution to the problem of change that seemed not only reasonable, but emotionally attractive. Yet it proved, finally and paradoxically, to be at once too great a departure from the traditional cosmos, and not enough of one. From the orthodox standpoint, of course, cosmic theism was an inadmissible attenuation of the Christian message; and from an historical standpoint it seems at least to have been an untenable one. It did not, as Fiske hoped that it would, point to a marriage of scientific and religious truth with any broad appeal. On the other hand Fiske's cosmic philosophy was, ironically, all too provincial a product of its own time. Casting its nets to enfold the universe, it captured simply a particular Victorian Weltanschauung--or so it seems in the present age of atrophied expectations. As history, Fiske's work could not let the past be itself because it geared the past to the demands of contemporary progress, while as prophecy it did not reach the spectre of radical discontinuity, of Henry Adams' "chaos," which rose over the end of the nineteenth century. In the succeeding age, the lesson might have been, a successful theism would have to recognize in its cosmos that which it could not command or encompass.

Footnotes

1. Milton Berman, John Fiske: the Evolution of a Popularizer (Cambridge: Harvard University Press, 1961), p. 220. (Hereinafter cited as Berman, John Fiske.)

2. Vernon Louis Parrington, Main Currents in American Thought: The Beginnings of Critical Realism in America 1860-1920 (New York: Harcourt, Brace and Company, 1930), p. 13. (Hereinafter cited as Parrington, Critical Realism.)

3. Russel B. Nye, "John Fiske and His Cosmic Philosophy," Papers of the Michigan Academy of Science,Arts and Letters, XXVIII (1942), 685. (Hereinafter cited as Nye,"Fiske.")

4. Jennings B. Sanders, "John Fiske," The Marcus W. Jernegan Essays in American Historiography. By His Former Students at the University of Chicago, Chapter VIII. Edited by William T. Hutchinson (New York: Russell and Russell, 1937), p. 144. (Hereinafter cited as Sanders, "John Fiske"); Berman, John Fiske, p. 13; John Spencer Clark, The Life and Letters of John Fiske, 2 volumes (Boston: Houghton Mifflin Company, 1917), I, 294, Fiske to Herbert Spencer, February 20, 1864. (Hereinafter cited as Clark, Life and Letters.) Clark notes that Fiske was very religious at fourteen, but that after he began to question orthodoxy, Henry Thomas Buckle "was the culminating influence which completely freed his mind from bondage to dogmatic theology" (pp. 66, 88, 114).

5. Ethel F. Fiske, ed., The Letters of John Fiske (New York: The Macmillan Company, 1940), p. 87, Fiske to Abby Morgan Brooks, March 30, 1862. (Hereinafter cited as Fiske, Letters); John Fiske, The Beginnings of New England: Or the Puritan Theocracy in Its Relation to Civil and Religious Liberty (Boston: Houghton, Mifflin

115

and Company, 1899), p. 33. (Hereinafter cited as Fiske, Beginnings of New England.)

6. John Fiske, A Century of Science and Other Essays (Boston: Houghton, Mifflin and Company, 1899), pp. 150-151. (Hereinafter cited as Fiske, Century of Science.)

7. H. Burnell Pannill, The Religious Faith of John Fiske (Durham: Duke University Press, 1957), p. 52. (Hereinafter cited as Pannill, Religious Faith.) Pannill, who emphasizes the transcendentalist element in Fiske's thought, offers the most extended treatment of his subject's religious views, and one which has been most useful in the preparation of this essay. John Spencer Clark points out Fiske's attraction to Emerson. Life and Letters, II, 255, 259. Among those most receptive to Fiske's views were members of the Free Religious Association, religious radicals who included such transcendentalists as Theodore Parker and Octavius Brooks Frothingham. Berman, John Fiske, p. 100.

8. Clark, Life and Letters, II, 477, 480-481.

9. Nye, "Fiske," 697-698.

10. Pannill, Religious Faith, pp. 52-53.

11. John Fiske, American Political Ideas Viewed from the Standpoint of Universal History (New York: Harper & Brothers, 1885), pp. 117-118. (Hereinafter cited as Fiske, American Political Ideas.)

12. John Fiske, Essays Historical and Literary, 2 volumes (New York: The Macmillan Company, 1902), II, 122. (Hereinafter cited as Fiske, Essays Historical and Literary.)

13. Fiske, Beginnings of New England, pp. 45-52.

14. Fiske, Essays Historical and Literary, pp. 121-122.

15. John Fiske, Excursions of an Evolution-ist (Boston: Houghton, Mifflin and Company, 1894), pp. 265-266, 288. (Hereinafter cited as Fiske, Excursions.)

16. Fiske, Beginnings of New England, pp. 58-59; John Fiske, Through Nature to God (Boston: Houghton, Mifflin and Company, 1899), pp. 65-66. (Hereinafter cited as Fiske, Through Nature.) J. D. Y. Peel points out the affinity of Calvinism and science, which he sees as a factor in Herbert Spencer's thought. "Calvinism is the most extremely transcendental form of Christianity, the remotest from immanentist, pantheistic conceptions of all nature as enchanted and God as coterminous with nature." Therefore, "only God was sacred and mysterious: there could be no barrier to the systematic investigation of the structure of nature, or to the wholesale alteration of it according to one's purposes. . . ." Herbert Spencer: The Evolution of a Sociologist (New York: Basic Books, 1971), pp. 103-104. (Hereinafter cited as Peel, Herbert Spencer.)

17. Fiske, Through Nature, pp. 20-23.

18. Fiske, American Political Ideas, p. 27.

19. Fiske, Essays Historical and Literary, p. 226.

20. Fiske, Beginnings of New England, p. 143.

21. Fiske, American Political Ideas, p. 27.

22. Fiske, Beginnings of New England, pp. 45-46.

23. Fiske, Century of Science, pp. 144-145.

24. Ibid., p. 144; Fiske, American Political Ideas, p. 25.

25. Fiske, Beginnings of New England, pp. 145, 149, 151, 246-247.

26. John Fiske, New France and New England (Boston: Houghton, Mifflin and Company, 1902), pp. 222-223. (Hereinafter cited as Fiske, New France); Fiske, Through Nature, pp. 144-145.

27. Fiske, New France, pp. 224-225, 331-332.

28. Fiske, Century of Science, pp. 148-150.

29. John Fiske, Outlines of Cosmic Philosophy. Based on the Doctrine of Evolution, with Criticism on the Positive Philosophy, 4 volumes. With an introduction by Josiah Royce (Boston: Houghton, Mifflin and Company, 1902), II, 132. (Hereinafter cited as Fiske, Cosmic Philosophy.) "The center of his concern was religious," Berman notes of Fiske. "Above all he wanted an explanation of the universe that would be both emotionally and logically compelling." Although Spencer's synthetic philosophy appealed to practical men in England, Edward L. Youmans realized that "this would not control American usage; 'nothing short of the Cosmic will satisfy the American spread-eaglism,'" he told Spencer. Berman, John Fiske, pp. 100-101.

30. Fiske, Cosmic Philosophy, I, 269.

31. Ibid., II, 341.

32. Ibid., IV, 229.

33. John Fiske, Darwinism and Other Essays. New edition, revised and enlarged (Boston: Houghton, Mifflin and Company, 1885), pp. 97-103. (Hereinafter cited as Fiske, Darwinism.)

34. John Fiske, The Idea of God as Affected

by Modern Knowledge (Boston: Houghton, Mifflin and Company, 1885), pp. 166-167. (Hereinafter cited as Fiske, Idea of God.)

35. Fiske, Through Nature, pp. 112-113.

36. Fiske, Idea of God, p. 159.

37. Fiske, Essays Historical and Literary, II, 283. Fiske sought a philosophical system which would provide for the 'scientific' establishment of convictions intuitively held," as Pannill notes. "The Cosmic Theism of John Fiske was rooted in an intuitive conviction about the significance of human life and consciousness." Religious Faith, pp. 85, 208.

38. Fiske, Cosmic Philosophy, IV, 104-105.

39. Ibid., I, 207, 209, 213.

40. Ibid., III, 353; IV, 351-352, 320. Philip P. Wiener suggests that Fiske "reveals an evangelical faith in an evolutionism that was to fuse science and the Protestant tradition of individualism against the 'static' claims of the revival of Catholicism, of the Comtean priesthood of positivistic sociologists, and of the more radical Jacobin atheism of the French communists." Evolution and the Founders of Pragmatism. With a foreword by John Dewey (Cambridge: Harvard University Press, 1949), p. 148. (Hereinafter cited as Wiener, Founders of Pragmatism.)

41. Fiske, Excursions, p. 282.

42. Fiske, Letters, 97, Fiske to Abby Morgan Brooks, March 16, 1863. Spencer was from a Dissenting background strongly influenced, as Fiske's was, by Calvinism. Peel believes that "Spencer and a number of other writers who shared his Dissenting origins and his deist/secularist opinions based their detailed historical and psychological theories on a necessaritarian

optimism which was demonstrably a transformation
of Calvinist themes. It is understandable enough
that just as predestination had been the response
of some men to radical social change in an earlier period, so a secular determinism was one response to equally disturbing changes in a later
one. Spencer's necessitarian scheme of evolution, and his general concern with certitude cannot be grasped otherwise." Herbert Spencer, pp.
7, 103.

43. The Personal Letters of John Fiske. A
Small Edition Privately Printed for Members of
the Bibliophile Society (Cedar Rapids: The Torch
Press, 1939), p. 134, Fiske to his mother, De-
cember 3, 1873. (Hereinafter cited as Personal
Letters.)

44. Fiske, Cosmic Philosophy, II, 205-206.

45. Fiske, Century of Science, p. 49; Fiske,
Cosmic Philosophy, II, 133.

46. Fiske, Cosmic Philosophy, II, 221.

47. Fiske, Essays Historical and Literary,
II, 251, 276. "From the parts to the totality,
from freedom to determinism--such has been the
drift of thought that science has laid upon us
and from which there is no easy escape," Parrington wrote. "Yet for the moment the rigid
determinism of the premise was overlooked and
man was accepted as the first-born and heir of
God's benevolent universe. . . . It was this
middle ground that Herbert Spencer came to
occupy in the minds of his American disciples--
holding to the older individualism with its
implications of anarchism, yet creating a cosmic philosophy that foreshadowed the eventual
dwarfing of the individual." Critical Realism,
pp. 192-193.

48. Fiske, Cosmic Philosophy, III, 307,
332-334.

49. _Ibid._, III, 327-328.

50. Fiske, _Through Nature_, pp. 6/-71, 76-79.

51. Fiske, _Cosmic Philosophy_, III, 125, 238; Fiske, _Idea of God_, pp. 160, 162-163.

52. John Fiske, _The Destiny of Man Viewed in the Light of His Origin_ (Boston: Houghton Mifflin and Company, 1884), pp. 113-114. Henry Steele Commager points out that with the lessening credibility of Enlightenment and Transcendentalist ideas, the evolutionary teachings of Spencer "gave new assurance of a universe governed by law and of the progressive destiny of man." Following Spencer, in this view, Fiske "lulled a generation of Americans into the conviction that there was no conflict between science and religion, helped them to sublimate their acquisitive economic practices into a philosophical system, furnished them a new basis for their belief in progress, and inculcated in them faith in the destiny of man." "John Fiske: an Interpretation," _Proceedings of the Massachusetts Historical Society_, LXVI (1936-1941), 333-334. J. Herman Randall, Jr. classifies Fiske among the "adjusters," or "transformers," who "used evolution to bolster up pre-Darwinian ideas" (and in a subgroup of "original advocates of a mechanistic evolution"). "The Changing Impact of Darwin on Philosophy," _Journal of the History of Ideas_, XXII (October-December, 1961), 437. Nye characterizes Fiske as evolution's prime apologist and philosopher in America. "Fiske," 686. Pannill shows that Fiske redefined teleology. "In his early works all purpose and design were rejected as investing the Deity with unwarranted anthropomorphic attributes. In his later works the 'teleology' which he was rejecting (purpose imposed from without the process) was distinguished from the 'teleology' which he was accepting (purpose which derived from the process itself). The latter kind could now be spoken of as the 'purpose of the Deity' since this Deity was imma-

nent in, though not exhausted by, the phenomena which made up the process. The assumption was that, in the light of this new teleology, the development of man's higher attributes was the clue to the meaning of the process and hence to the nature of the Being revealed in the process. Thus the higher attributes of man really indicated the metaphysical nature of God." Religious Faith, p. 169.

53. Fiske, Darwinism, pp. 6-7. Christians "faced the problem of finding a meaningful place for God in a world which seemed self-determining. The concept of immanence that attracted Fiske was the most widely accepted solution of this problem. . . . Immanence--seeing God as present in all parts of the process--made the universe more habitable to man." Berman, John Fiske, pp. 193-194.

54. Fiske, Essays Historical and Literary, II, 284.

55. Personal Letters, p. 125, Fiske to his wife, November 18, 1873.

56. Fiske, Through Nature, p. 115.

57. Fiske, Idea of God, p. 163.

58. Fiske, Century of Science, pp. 62-63. Fiske's religious ideas appealed to certain types of Protestants, Berman notes, including many conservative Unitarians (more liberal Unitarians found little new in them.) "Among Calvinists, as among Unitarians, Fiske won the greatest praise from those interested in healing denominational differences. His work lacked sufficient rigor to appeal to those actively engaged in modifying doctrine and he was far too naturalistic to satisfy the most rigidly orthodox, who ignored him. But those seeking a middle path were much encouraged by Fiske's optimistic view of the nature of the universe and by his solemn assurances that sci-

ence supported the best part of religious beliefs. From this middle group Fiske drew his
most ardent supporters." John Fiske, pp. 176,
185-186.

59. Fiske, Cosmic Philosophy, I, 273.

60. Ibid., IV, 298.

61. Ibid., IV, 295-296.

62. Ibid., IV, 250-252.

63. Fiske, Excursions, pp. 303-304.

64. Fiske, Cosmic Philosophy, IV, 256-259.

65. Ibid., IV, 233, 237, 248, 288.

66. Ibid., IV, 193.

67. Fiske, Through Nature, pp. 166, 173.
Fiske "redefined the 'anthropomorphism' which he
was rejecting in such a way as to exclude from
the definition,for all practical purposes, the
higher attributes of man. The anthropomorphism
involved in speaking of God in 'psychical' or
'ethical' terms was now considered to be a legitimate part of the theistic position." Pannill,
Religious Faith, p. 168.

68. Fiske, Cosmic Philosophy, IV, 364;
Fiske, Idea of God, p. 163.

69. John Fiske, Life Everlasting (Boston:
Houghton, Mifflin and Company, 1901), pp. 85-86;
John Fiske, The Unseen World, and Other Essays
(Boston: Houghton, Mifflin and Company, 1876),
pp. 55-57 and passim.

70. Fiske, Cosmic Philosophy, III, 275-276,
282-286.

71. Ibid., III, 286-287; Fiske, Darwinism,

p. 143.

72. Wiener, Founders of Pragmatism, pp. 133-134.

73. Fiske, Cosmic Philosophy, III, 255-257.

74. Ibid., III, 265.

75. Ibid., I, 217; III, 268-272. In refuting this position, William James remarked that "all this comes from Mr. Fiske's not distinguishing between the possibles which really tempt a man and those which tempt him not at all. Free-will, like psychology, deals with the former possibles exclusively." James, The Principles of Psychology, 2 volumes (Dover Publications, 1950), II, 577.

76. Fiske, Cosmic Philosophy, III, 276.

77. Ibid., II, 252-253.

78. Clark, Life and Letters, I, 311.

79. Fiske, Through Nature, pp. 149-151; Fiske, Excursions, pp. 274-275; Fiske, Darwinism, p. 69.

80. John Stephen Martin, "Henry Adams's 'Dynamic Theory of History' and the New England Dialectic of Necessity," (unpublished Thesis Submitted to the Graduate Faculty of the University of Georgia in Partial Fulfillment of the Requirements for the Degree of Master of Arts, 1961), pp. 58-59, 63, 68-71.

81. Fiske, Essays Historical and Literary, II, 73, 76, 81.

82. Fiske, American Political Ideas, p. 6.

83. Fiske, Through Nature, pp. 114-115.

84. Fiske, Cosmic Philosophy, III, 295, 298, 304-305.

85. Fiske, Through Nature, pp. 100-105; Fiske, American Political Ideas, pp. 106-107; Fiske, Excursions, pp. 222, 232. "The Fiskean optimism spoke so convincingly to the mass of 'emerging Americans' because it so easily identified an indicated peaceful, industrial democracy with the religious ideal of the Kingdom of God." Pannill, Religious Faith, p. 227.

86. Sanders, "John Fiske," p. 166.

87. Fiske, Essays Historical and Literary, II, 22.

88. Fiske, American Political Ideas, pp. 103-104; Fiske, Darwinism, p. 242.

89. Fiske, American Political Ideas, p. 115; John Fiske, Unpublished Orations. "The Discovery of the Columbia River and the Whitman Controversy;" "The Crispus Attucks Memorial;" and "Columbus Memorial." (Boston: Printed for Members only. The Bibliophile Society, 1909), p. 40.

90. Fiske, Essays Historical and Literary, I, 273.

91. Fiske, Cosmic Philosophy, IV, 54-56; III, 105.

92. Ibid., III, 290-291.

93. Ibid., IV, 321, 327, 329-335, 342.

94. Ibid., IV, 369.

95. Ibid., IV, 357-358, 362. Unlike Spencer, Berman notes, Fiske "had little interest in fostering social change. . . ." "It is a measure of the difference between England and America that a social philosophy designed to validate

change should become the mainstay of American conservative thought in the latter part of the nineteenth century." John Fiske, p. 100.

96. Fiske, Cosmic Philosophy, IV, 38-39.

97. Ibid., IV, 27; III, 306.

98. Fiske, Through Nature, pp. 23-29.

99. Fiske, Cosmic Philosophy, I, 272-273.

CHAPTER III

JOSIAH ROYCE: THE COMMUNITY OF THE UNIVERSE

Of the figures considered in this study, Josiah Royce (1855-1916) was the youngest, and was alone not a New Englander by birth. Yet intellectually Royce fits most comfortably between Bancroft and Fiske, who in their disparate ways adapted traditional Protestant assumptions to new political and scientific ideas, and William James and the Adams brothers, in whom the earlier certitudes gave way to distinctly twentieth century doubts. In one critical way, indeed, Royce represents the most complete expression of our theme: the persistence and dissolution of religious faith in mundane forms of thought. For Bancroft and Fiske, progress, democracy, and evolution had been the terms of such secular theology; the Californian used the philosophically larger canvas of German idealism, adapted to American needs. The sense of cosmic harmony and purpose, which Bancroft and Fiske sought to find through history and evolution, took on with Royce such an apparent philosophic coherence that, like the "one-hoss shay" of the elder Holmes, it could only go to pieces all at once. (The image better describes the fate of Roycean idealism than that of Calvinism, to which Holmes applied it; the breakup of Calvinism was far less sudden.) But it was in its own way a fine contrivance, and

127

one which is far even now from seeming wholly antique.

A man less imbued with cosmic optimism would have died in despair. The end of Royce's life came during a war which has generally been viewed as a frightful chasm between the nineteenth century and the twentieth, and although it is easy to locate the philosophical divide at an earlier date, World War I was a massive blow to the assumptions of Royce's thought as it was to that of the West generally. Royce hoped that the outcome of the war would vindicate his philosophy through the achievement of a true global unity, and the bitterness of his reaction against the Germans derived from his apprehension that they were helping to make the world very unsafe for his cardinal principle of community. It had been the Germans, primarily, who had taught Royce his philosophy; now, it appeared, they had betrayed it and him. They had been disloyal. But the larger and more poisonous disloyalty was that of the West generally to the Roycean vision of a harmonious cosmos which was the expression of the manifold communal will of the Absolute. And to the extent that this described an ideal of western civilization, the disloyalty was older than the war, and deeper than Royce imagined.

i.

Like many of his generation, Josiah Royce rejected familial Calvinism (even though represented in this case by his beloved mother, Sarah Royce), while retaining the moral and theistic imperatives which it had embodied. These found definite formulation during his graduate studies in Germany in 1875-1876, which made of him "a German romanticist in literature, a German idealist in philosophy." Academically, Royce has been placed in the tradition of post-Kantian idealism. Critics have particularly noted parallels with Immanuel Kant himself: that of

128

Kant's "duty for duty's sake" with Royce's "loyalty to loyalty," for example, or or Kant's
"kingdom of ends" with Royce's "community of interpretation."[1] There was a similar dualism.
Royce distinguished between the "world of description" and the "world of appreciation," terms
which were comparable to Kant's "phenomena" and
"noumena." "The world of description," Vincent
Buranelli explains, "is. . .governed by natural
law, necessity, regularity, repetition. It is
supremely the world of science where reign the
principle of causation, the uniformity of nature,
the conservation of mass and energy." The world
of appreciation, on the other hand, is "the world
of value judgments, of aesthetic reactions, of
sensory feelings."[2] The world of appreciation is
beyond causation, except as it embodies its own
justification for being what it is. It is thoroughly a world of freedom; "its own significance
is what occasions it thus to express itself."
The laws, necessity, causation, and uniformity
of the physical universe "belong, not to its inner nature as such, but to the external show of
this nature." Therefore,

> all physical causation is only the
> describable translation of the inner
> meaning of things into terms of re-
> lations among bodies. The relations
> of the world of appreciation, which is
> the true world, to the world of de-
> scription, which is its show, are
> therefore themselves in no wise re-
> lations of cause and effect. I as ob-
> server, interpreting the true world
> in terms of our human forms and the
> categories of theoretical science, am
> bound to see, in the world as thus in-
> terpreted, rigid laws of causation.
> But the laws thus seen are symbols of
> deeper truth, and not the physical
> effects of this truth. This deeper
> truth itself is not causal. It is
> only such truth as, in order to be

129

> describable, must show the aspect that
> the laws of causal connection in our
> experience interpret in their own im-
> perfect way.[3]

Bound in the temporal order of things, then, we
are free in the eternal order. Causation for
Royce was not so deep or fundamental as Being itself, and the world ultimately "is what it is.
So the Logos,from eternity, and in one organic
all-embracing act, constitutes his system of ap-
preciative truth."[4]

Royce reasonably objected to being defined
too narrowly as a Kantian, Hegelian, Spinozist,
or by any such label. "I should describe the
sort of Idealism that I hold as a sort of 'post-
Kantian, empirically modified, Idealism,'"he suggested informally in 1896, "'somewhat influenced
by Hegelian, but also not uninfluenced by Schop-
enhauerian motives, with a dash of Fichte added.'"[5] On balance, it is fair to regard him as
a "Germanized American thinker."[6] But the American part of the formula was essential; his
thought was couched sufficiently in his native
accents that it has been possible to view him as
his nation's "ideal interpreter and spiritual
guide," and as "America's national philosopher"
more nearly even than William James. "Very few
thinkers," Jacob Loewenberg noted, "ever have
with Royce's passion and persistence fused their
technical interests with the problems of their
country."[7] After all, the national character
contained an idealizing and universalizing pole
as well as a practical and pragmatic one, and if
James inspired the practical American, Royce addressed himself as much to the American idealist.

In either case, however, the result was a
species of practical idealism which seems characteristically American. For an idealist, Royce
had notably mixed emotions about transcendentalism, which he considered an international movement originating in Europe and spreading "even

into our own country." Transcendentalism had expressed, he thought, "a single great idea: the
idea that in the free growth and expression of
the highest and strongest emotions of the civilized man might be found the true solution to the
problem of life." He was painfully aware that
the movement had been superseded by "a dangerous
practical materialism." Yet the transcendentalism of the earlier nineteenth century seemed
finally to him too subjective and introspective,
and he could only hope for the rise of a broader
transcendentalist movement that would "not run
to waste and be lost in the deserts of sentimental melancholy."[8] (It might be pointed out
that in the American transcendentalist school at
its most impressive, in Thoreau and much of Emerson, there is a determination similar to Royce's
to root the ideal in the practical. Royce could
have drawn more heavily upon this American tradition than he did, but when he became personally
acquainted with it after the Civil War, its force
had largely been dissipated.)

The effort to bind the transcendent to the
mundane was at the center of Royce's thought.
"What you experience God experiences. The difference lies only in this, that God sees in unity
what you see in fragments."[9] This proposition
defined his idealism, and it was intended to put
equal weight on the holistic and the fragmentary.
"If idealism means anything," he insisted, "it
means a theory of the universe which simply must
not be divorced from empirical considerations, or
from the business of life. . . . It is, and in
its best historical representatives always has
been, an effort to interpret the facts of life."[10]

As Royce sought in his philosophy to relate
the ideal to the concrete, so in his political
and historical thinking he was intrigued by the
confrontation of the idealist with practical problems. In studying the history of his native
state of California, he became acutely conscious
of the collision of ideals with practical exigen-

131

cies, and of the confrontation, even the self-confrontation, of the idealistic with the practical American. "The Idealist," he perceived, "gets into conflict with the sheriff;the Higher Law has to face the processes of the courts; a company of homeless wanderers have to solve, in a moment, a critical problem of civilization." Royce fully appreciated this common-sense duality of everyday life. "In the night we deal, if we like, with the world, the universe, and God," he noted. "In the morning we have to deal with such things as the Sheriff, the Mayor and the writs of the County Court. . . ."11 But the aim of his philosophy was to place the sheriff in the universe, and find in plurality the true concomitant of unity.

Insisting upon the practical and immediate dimension, Royce was contemptuous of what seemed to him the merely visionary. While acknowledging the valuable function which had been performed by the radical abolitionists, for example,Royce found them rather too detached from reality:

> This Infinite that they worshipped was, however, in his relations to the rest of the world, too often rather abstract, a Deus absconditus, who was as remote from the imperfections and absurdities of the individual laws and processes of human society, as he was near to the hearts of his chosen worshippers. From him they got a so-called Higher Law. As it was ideal, and, like its author, very abstract, it was far above the erring laws of men, and it therefore relieved its obedient servants from all entangling earthly allegiance. If the constitution upon which our sinful national existence depended, and upon which our only hope of better things also depended, was contradicted by this Higher Law, then the constitution was a "league with hell," and anybody could set up for himself, and he and the In-

132

finite might carry on a government of their own.[12]

Royce believed strongly that the ideal must be recognized as existing, however partially and haltingly, in the social order; otherwise the ideal became mere abstraction. Thus he held that "patient loyalty to the actual social order is the great reformer's first duty; that a service of just this erring humanity, with its imperfect and yet beautiful system of delicate and highly organized relationships, is the best service that a man can render to the Ideal. . . ."[13]

There was in this a clear and acknowledged pragmatism which furnishes a notable common denominator between Royce and William James, even though it was worked out in different philosophical systems. Certainly the large measure of agreement between the two is lost in any facile contrast between the Monist and the Pluralist. Royce explicitly agreed with James that "no truth is a saving truth--yes, no truth is a truth at all unless it guides and directs life. . . . On the other hand," he added, "the will is a collection of restless caprices unless it is unified by a rational ideal." Adapting a Jamesian proposition, he suggested that a truth, insofar as it works, shows itself to be "an eternal truth." But such a truth, he insisted, was to be judged on the basis of a larger experience than that of the individual life; "whatever you regard as a genuine test of the workings of your ideas is some living whole of experience above the level of any one of our individual lives."[14]

Royce was thus insistent on applying pragmatism on a social and ideal plane. "We need unity of life," he said. "In recognizing that need my own pragmatism consists." To a remarkable degree, he did succeed in combining the idealist and pragmatic positions. He perceived no basic difficulty in this, however; he believed that the leading idealists were all pragmatic in the sense that they emphasized the relation of

133

truth to action, and conversely that James himself had gravitated toward idealism late in his career.[15] There was at least one factor, he believed, which tied pragmatism conclusively to absolute idealism:

> The pragmatist who denies that there is any absolute truth accessible has never rightly considered the very most characteristic feature of the reasonable will, namely, that it is always counselling irrevocable deeds, and therefore is always giving counsel that is for its own determinate purpose irrevocably right or wrong precisely in so far as it is a definite counsel.[16]

Royce was unequivocal: "I am both a pragmatist and an absolutist," he proclaimed, "and. . .I believe each of these doctrines to involve the other, and. . .therefore I regard them not only as reconcilable but as in truth reconciled."[17]

Although they have served as opposed symbols of idealism and pragmatism, monism and pluralism, there is then an intimate confluence in the ideas of Royce and James. From the present perspective they can be seen to represent differing possibilities within the same broad cast of mind. Above all, perhaps, they insisted on human life as a cosmic moral drama, in which novelty, risk, and struggle were realities, and in which the individual had a margin of freedom. Both were relational thinkers, James developing a philosophy of "co-," as he called it, and Royce the tighter concept of "community." Both came to emphasize variety and diversity; in that sense Royce as well as James was a pluralist. If James and Royce represented respectively the particularizing and the universalizing sides of the national character, yet both sought the middle ground where particular and general, unity and multiplicity, met.

Above all, the two thinkers shared a cosmic perspective which in each case was marked by a religious temperament, and, in different ways, sought confluence with some sort of higher consciousness. With Royce this was expressed in the "Absolute," as a universal community. James was a less certain theist, and in any event admitted no absolute. As Royce interpreted the Jamesian position, the individual's "deeper ideals always depend upon viewing life in the light of larger unities than now appear, upon viewing yourself as a coworker with the universe for the attainment of what no present human game of action can now reveal." Thus James's ethical maxims won their way "to a resolute interpretation of human life as an opportunity to cooperate with the superhuman and the divine. . . ." At bottom, Royce felt, these ethical maxims assumed certain absolute truths.[18] And certainly it is difficult to deny an irreducible element of moral absolutism in James; indeed, his pluralistic system was designed to ensure the integrity of good and evil as distinct and opposed qualities.

Although the correspondences in their thought now in some ways loom larger than their differences, the divergent emphases in James and Royce are essential to their meaning for the twentieth century. Ultimately James is a pluralist, while Royce is a monist. James's emphasis is on the individual where Royce's is on the community. This comes out most clearly in their views on religion. Religious truth for James is emphatically individual; for Royce it is social. Royce was firm in his view that "James is indeed wrong. . . to neglect the social roads that lead toward the experience of what we take to be divine." The younger man insisted that "normally the way to salvation, if there be any such way, must lead through social experience."[19] James looks toward an existentialist perspective, toward the modern sense of living on the "perilous edge"; Royce with his universal community has an affinity with the equally modern straining after a renewed holistic sense of the universe. Royce remarked of his colleague that "he understood, he shared, and he also transcended the American spirit."20 The assessment could serve as well for Royce; between them the philosophers of community and pluralism expressed an old hunger for the frontier and an old hope of a truly harmonious society, and looked beyond the narrower manifestations of these American concerns to the projected point at which they met.

One great endeavor of nineteenth century thought, in which James and Royce shared, was to encompass traditional values in an intellectual system commensurate with the expanded dimensions of the cosmos. This proved ultimately beyond the very considerable abilities of the century; perhaps it was impossible. The constructs, more fragile even than Henry Adams' cathedrals, could not bear the weight. Quantity overwhelmed order. Royce ridiculed Spencer's attempted unification of knowledge as a case of trying to find a bag big enough to hold all the facts, and it would be possible to make a similar charge against Royce in the mode of philosophy. But it is the effort that commands attention and respect. Later, from the smug viewpoint of disillusionment, the Victorian world looked only absurd and hypocritical in attempting to paper over the fissures which had opened in its civilization. Yet in many ways the failing effort to conserve and interpret the sense of a cosmos in which humanity was at home seems more interesting and instructive today than the scientific reductionism, arid instrumentalism, and ideology-mongering which succeeded.

Royce's presentation of this sense of the cosmos remains a challenge in its very comprehensiveness. It remains particularly a challenge in American thought, as it draws together the American polarities of individualism and theological absolutism, and finds for them a principle of mediation, or interpretation, in the concept of

136

community. There is a sense, indeed, in which Royce's vision of community is a most radical challenge to the characteristically atomistic American way of looking at the world. In this respect he could yet prove a hinge to the thinking of the late twentieth century. An age inured to dissonance will find little truth in cosmic harmonies, as an atomistic society will find little meaning in a Roycean philosophy of loyalty. But the revolt against the disjunctive and fragmentary might look upon the idea of universal community with new interest.

ii.

"Community" became Royce's central concept. Ultimately and preëminently religious in nature, it was also the logical expression of the "essentially relational" character of Royce's thought. "He hunts for orders, classes, groups, and communities that will unify individual things and persons," Buranelli notes. "He constructs a pattern of philosophical explanation in which everything finds its proper place in relation to everything else."[21] Thus the theme of Royce's California was the early struggle to achieve community in that state, teaching, the author thought, "a lesson in reverence for the relations of life."[22]

What precisely is the community? Royce was emphatic that "a community presents itself to our minds both as one and as many; and unless it is both one and many, it is no community at all." Consequently he rejected an atomistic in favor of an organic model:

> A community is not a mere collection of individuals. It is a sort of live unit, that has organs, as the body of an individual has organs. A community grows or decays, is healthy or diseased,

is young or aged,much as any individual
member of the community possesses such
characters. Each of the two, the community or the individual member, is as
much a live creature as is the other.
Not only does the community live, it
has a mind of its own,--a mind whose
psychology is not the same as the
psychology of an individual human being. The social mind displays its
psychological traits in its characteristic products,--in languages, in cus-
toms, in religions,--products which an
individual human mind, or even a collection of such minds, when they are
not somehow organized into a genuine
community,cannot produce. Yet language,
custom, religion are all of them genuinely mental products.[23]

For Royce it was one of the most significant of
truths "that a community, when unified by an active indwelling purpose, is an entity more concrete and, in fact,less mysterious than any individual man, and that such a community can love
and be loved as a husband and wife love; or as
father or mother love." Indeed, he believed,"a
highly organized community is as truly a human
being as you and I are individually human."[24]

During the First World War, Royce expressed
a hope for a future community of mankind which
would be neither a mere collection of individuals
nor mere masses of people. He called this the
"Great Community." Although himself somewhat
carried away by the anti-German spirit of the
war, he at least cut through some of the simplic-
ities of Allied propaganda. "Liberty alone never
saves us," he pointed out. "Democracy alone never
saves us. Our political freedom is but vanity
unless it is a means through which we come to
realize and practice charity in the Pauline sense
of that word." Charity, as Royce had noted,
meant community.[25] He had long held, furthermore,
that there was an ideally universal community,

138

"To this community in ideal all men belong;" he explained, "and to act as if one were a member of such a community is to win in the highest measure the goal of individual life. It is to win what religion calls salvation." The universal community meant, in sum, "man viewed as one conscious spiritual whole of life."[26]

On a more mundane--yet at the same time still spiritual--level, the principle of community could be expressed politically. Convinced of "the sacredness of a true public spirit," Royce closed his _California_ with a succinct expression of history's "old and simple" lesson:

> It is the State, the Social Order, that is divine. We are all but dust, save as this social order gives us life. When we think it our instrument, our plaything, and make our private fortunes the one object, then this social order rapidly becomes vile to us; we call it sordid, degraded, corrupt, unspiritual, and ask how we may escape from it forever. But if we turn again and serve the social order, and not merely ourselves, we soon find that what we are serving is simply our own highest spiritual destiny in bodily form. It is never truly sordid or corrupt or unspiritual; it is only we that are so when we neglect our duty.[27]

Royce's paean to the divinity of the state does not mark him as a statist in any secular or totalitarian sense. The "State" for Royce is the community in its political aspect, and his estimation of it one more manifestation of his "reverence for the relations of life." Royce did run notably counter here not only to the Protestant axis between God and the individual, but even to the transcendentalist view, which although it emphasized the interconnectedness of life, entirely denigrated social and political institutions as interfering with the transcendent consciousness.

There had of course long been an ideal of America as a harmonious community,and a nationalistic sense of the mission of the American community in the world. But more thoroughly than any previous American thinker, Royce made a philosophy of community, seeking to join consciousness in its individual, social and cosmic phases. The parts of the triad were equal and interdependent. Thus Royce believed that self-conscious functions were always also social functions. The customary opposition between egoism and altruism seemed to him overly abstract, and indeed false. "As a fact," he argued, "a man becomes self-conscious only in the most intimate connection with the growth of his social consciousness. These two forms of consciousness are not separable and opposed regions of a man's life; they are thoroughly interdependent." One could be conscious of oneself only in relation to one's (real or ideal) fellow; one could not "really will to preserve the Ego, without also willing to preserve and to defend some sort of Alter, and some sort of relation to my fellow who is this Alter, and upon whom my conscious Ego depends for its very life." Even the murderer acted for a social end--e.g. honor, property, power; bad altruism was not identical with egoism. A man existed as a man only in human relationships; "the ethical problem is not: Shall I aim to preserve social relations? but: What social relations shall I aim to preserve?" Nor could we know our own inner life apart from "an essentially social contrast with other minds. . . ." ("I am I in relation to some sort of a non-Ego.") Even our relations with nature involved "a more or less social contrast between our life and the life of nature," our conception of physical reality being actually derived from our conception of "social fellow-beings."28 In the most profound sense, then, man lived in community.

So did God. The "Absolute" was nothing less
than a universal community, comprising "a vast
society of finite beings."[29] In this way Royce
communalized American Protestant pietism. The
ideal which sought through personal regeneration
to identify the individual's will with that of
God was superseded by the ideal of the Absolute
as a community of wills. Finite and infinite
were fulfilled through each other. God's life
"sees the one plan fulfilled through all the manifold lives, the single consciousness winning its
purpose by virtue of all the ideas, of all the
individual selves, and of all the lives. No finite view is wholly illusory. Every finite intent taken precisely in its wholeness is fulfilled in the Absolute."[30] In sum, the

> Absolute purpose is not only One, but
> also infinitely complex, so that its
> unity is the unity of many Wills, each
> one of which finds its expression in
> an individual life, while these lives,
> as the lives of various Selves have an
> aspect in which they are free, in so
> far as each, while in many aspects de-
> termined, is still in its own measure
> a determiner of all the rest. . . .
> Free, in its own degree, is every indi-
> vidual will amongst all the wills that
> the world-life expresses, because ev-
> ery such will, as unique, is in some
> respect, underivable from all the
> others.[31]

Royce placed great emphasis on this uniqueness of the individual will, for it was characteristic of "absolute idealism" that it insisted
upon, in a certain sense, an absolute individualism. Will, Royce believed, determined the consciousness of individuality. "The individual is,
primarily, the object and expression of an exclusive interest, of a determinate selection."[32]
Furthermore, he thought, "the individualizing
will of any person, as this person, is expressed,

141

from moment to moment, in his more or less conscious intention to view his life as a struggle towards, and consequently as a contrast with, his ideal goal."[33] This resembles William James's notion of the meaning of life as the fight for a personal ideal, but for Royce the purpose of the individual is joined to the purpose of the Absolute..

Individuality is elusive, Royce realized; "an individual is a being that no finite search can find." Rather, it appeared, "only an infinite process can show me who I am." He attempted to show that "the only solution of this mystery lies in conceiving every man as so related to the world and to the very life of God, that in order to be an individual at all a man has to be very much nearer to the Eternal than in our present life we are accustomed to observe."[34] Yet he found in individuality an ultimate reality:

> The individuality of every man appears at once as the most reasonable and as the most unreasonable feature about him--the most reasonable because what we most value in humanity, what love most emphasizes, what our social longing most idealizes, what our rational passion of liberty most insists upon is the individual human being, so that whatever gives our reasonable life its value, its friends to love, its task to perform is something individual. Yet, on the other hand, the individuality of everybody appears also as the unreasonable aspect of human nature in so far as individuality means whim, caprice, waywardness, oddity, eccentricity--in brief, whatever about any human being involves rebellion against order and intrusion upon the will of one's fellows. Thus our world of experience is a synthesis of what appear to us at present rational and irration-

al features. The history of society,
and in particular of religion, of science, and of philosophy, appears to us
as a warfare of reason and unreason.[35]

The individual was both teleologically and
morally unique. Given a unique whole (the Absolute), "every fragment and aspect, just by virtue
of its relation to the whole is inevitably unique.
. . . If the absolute knowledge sees the whole
as a complete fulfillment of purpose, then every
fact in the world occupies its unique place in
the world." Therefore, "we finite beings. . .
are unique and individual in our differences,
from one another and from all possible beings,
just because we share in the very uniqueness of
God's individuality and purpose." Indeed, the
moral law addressed "one great command. . .to
the individual in regard to the individual's own
self-cultivation. This command is 'Be unique,
as your Father in heaven is unique.'"[36] Concomi-
tantly, the true individual was the moral individual, for

the term "person," in its metaphysical
sense, can mean only the moral individual, i.e. the individual viewed as
meaning or aiming towards an ideal,
good or relatively bad, angelic or
relatively diabolical, lawful or relatively anarchical; for only the moral
individual, as a life lived in relation
to a plan, a finite totality of experience viewed as meaning for itself a
struggle towards conformity to an ideal,
has, in the finite world, at once an
all-pervading unity, despite the unes-
sential accidents of disease and of
sense, and a single clear contrast, in
its wholeness, to the rest of the universe of experience.[37]

There is, then, a social dimension to Royce's
system which keeps it from being merely obsessed
with the individual's relation to the Absolute.

143

In an ideal sense, a man must extend his life, and it is this extension of individuality which makes the community possible. Royce's method, as he himself remarks, "encourages a man to interpret his own individual self in terms of the biggest ideal extension of that self in time which his reasonable will can acknowledge as worthy of the aims of life." There is actually, as Jacob Loewenberg noted, a twofold extension of the individual, "temporal and social," in time and in space; "the very essence of the community depends upon the power of individual selves to extend their lives without definable limit." The self in this sense, another critic adds, is infinite; "our purposes, if completely embodied, would make us identical with the primal being."[38]

This sense of the limitless extension of the self sets Royce sharply apart from non-theistic thinkers. "I can be genuinely in love with the community," he believed, "only in case I have somehow fallen in love with the universe."[39] There is no more succinct and characteristic statement of his philosophy, interpreting as it does a basically traditional and religious feeling into modern terms of "ultimate concern."

Heterogeneity was essential to the universal community. Royce held his Absolute to be "the unity of many Wills, each one of which finds its expression in an individual life. . . ."[40] The philosophy of community was a way of reconciling the unity and multiplicity which Henry Adams found irreconcilable. If ultimately a monistic idealist, Royce went as far as he could to make his system one of plurality and variety, with the fundamental intention of preserving the uniqueness of the individual without compromising the absoluteness of the Absolute. The gist of the matter was that, for Royce, the Absolute did not swallow up the finite, but was present in the finite:

144

The very simplest view of any finite
fact already makes it a positive part
of the unique divine experience, and
therefore, as this part, itself unique.
A still deeper view recognizes any
finite will, say your own present will,
as a stage or case of the expression
of the divine purpose at a given point
of time; but this expression, too, is
once more unique. And this expression
is also in one aspect no other than
what you find it to be, to wit, your
own conscious will and meaning.[41]

Unity and multiplicity were thus interdependent concepts for Royce. The Absolute joined and
related human lives, while at the same time it
nurtured their variety. Royce believed that "the
uniqueness of the Absolute Individual, his inclu-
sive unity, his freedom, his self-possession,
hinders in no whit the included variety, the relative separateness, of the finite moral individuals, who, in their own grade of reality, are as
independent of one another, in the interlinked
contents of their lives, as the moral order requires."[42]

Royce interpreted evolution in this fashion.
As with others of his generation, he was deeply
influenced by the currents of evolutionary
thought, but he discerned within the doctrine of
evolution a fundamental conflict. Was evolution
to be interpreted in the light of mechanistic determinism, as a sequence in a rigid train of
causation, yet verifiable only empirically? Or
did evolution comprise an ideal whole, in which
absolute purpose was at work? Royce solved the
problem with a dualism; evolution might be regarded as a series of events linked by material
necessity, he decided, yet the process as a whole
viewed as teleological and ideal.[43] The dualism
was compatible with his sense of the process of
evolution as one of increasing heterogeneity.
This to an extent paralleled the formula of Spen-

145

cer and Fiske which traced the development of coherent heterogeneity from incoherent homogeneity,
but Royce's system seems more authentically pluralistic. Evolution was for him "not the history
of the growth of life from the lifeless, but the
history of the differentiation of one colony, as
it were, of the universal society from the parent
social order of the finite world in its wholeness." Put another way,

> What value human life may get we in a
> measure know. But we certainly do not
> know that the nature-experience whose
> inner sense is not now communicated to
> us is in the least lower or less full
> of meaning. Our human evolution is,
> as it were, simply the differentiation
> of one-nature dialect, whereby a group
> of finite beings now communicate to-
> gether. We have no right to call the
> other tongues with which nature speaks,
> barbarous, because in our extraordinary
> isolation from the rest of nature, we
> have forgotten what they mean.[44]

Royce's idealist interpretation of evolution attempted to make room for novelty. If evolution
were describable only in terms of natural law,
all would be contained in the beginning, novelty
would be illusory, and there could be no true
ethical process. Contrary to James, to whom an
Absolute was incompatible with any such interpretation, Royce believed that his idealism, pos-
iting an ethical process distinct from natural
process, preserved both the novel and the ethical.

Royce's psychological thought showed the
same impulse to bring disparate elements into
balance and ultimate order: past and future,
continuity and change, heredity, environment,
and spontaneity:

> The environment and the inherited

146

tendencies of an organism determine at
any moment specific acts. The already
acquired habits of the organism determine how these specific acts shall
be based upon former actions. So far,
however, the environment appears as the
one source of whatever novelties are to
appear in conduct; while the organism
appears disposed to persist in its former modes of conduct, or to repeat such
actions as its ancestral tendencies,
its experience, and its docility, predetermine. But if, amongst the various
reactions of the organism, there are
such as take the form of a restless
search for novelty of environment and
of conduct, then novelties will appear
in the actions of the organism--novel-
ties which are due, in an important
measure,to the tendencies which the
organism itself has inherited. And yet
the resulting acts will not be mere
repetitions of ancestral acts, because
they will have resulted from novel relations to an environment. It thus
comes to be the case with the organism
and with the mind, as it is with the
emigrant to a foreign country. In the
new country he lives a new life, and
not the life of his ancestors. This
result is indeed due to the new environment. Yet the new environment would
never have come to him if he had not
wandered. And he would never have wandered had it not been the result of a
restlessness that was his own.[45]

The lessons of evolution and psychology for
Royce, then, were the lessons of variety, novelty, and differentiation; yet he gave equal weight
to the principle of continuity. Heredity and
environment were determinants, but of such sort
as to foster a type of spontaneity. Far from the
iron determinism of some social Darwinists, this
was a view which restated the old ideal of order-

ed and harmonious liberty in the light of nineteenth century evolutionary thought.

In Royce's concern for order, social relations, and continuity there was a clear and fundamental conservatism. This was not incompatible
with his conventionally or more than conventionally liberal position on civil liberties, race
relations, and other such social and political
questions. It was a conservatism which rested on
the assumption of the continuous and related nature of experience. The problem with which it
concerned itself was that which Royce designated
"interpretation," of the translation of past into
future with justice to the claims of both. This
represented a concern potentially as progressive
as it was conservative, but Royce's strong emphasis on order as the end of social evolution
tended to place him more comfortably within the
Burkean tradition.

A native of California, which was not far
removed from frontier conditions during his youth,
Royce was acutely conscious of the eternal struggle between order and disorder. His history of
the state described "the evolution of California
from disorder to unity, from lynch law to justice,
from miners' meetings to local government." California thus became a "sociological laboratory,"46
in which to study the struggle between "every conservative tendency and the forces of disorder."
This struggle, Royce saw, is never entirely won,
for "anarchy is a thing of degrees, and its lesser degrees often coexist even with the constitu-
tions that are well-conceived and popular." His
bias in California was for the claims of society.
The social process, he explained, consists in
"the struggle of society to impress the true dignity and majesty of its claims on wayward and
blind individuals, and the struggle of individual
man, meanwhile, to escape, like a fool, from his
moral obligations to society." Californians
learned from repeated experience the "fearful effects" of irresponsible freedom, and the necessi-

148

ty of social order. Family, school, and church
were preeminently needed as conservative social
forces. The danger in popular sovereignty, Royce
felt, was not passion but apathy--"its corrupt
love of ease, its delight in old and now meaningless phrases, and in the men who use these
phrases. Such men do not destroy the existing
social order, but while preserving it from sudden
injury, they fatten themselves upon the slow decay that goes on it its less vigorous forces."[47]

Royce strikes a particularly Burkean note in
his conception of the temporal dimension of the
community, so reminiscent of the Whig's dictum
that society is a partnership, not merely between
those who are living, but between those who are
living, those who are dead, and those who are yet
to be born. The true community, Royce pointed
out, "is essentially a product of a time-process.
. . . Its more or less conscious history, real
or ideal, is a part of its very essence. A community requires for its existence a history and
is greatly aided in its consciousness by a memory." Past and future are parts of the same
whole,and each moment makes its unique contribu-
tion to the "symphony" of history. The "equal
'ideality' of past and future. . .logically forbids conduct to   act with reference to a limited portion of time or to a limited being or group
of beings. . . ." His own method, he noted, "encourages a man to interpret his own individual
self in terms of the largest ideal extension of
that self in time which his reasonable will can
acknowledge as worthy of the aims of life."[48]

Royce's sense of social coherence and continuity naturally fitted him for a certain com-
fort within the Anglo-American constitutional
tradition; he could admire "that ancient proceed-
ing of compromise in place of adherence to abstract principle which has been all along so characteristic of the Anglo-Saxon in his political
life."[49] But the precariousness of this spirit
was clear enough to keep Royce from being at ease

in Zion. He recognized the stains on late nineteenth century American society wrought by racial
prejudice and political corruption. (He thought,
however, that in a newly developing country it
was sometimes more prudent to tolerate a degree
of corruption than to encourage "political offi-
ciousness.")[50] He looked back on the Mexican War
as a venture in international immorality by the
United States, and expressed the hope that if the
nation again decided "to serve the devil, it will
do so with more frankness, and will deceive itself less by half-conscious cant." The same
spirit could transform the conservative into the
zealot. Near the end of his life (but before
American entry) he was sufficiently swept along
by the tide of World War I propaganda as to equate
the possible victory of Germany with "the triumph
of Satan." Rather than yield up its ideal, it
now seemed to him, it would be better for mankind
"that war should rage, with all its horrors, so
long as humanity lasts. . . ."[51] The conservative function of "interpretation" was extinguished
in the light of this Manichean vision.

This was a crusading spirit ordinarily submerged in Royce's impulse to include, to relate,
to create a community. To be sure, he insisted
on the absolute and irrevocable quality of evil
(with which he had come to identify the leaders
of Germany), but in his "world of appreciation,"
eternity encompassed and reconciled normally opposed political positions. In the "world of description," he recognized change as an inelucta-
ble fact of life. In 1880, indeed, he characterized his own time as revolutionary. But while
radicalism and conservatism could only mean divergent attitudes toward this revolutionary
change, Royce perceived an ultimate bond between
them. For the sincere revolutionary, he thought,
destruction was only a prelude to reconstruction,
and thence to the conservation of that which was
to be reconstructed. His thesis was "that conservatism and radicalism are examples of a single
tendency of voluntary progress, the tendency,

150

namely, to satisfy changing needs with the least possible change of plan, to gain as much new experience as possible with the least alteration of the ways of gaining it."[52]

Royce offered here no great insight into politics, but he did suggest the range of his relational thought and its central notion of community. Community itself was at once a profoundly conservative and a profoundly radical idea. It denoted both the traditional familiar grouping of the sort that Royce sought to reconstitute as "provincialism," and the Utopian, never fully attainable ideal of his "Beloved Community." Community was a dream of the past and a dream of the future, the uniting principle between Burkean and millenarian. It nurtured and governed the individual, and yet in the vein of romantic radicalism was the field for the fully extended life of the individual.

Royce's advocacy of provincialism lets us glimpse the community principle on a concrete level. A province, in his definition, was a community compact enough to possess its own traditions, ideals, and aspirations. It was, he thought, essential to civilization. Provincialism combatted the "levelling tendency," and although the latter term was an old fashioned one, Royce's application of it was very modern:

> By the levelling tendency in question I mean that aspect of modern civilization which is most obviously suggested by the fact that, because of the ease of communication amongst distant places, because of the spread of popular education, and because of the consolidation and of the centralization of industries and of social authorities, we tend all over the nation, and, in some degree, even throughout the civilized world, to read the same daily news, to share in the same general ideas,

> to submit to the same overmastering
> social forces, to live in the same
> eternal fashions, to discourage indi-
> viduality, and to approach a dead level
> of harassed mediocrity. . . . The vast
> corporation succeeds and displaces the
> individual. Ingenuity and initiative
> become subordinated to the discipline
> of an impersonal social order.[53]

The trend toward social consolidation had become
so strong, Royce was persuaded, that the pursuit
of the ideal must be carried to a new realm--the
"realm of real life," of the province. "There,"
he suggested, "must we flee from the stress of
the now too vast and problematic life of the nation as a whole. . . . Freedom," he thought,
". . .dwells now in the small social group, and
has its securest home in the provincial life.
The nation by itself, apart from the influence
of the province, is in danger of becoming an incomprehensible monster in whose presence the
individual loses his right, his self-consciousness, and his dignity. The province must save
the individual."[54]

Royce was accordingly repelled by "the great
industrial forces, the aggregations of capital,
the combinations of enormous physical power, em-
ployed for various social ends. These vast social forces are like the forces of nature," he
remarked. "They excite our loyalty as little as
do the trade-winds or the blizzard. . . ." Citing Hegel's "self-estranged social mind," Royce
emphasized that it was necessary to educate "the
self-estranged spirit of our nation to know itself better." We needed "a new and wiser provincialism," for,he maintained, provincial loyalty "is the best mediator between the narrower
interests of the individual and the larger patriotism of our nation."[55]

The province was an alternative to atomistic
individualism and to collective mass society, conditions which Royce perceived to be ultimately

identical. Viewing the modern forces which detach men from their fellows at the same time that they nurture large social combinations, it was apparent to him

> that <u>individualism and collectivism are tendencies, each of which, as our social order grows, intensifies the other</u>. The more the social will expresses itself in vast organizations of collective power, the more are individuals trained to be aware of their own personal wants and choices and ideals, and of the vast opportunities that would be theirs if they could but gain control of these social forces.[56]

This individualist-collectivist society was in a perverse way the reflection of the guiding Protestant paradox of the liberated individual who was a slave to the omnipotent God. In the modern secular version, the liberated individual was a slave to vast and impersonal forces beyond his control. And the latter dispensation, at least, was not such as to favor real individuality. "Individualistic communities," Royce observed, "are almost universally, and paradoxically enough, communities that are extremely cruel to individuals."[57]

The whole weight of Royce's philosophy was behind his conclusion that "chasms do not individuate." Individuation resulted not from separation, but from the manifold fulfillment of the will of the Absolute. It was this will, "in freely differentiated, various, and unique forms, that appears as identical with the various individual finite wills, but <u>so</u> appears in them that the total constitution of this world of wills embodies the one Divine Will wherein all these free elements are united, organised, harmonized." This conception did not permit finite individuals to be "confounded with one another" in a collectivist, or even in a democratic, manner. George

153

Bancroft had envisioned democracy as a rolling ocean. Royce rejected the image, adapting an older one to his purpose. Individuals, he said, "do not slip as dewdrops into any sort of shining sea. They are individuals, constitutive of an individual [the Absolute] . And the 'City of God' is God, while its citizens are free and finite individuals." The many wills harmonized with the whole, the best type of unity being a unity which "consists of elements which embody a universal type, but which are not exhaustively predetermined either by that type or by one another." No greater degree of dependence was required; on the other hand, "a world of individuals more separate than this, more endowed with absolute caprice than this, would be a world of anarchy, no 'City of God,' but a moral hell."58

Consequently Royce took a wary view of individual freedom. He saw no value and much danger in freedom as "limitless eccentricity, individuality without other aim than to be peculiar. . . ."59 This was futile. "Everybody," he remarked, "has tried to realize the ideal of individualism, this ideal of a happy or satisfied self, either for himself or for some loved one; and everybody finds, if he tries the thing long enough, what a hollow and worthless business it all is."60 Nor did it help to lump individuals together, no matter on how apparently equitable a basis. "Since the detached individual is essentially a lost being," he pointed out, "you cannot save masses of lost individuals through the triumph of mere democracy. Masses of lost individuals do not become genuine freemen merely because they all have votes."61 Royce accordingly distrusted the use of "freedom" as a shibboleth of mass political movements. "Human freedom," he emphasized, "is a personal affair. Man cannot be free; men must be." Whether on the individual or the social plane, the desire for freedom was doomed to disappointments. Demanding freedom from restraint, the personal will demanded equally its expression in a social life full of re-

154

straints. The will to be free, he observed, "asserts itself in all sorts of self-surrendering, self-entangling ways," as when "the will of the people seeks freedom, and therefore accepts ere long the rule of despots or, in our age and land, the rule of the 'bosses.'"[62]

Royce was particularly appalled by the philosophic and practical individualism of his own time. The earlier romantic individualism at least had "always sought great heart experiences, and generally believed in them. . . ." The individualism of German romanticism, in particular, had been constructive and not merely iconoclastic. "Individualism is indeed always strongly negative," Royce asserted, "but the individualism of that time had its hearty positive enthusiasms, and often hugged its very illusions." Modern individualism, on the other hand, was characterized by "a more drastic and contemptuous tone," its more extreme advocates seeming to delight in making "pyramids of the skulls of their enemies." As exemplified by Friedrich Nietzsche, it seemed finally "a restlessly intolerant and muscular individualism which despises its own sufferings, an idealism without any ideal world of truth, a religion without a faith, a martyrdom without prospect of a paradise. . . ." As such it was unacceptable to Josiah Royce.[63]

No more acceptable, in the long run, was the Spencerian philosophy, with its strange mixture of individualism and cosmic determinism. It appears that Herbert Spencer may for a time have captivated Royce, but if so his enthusiasm rapidly and drastically waned. He continued to respect Spencer as a humane man, and as one with a secure and significant place in the history of English thought. But Spencer was too much the facile generalizer to satisfy his American colleague. "If you found a bag big enough to hold all the facts," he complained, "that was an unification of science. . . . Spencer's theory of evolution does not determine the relations of the

155

essential processes of evolution to one another, does not define their inner unity, and does not enable us to conceive a series of types of evolutionary processes in orderly relations to one another."[64]

Royce found a certain naïveté at the bottom of Spencer's thought, a "childlike ignorance" that there was any ethical problem inherent in evolution.[65] Furthermore, he decided that Spencer, although an individualist, could appreciate only an individual of his own particular stripe. His temperament suited to generalities, and "a lover of humanity in the abstract, Spencer was peculiarly destitute of any large power to appreciate individuals." In short, the Englishman failed adequately to relate the individual to the general, especially from the ethical standpoint. The failure was educational, however; thus Royce noted Spencer's conviction that a coherent theory of nature

> would furnish a systematic and complete foundation for his own never changing individualistic ethics, and for his sturdy, old-fashioned British liberalism. In this way, the main work of Spencer's life came to be an effort to bring into synthesis an organic theory of the unity of the evolutionary process, with a doctrine regarding the freedom and the rights of the individual which had come down to him from an age when evolution and the organic unity of things had indeed interested Englishmen but little. This particular synthesis of organic evolution with individual independence remains one of the most paradoxical, and consequently most instructive, features of Spencer's teaching.[66]

The indictment was not only of Herbert Spencer, but of the whole Anglo-American school of thought which attempted to combine political and economic individualism with a cosmic determinism which was the negation of individuality.

Royce's own view of the problem of individuality held it to be tantamount to the problem of freedom. "If I am I and nobody else, and if I am I as an expression of purpose," he argued, "then I am in so far free just because, as an individual, I express by my existence no will except my own." We are free, then, to the extent that we consciously and uniquely will, according to Royce.[67] "Individuality, contingency, freedom,-- these, he supposed, ". . .are profoundly inter-related categories. Necessity concerns the finite interrelationships of thought. . . . But, as an object of exclusive interest, the true individual of the ultimate real world is a fact that expresses the free interest, or Love, of the Absolute as will."[68] This left the practical difficulties of reconciling the unique individual will with the purposes of the community.

Royce offered one solution with his philosophy of loyalty. It was after all loyalty which held the community together, loyalty as "a practical faith that communities, viewed as units, have a value which is superior to all the values and interests of detached individuals."[69] To love the community was to be loyal, and loyalty, he believed,was "the heart of all the virtues, the central duty amongst all duties." He regretted that in his own time Americans had seemed to forget the virtue of loyalty, and had neglected to cultivate it in their social order.[70]

More precisely, Royce defined loyalty as "the Will to Believe in something eternal, and to express that belief in the practical life of a human being." Whoever sought any universal truth was being loyal to a cause. Such a cause was outside of the individual, but personal as well as superpersonal--". . .not only another than his private self; it is in a sense his larger

self. . . . Loyalty is a sort of possession. It
has a demonic force which controls the wayward
private self. The cause takes hold of the man,
and his organism is no longer his own, so long
as the loyal inspiration is upon him." The genuinely moral attitude seemed to Royce then to be
always one of loyalty; he felt, indeed, that
"the whole moral law is implicitly bound up in
the one precept: Be loyal." He preferred even
blind loyalty "to the sort of thoughtless individualism which is loyal to nothing."[71]

Loyalty, Royce thought, fulfilled the individual, teaching him to assert himself through
devotion to his community. It touched the whole
personality. "Loyalty has its elemental appeal
to my whole organism," he remarked. "My cause
must become one with my human life. Yet all this
must occur not without my willing choice. I must
control my devotion. It will possess me, but
not without my voluntary complicity; for I shall
accept the possession."[72] The concept of loyalty
thus fitted well with his belief in freedom of
choice within the ideal whole. "All the highest
forms of the unity of the spirit, in our human
world, constantly depend, for their very existence, upon the renewed free choices, the sustained loyalty, of the members of communities," he
pointed out.[73]

The philosophy of loyalty fitted closely and
explicitly too with Royce's religious vision. It
was a thesis of his The Problem of Christianity
that "the religion of loyalty, the doctrine of
the salvation of the otherwise hopelessly lost
individual through devotion to the life of the
genuinely real and Universal Community, must survive, and must direct the future both of religion
and of mankind, if man is to be saved at all."
Loyalty, he believed, involved "at least a latent
belief" in the superhuman, for religion in its
highest forms was "the interpretation both of the
eternal and of the spirit of loyalty through emotion, and through a fitting activity of the imag-

ination."[74] Royce in fact identified loyalty with Christian love, or grace; "the power that gives to the Christian convert the new loyalty," he observed, "is what Paul calls Grace." In a broader religious context, he suggested that "without loyalty, there is no salvation." All the loyal, he concluded, are, and always have been, "one genuine and religious brotherhood";"I call the community of all who have sought for salvation through loyalty   the Invisible Church."[75]

The same principle could be extended to more mundane areas. It seemed clear, for example, that the triumph of science had been due largely to loyalty to the general cause of science. The political implications seemed even more obvious; for Royce loyalty to the state partook of the universal and religious significance of loyalty. In the strenuous mode of the time, he proclaimed that "every patriotic song which deifies one's country, every other form of the religion of patriotism, exemplifies the experience of the devoted lover of his country by teaching that it is 'man's perdition to be safe' in case his social world calls for the sacrifice of his life, and that salvation comes through service."[76]

Loyalty meant necessarily the possibility of treason, and Royce did not shrink from defining it. "All deeds are indeed irrevocable," he acknowledged. "But the only traitorous sin against the light is such that, in advance, the traitor's own free acceptance of a cause has stamped it with the character of being what his own will had defined as his own unpardonable sin. . . . There was a moment when he freely did whatever he could to wreck the cause that he had sworn to serve." Treason thus banished to the "hell of the irrevocable," for "the guilt of a free act of betrayal is as enduring as time."[77]

The major apparent difficulty with the philosophy of loyalty is the strong possibility that loyalties will conflict. Royce's solution to this problem was the precept of loyalty to loyalty; that is, one should act in such a way that "there shall be more of this common good of loyalty in the world than there would have been, had you not lived and acted." Thus, "the spirit of our true loyalty is never opposed to the existence of our neighbor's loyalty." Loyalty to loyalty was the one cause that all had in common.[78]

> The traditional view of loyalty has associated the term, in the minds of most of you, with moral situations in which some external social power predetermines for the individual, without his consent, all the causes to which he ought to be loyal. Loyalty so conceived appears to be opposed to individual liberty. But in our philosophy of loyalty there is only one cause which is rationally and absolutely determined for the individual as the right cause for him as for everybody,-- this is the general cause defined by the phrase loyalty to loyalty. The way in which any one man is to show his loyalty to loyalty is, however, in our philosophy of loyalty, something which varies endlessly with the individual, and which can never be precisely defined except by and through personal consent. I can be loyal to loyalty only in my own fashion, and by serving my own personal system of causes.[79]

Royce's advocacy of the community, then, was not rooted in nostalgia; he did not plead for the restoration of the traditional village community, as often repressive and demanding of conformity as that was. He proposed community based not on caste and inheritance, but on voluntary loyalty-- a loyalty, furthermore, tolerant of other loyalties, according to the cardinal principle of loyalty to loyalty. Royce here suggested a way by which conservatism in the Burkean vein might be divested of the undue coerciveness of tradition, to be rendered in this way, perhaps, truly applicable to American society for the first time. In the Hegelian mode which critics have noted in Royce's _California_, the voluntary community might then emerge as the synthesis of traditional and atomistic types of society, and loyalty mediate between prescription and anomie.[80] But essential to such possibilites was the religious principle which animated Royce's conception of community, viewed on the level of the province as on that of the universe.

iii.

In constructing his philosophy of community, Royce had borrowed from Charles Sanders Peirce a triadic scheme of cognitive process, involving not only perception and conception, but also interpretation. Perception had "its natural terminus in some object perceived," and was therefore "intolerably lonesome"; conception by itself was open to the charge of being sterile; but interpretation was a social process, mediating between diverse ideas or sensations, and between perception and conception themselves, as an essential part of understanding. Indeed, Royce argued,"the real world is the Community of Interpretation which is constituted by the two antithetic ideas, and their mediator or interpreter, whatever or whoever that interpreter may be." (He noted the resemblance of this idea to the Hegelian dialectic, but argued that Peirce had not been notably influenced by Hegel, and that in any case "Peirce's concept of interpretation defines an extremely general process, of which the Hegelian dialectical triadic process is a very special case.")[81]

Royce further developed this insight of Peirce, applying it to the life of the community

161

as it existed in time. The temporal dimension
was indispensable, for in his understanding a
complete community was one both of memory and of
hope. One lived in the past and the future as
well as in the present, and necessarily incorporated something of both into one's life. "The
time process, and the ideal extensions of the
self in this time-process," he thought, "lie at
the basis of the whole theory of this community."
Royce acknowledged his "world of interpretation"
as fundamentally historical and teleological.
"The pursuit, the search for the goal, the new
interpretation which every new event requires,--
this endless sequence of new acts of interpretation,--this constitutes the world," he concluded.
"This is the order of time."[82]

The community of interpretation, then, expressed "a system of essentially social relations"; it was "the coherent life which includes
past present and future, and holds them reasonably together, . . . [and] in which the present,
with an endless fecundity of invention, interprets the past to the future. . . ."[83] But for
Royce the social, in the highest sense, meant
the divine. For the nature of deity itself, it
seemed to him, could best be understood "in the
form of the Community of Interpretation, and
above all in the form of the Interpreter, who
interprets all to all, and each individual to
the world, and the world of spirits to each individual." He believed that "in such an interpreter, and in his community, the problem of the
One and the Many would find its ideally complete
expression and solution. . . . In him the Community, the Individual, and the Absolute would be
completely expressed, reconciled, and distinguished." There was no real world, Royce thought, unless both the interpreter and the community were
real. "The history of the universe, the whole
order of time, is the history and the order and
the expression of this Universal Community."
While the world of interpretation was historical
and teleological, the ideal goal was never reached

at a given point in time. The "pursuit of the goal," he concluded, "this bondage of the whole creation to the pursuit of that which it never reaches,--this naturally tragic estrangement of this world from its goal,--this constitutes the problem of the universe." But he added that "the whole order of time, the process of the spirit, is interpreted, and so interpreted that, when viewed in the light of its goal, the whole world is reconciled to its own purposes."[84]

The greatest task of interpretation was religious not only in form but in content. This was the interpretation of Christianity, essential to the historic life of western civilization, yet drastically weakened by the challenges of rationalism and science. The difficulty, as Royce realized, was not in working out plausible compromises, as between Darwin and Genesis, with the intent of preserving the spirit while sacrificing the strict letter. Such compromises were often eminently reasonable, satisfying moral and even aesthetic sensibilities. Yet so far at least as American Protestantism was concerned, they seemed always to vitiate Christianity. There was no logical stopping place in the process of rationalization, and there appeared by the early twentieth century to be only the stark alternatives of an atavistic fundamentalism and a sterile theological liberalism that had scarcely the properties of religion. Whether Royce solved the problem more persuasively than other thinkers who have struggled with it, including the neo-orthodox school and the Christian existentialists, is doubtful; certainly his influence has been far less. But it was fully commensurate with the direction of his life and career, as well as with the needs of his time, that his last major effort of systematic thought should be The Problem of Christianity, first delivered in lecture form, and then published in 1913. It is now perhaps his most interesting work.

In treating with Christianity, as elsewhere

in his philosophy, Royce's great project was to conjoin the concrete and individual with the ideal and universal. "Community" was the medium through which he tried to accomplish this. Royce departed drastically from the Protestant spirit in holding the central idea of Christianity to be not its founder, but the church itself. He attributed the first self-realization of its own essence to the Christianity of the Apostle Paul. Christian love, with Paul, had taken on the form of loyalty, defined as "the thoroughgoing and loving devotion of an individual to a community." This was "Paul's simple but vast transformation of Christian love."[85] Grace, according to Bancroft, had been rendered by Jonathan Edwards as universal love, but according to Royce's interpretation Paul had taken the further step seventeen hundred years previously of transforming love into loyalty.

If his idea of the church seems Catholic in spirit, Royce remained a Protestant in holding the historic church to have departed fundamentally from the ideal of the Christian community. Indeed, no particular church had ever realized the ideal, and the true church, consequently, remained an invisible one. This universal community was, in fact, the Kingdom of Heaven. Royce acknowledged that the church as a disembodied idea was far from satisfying human needs, and as always his intent was to discover the practical meaning of the ideal.

Royce pointed out that his own concern was with religious experience on the social plane, as distinguished from William James's emphasis on individual religious experience. Indeed, for Royce, it was the community which saved. But this was a very special kind of community, to which he attached the name, "The Beloved Community." He was emphatic that no mere aggregation of individuals sufficed. He attributed to Paul the doctrine that "Man's fallen state is due to his nature as a social animal. This nature is such that you can train his conscience only by

164

awakening his self-will." But self-willed individualism, he reiterated, was only the concomitant of collectivism:

> In general, and upon high levels of
> human intelligence, when you train
> individualism, you also train col-
> lectivism; that is, you train in the
> individual a respect for the collec-
> tive will. Amd it belongs to Paul's
> very deep and searching insight to
> assert that these two tendencies--
> the tendency towards individualism,
> and that towards collectivism--do
> not exclude, but intensify and in-
> flame each other.

This was so because the training of the individual, although breeding respect for the law as the expression of collective will, also makes him conscious of personal drives which war against the collective will. Whatever the result in outward conduct, "it inevitably leads to an inner division of the self, a disease of self-consciousness, which Paul finds to be the curse of all merely natural human civilization." This natural community is a community of sin.[86]

The only escape from this community of sin is loyalty, i.e. the individual's "love for an united community, expressed in a life of devotion to that community." The difficulty is that the Beloved Community is the union of members who love it, but in order for them to love it, there must first be something to love. The community appears then beyond the unaided ability of man to achieve. With the ground thus prepared, Royce can keep his doctrine of the Beloved Community from becoming merely another secular call to uplift. For a special intervention is needed to bring the community into being, that attributed by Christianity to its founder. Christ was the means of grace; "He both knew and loved his community before it existed on earth; for his fore-

165

knowledge was one with that of the God whose will he came to accomplish."[87]

Royce believed that Christianity was distinguished by the thoroughness with which it grasped the idea of community:

> The Individual and the Community. . . .
> This pair it is which, in the first
> place, enables Christianity to tell the
> individual why, in his natural isola-
> tion and narrowness, he is essentially
> defective,--is inevitably a failure, is
> doomed, and must be transformed. . . .
> This is why, for Christianity, the sal-
> vation of man means the destruction of
> his natural self,--the sacrifice of
> what his flesh holds dearest,--the ut-
> ter transformation of the primal core
> of the social self. I say: it is the
> merely natural relation of the individ-
> ual to the community which, for Chris-
> tianity, explains all this. Here are
> two levels of human existence. The in-
> dividual, born on his own level, is
> naturally doomed to hatred for what be-
> longs to the other level. Yet there, on
> that higher level, his only salvation
> awaits him.[88]

The community, moreover, preserves a balance between the individual and the whole; it "presents itself to our minds both as one and as many; and unless it is both one and many, it is no community at all."[89]

Royce's idea of salvation by the community was a sharp departure from the traditional Protestant insistence on salvation as a transaction directly between God and the individual, and the concomitant sharp dichotomy between individualism and arbitrary social power. Twentieth century experience and thought have tended to bear out Royce's contention that genuine individuality

166

flourishes within a community. He was not, however, deluded into believing that a community could be constructed through any facile kind of social engineering. Without insisting upon the supernatural element of Christian theology, he saw that loyalty, in his sense, depended upon an "x" factor transcending mundane human relationships. "Knowledge of the community," he insisted, "is not love of the community. Love, when it comes, comes as from above."[90] This, of course, was Royce's version of the old Christian idea of grace. Again, one could be truly in love with the community only if one were also in love with the universe.

This proposition is the key to Josiah Royce, and furnishes at least an insight into his age, in which to many of the most discerning the cosmos could no longer be seen as subservient to human purpose--mirrored in divine will--but which could still seem hospitable to it. Royce's conception of the Absolute as universal community was an appropriate expression of religious sensibility in a world distrustful of hierarchy but still insistent on teleology. If such an Absolute was far removed from the Calvinist God of his mother, Royce's conjoining of cosmos and community was also far removed from later canons which held the universe to be alien to man and to whatever community he might construct. The Christian precepts of love of God and love of neighbor provided the basis for a theology of community which claimed a solution to the nineteenth century problem which presaged the twentieth century problem of an alien universe--the riddle of the One and the Many. William James and Henry Adams would doubt the efficacy of such a solution.

Footnotes

1. Vincent Buranelli, Josiah Royce (New York: Twayne Publishers, 1964), pp. 51, 63, 83. (Hereinafter cited as Buranelli, Royce.) John Clendenning describes Royce as "America's only international representative of post-Kantian idealism." The Letters of Josiah Royce. Edited with an Introduction by John Clendenning (Chicago: University of Chicago Press, 1970), p. 9. (Hereinafter cited as Royce, Letters.) Bruce Kuklick classifies Royce among the "Cambridge pragmatists," and notes that their pragmatism was a form of neo-Kantianism drawing from a set of connected doctrines: "a constructionalist epistemology stressing the changing character of our conceptual schemes; a commitment to a variety of voluntarism; a Kantian concern with the nature of possible experience; an adherence to the idealist principle that existence does not transcend consciousness; a distrust of traditional British empiricism; a recognition of the importance of logic for philosophy; an uncomfortableness with the dichotomy between the conceptual and the empirical; a refusal to distinguish between questions of knowledge and of value; an emphasis on the relation of philosophy to practical questions; and a desire to reconcile science and religion." Josiah Royce: An Intellectual Biography (Indianapolis: Bobbs-Merrill, 1972), p. 2. (Hereinafter cited as Kuklick, Royce.)

2. Buranelli, Royce, pp. 130-131. "Kant appeals to the two worlds of phenomena and noumena, the former rigidly controlled by scientific laws, the latter marked by freedom and ethical conduct. Royce appeals to the two worlds of description and appreciation. But for Royce it is actually a single world viewed from different perspectives. His is a double-aspect theory." Ibid., p. 129.

3. Josiah Royce, The Spirit of Modern Philosophy (Boston: Houghton Mifflin, 1892), pp.

168

413-416, 419. (Hereinafter cited as Royce, Spirit of Modern Philosophy.)

4. Josiah Royce, Studies of Good and Evil, A
Series of Essays Upon Problems of Philosophy and
of Life (Hamden, Connecticut, 1964), p. 168.
(Hereinafter cited as Royce, Good and Evil); Josiah Royce, The World and the Individual, 2 volumes (New York: Macmillan, 1900-1901), I, 469.
(Hereinafter cited as Royce, World and the Individual); Royce, Spirit of Modern Philosophy,
p. 429.

5. Royce, Letters, p. 346. Royce to Frank
Thilly, May 6, 1896.

6. Buranelli, Royce, p. 63. "The influences
which most profoundly molded his thought," John
McCreary believed, "were those received from his
studies of Lotze, Schopenhauer, Kant, and Schel-
ling. His great work, The World and the Individual, reveals a profound study of the thought of
Hegel, of Indian philosophy, and of scholasti-
cism." "The Religious Philosophy of Josiah
Royce," The Journal of Religion, XXX (April,
1950), 117. (Hereinafter cited as McCreary, "Religious Philosophy of Josiah Royce.") Critics
have appreciated Royce's importance and influence. "He is mentioned as a contributor to modern logic by Russell and Lewis,"Buranelli notes.
"His metaphysics helped to fashion the existentialism of Marcel. His philosophy of the community is like that of Buber, his dialectical theology like that of Barth, Niebuhr, and Hocking."
Buranelli, who believes that James did not break
a trail for later thinkers as Royce did, suggests
that the latter should rank only after Charles
S. Peirce as an American philosopher. Royce,
pp. 146-147. A somewhat different view is taken
by Morton White. "Royce's philosophy was one
against which many social thinkers and philosophers rebelled at the turn of the twentieth cen-

tury, but it did not go down without a struggle,"
Morton concludes. "It was encased in thick-
plated armor since it was formidably protected
by the use of mathematical logic, a philosophy
of science, a theory of meaning, and modern biology; it lived in the mighty fortress of Christianity; it had its links with the American
tradition; it was formulated in the rolling peri-
olds of a powerful preacher. But, as the saying
goes, the bigger they are, the harder they fall;
and when the mighty Royce fell, it was as if the
temple of American philosophy itself had collapsed." Science and Sentiment in America:
Philosophical Thought from Jonathan Edwards to
John Dewey (New York: Oxford University Press,
1972), p. 239. (Hereinafter cited as White,
Science and Sentiment.)

7. Jacob Loewenberg, "Josiah Royce: Interpreter of American Problems," University of
California Chronicle, XIX (n.d.), pp. 3-4.

8. Josiah Royce, Fugitive Essays. With an
Introduction by Dr. J. Loewenberg (Cambridge:
Harvard University Press, 1920), pp. 305, 319-
321. (Hereinafter cited as Royce, Fugitive Essays.) "Royce's Absolute had many similarities
to Emerson's Over-Soul," Ralph Henry Gabriel
points out. "Because God is in man, Emerson
thought human nature divine. For Royce, in his
last days, the Absolute was the completion of the
Great Community. . . . Emerson sometimes spoke
of the Over-Soul as a universal Mind of which the
mind of man is a part. Royce's Absolute was more
than universal Mind; he was universal Will including the minds and wills of living men and, at
the same time, supplementing and completing them."
The Course of American Democratic Thought. Second Edition (New York: Ronald Press, 1956), pp.
313-314. (Hereinafter cited as Gabriel, American
Democratic Thought.)

9. Royce, Good and Evil, p. 17.

10. _Ibid._, pp. iii-iv.

11. _Ibid._, pp. 299, 336.

12. _Ibid._, pp. 324-325.

13. _Ibid._, p. 325.

14. Josiah Royce, _The Sources of Religious Insight. Lectures Delivered Before Lake Forest College on the Foundation of the Late William Bross_ (Edinburgh: T. & T. Clark, 1912), pp. 144-150. (Hereinafter cited as Royce, _Sources of Religious Insight._)

15. Josiah Royce, _The Philosophy of Loyalty_ (New York: Macmillan, 1908), p. 341. (Hereinafter cited as Royce, _Loyalty_); Josiah Royce, _Lectures on Modern Idealism_ (New Haven: Yale University Press, 1923), pp. 85-86. (Hereinafter cited as Royce, _Modern Idealism_; Josiah Royce, _The Problems of Christianity_. With a new introduction by John E. Smith (Chicago: University of Chicago Press, 1968), pp. 240-242. (Hereinafter cited as Royce, _Problem of Christianity._)

16. Royce, _Sources of Religious Insight_, p. 157.

17. Royce, _Modern Idealism_, p. 258.

18. Josiah Royce, _William James and Other Essays on the Philosophy of Life_ (New York: Macmillan, 1912), pp. 38, 40-41. (Hereinafter cited as Royce, _William James._)

19. Royce, _Sources of Religious Insight_, pp. 74-75.

20. Royce, _William James_, p. 36. Buranelli notes of Royce and James that "they were able to come to grips with one another because of the extent to which they agreed. Both were practical, empirical, and averse to wayward romantic philos-

171

ophizing. Both were voluntarists who allotted a
commanding function to the will in the formation
of rational judgments. The point at issue between them was the metaphysical system that best
accounted for the practical, the empirical, and
the voluntaristic. Their differences could not
be resolved because, while Royce remained an absolute idealist of the post-Kantian type, James
was trying to disintegrate both absolutism and
idealism with the solvent of pragmatism." Royce,
pp. 72-73. "As Royce later called his doctrine
Absolute Pragmatism, we may interpret James as
a pluralistic idealist," Kuklick concludes.
Royce, p. 5.

21. Buranelli, Royce, p. 106.

22. Josiah Royce, California from the Conquest in 1846 to the Second Vigilance Committee
in San Francisco. A Study of American Character
(Boston: Houghton Mifflin, 1886), p. 500. (Hereinafter cited as Royce, California.)

23. Royce, Problem of Christianity, pp. 235,
80-81.

24. Ibid., pp. 94, 122.

25. Josiah Royce, The Hope of the Great Community (New York: Macmillan, 1916), p. 52. (Hereinafter cited as Royce, Great Community.)

26. Royce, Problem of Christianity, pp. 85,
218.

27. Royce, California, pp. 465, 501. Earl
Pomeroy discusses Royce's work as a historian.
He notes that although Royce wrote no history in
his later career, "his philosophy became increasingly social, and the relationship between his
cosmology and his interest in themes that he ex-
plored in his historical writing became closer or
at least clearer." "Josiah Royce, Historian in
Quest of Community," Pacific Historical Review, XL

(February, 1971), 5.

28. Royce, Good and Evil, pp. 201-205.

29. Royce, World and the Individual, I, 414.
"Royce's Absolute," Jacob Loewenberg points out,
"is preeminently a social concept. It is this
social character of Royce's Absolute--often over-
looked--which distinguishes it from the simple
and undifferentiated and unutterable One of the
mystic. . . . Unity and multiplicity are for him
interdependent concepts. The Absolute has the
unity of a social organism; it is the complete
integration of a complexity and variety of purposes, wills, and ideals." Royce, Fugitive Essays, pp. 11-12.

30. Royce, World and the Individual, I, 426-
427. "The concept of an individual in the full
sense is a limiting concept not corresponding to
any fact of our conscious experience. . .," Royce
wrote. "Our goal is the envisionment of the one
real individual, viz., the whole universe." Royce,
Letters, p. 341. Royce to Mary Whiton Calkins,
spring, 1896. McCreary suggests that Royce was
"striving, perhaps more or less consciously, to
retain whatever security there may be for ethical and religious values in the theistic position,
while maintaining at the same time a philosophy
which was in fine pantheistic. It appears as
though he was desirous of utilizing the strength
of theism within a pantheistic framework." "Religious Philosophy of Josiah Royce," 124.

31. Royce, World and the Individual, II,
335-337.

32. Ibid., I, 460.

33. Josiah Royce, Joseph LeConte, G. H. Howison, and Sidney Edward Mezes, The Conception of
God. A Philosophical Discussion Concerning the
Nature of the Divine Idea as a Demonstrable Reality (New York: Macmillan, 1898), p. 316. (Here-

inafter cited as Royce, Conception of God.) Buranelli notes that Royce "sounds like an existentialist when he talks about the self making itself. . . ." Royce, p. 125.

34. Josiah Royce, The Conception of Immortality (New York: Greenwood Press, 1968), pp.
28, 5. (Hereinafter cited as Royce, Conception
of Immortality.) "Royce was the first American
thinker to front squarely the apparent contradiction between the first and the second doctrine
of the democratic faith, between the postulate of
a fundamental law and that of the free individual." Gabriel, American Democratic Faith, p. 307.

35. Royce, Modern Idealism, pp. 246-247.

36. Royce, Conception of Immortality, pp.
66-68; Royce, Good and Evil, p. 249.

37. Royce, Conception of God, p. 292.

38. Royce, Problem of Christianity, p. 270;
Royce, Fugitive Essays, pp. 25-26; Buranelli,
Royce, p. 128. John E. Smith characterizes Royce's self as a "time-spanning unity." Royce's
theory of the individual person, Smith thinks, is
the part of his thought which best survives criticism and gives most insight for the present.
Themes in American Philosophy: Purpose, Experience, and Community (New York: Harper & Row,
1970), pp. 109-110.

39. Royce, Problem of Christianity, pp. 269-
270.

40. Royce, World and the Individual, II,335.
"The trend in Royce's thought is clear: It was
away from a more abstract unity towards a more
sharply defined pluralism. His growing dread of
the mass mentality, his insistence on the freedom of the individual mind, his prophetic insight
into the dangers of Leviathan and his devotion to
the province, all were brought to the clearest

utterance in the doctrine of the community. It
is not fair to Royce's intent to make him a cham-
pion of increasing federal power as the late
President Roosevelt once tried to do." James
Harry Cotton, Royce on the Human Self (Cambridge:
Harvard University Press, 1954), p. 263.

41. Royce, World and the Individual, I, 464-
465.

42. Royce, Fugitive Essays, p. 12; Royce,
Conception of God, p. 273.

43. Royce, Spirit of Modern Philosophy, pp.
425-426. Morton White points out that "the nineteenth century regarded change and the flow of
things as the most interesting feature of the universe. Karl Marx himself was not more insistent
about this than Royce." Science and Sentiment,
p. 230.

44. Royce, Good and Evil, pp. 207, 232.
Royce elsewhere noted that in "voluntary progress,
as distinguished from physical evolution, there
was a tendency toward unity and homogeneity of
actions considered in reference to their ends.
. . ." Fugitive Essays, pp. 129-130.

45. Josiah Royce, Outlines of Psychology: an
Elementary Treatise with Some Practical Applications (New York: Macmillan, 1908), pp. 318-319.

46. Buranelli, Royce, p. 40.

47. Royce, California, pp. 246, 271, 273,
375, 398, 497-498.

48. Royce, Problem of Christianity, pp. 243,
270; Royce, Spirit of Modern Philosophy, p. 431;
Royce, Fugitive Essays (introduction by Loewenberg), p. 25. Compare Royce's "symphony of history" with Bancroft's "celestial poem."

49. Royce, California, p. 259.

50. Josiah Royce, Race Questions, Provincialism, and Other American Problems (New York: Macmillan, 1908), p. 47 and passim. (Hereinafter cited as Royce, Race Questions); Royce, California, p. 498. Royce was not a reactionary. He appreciated, as he wrote in 1880, that "the Revolution of the past hundred years has expressed especially the need of the individual for fuller life, and for a better knowledge of his place in the universe." But he thought that the revolution had been blind in its optimism. "In our time, our duty is to correct this optimism by recognizing the ever-present fact of evil in the world." He thought that radicalism was apt to have too negative a quality: "the innovator talks of Liberty, of Nature, of Equality, as if with these barren ideas the whole complexity of life could be measured. Forgetting the negative character of the notions he recommends, forgetting that Nature seems only the absence of voluntary interference, Liberty the absence of restraint, Equality the absence of definite moral relations. . . ." Fugitive Essays, pp. 94, 90, 81.

51. Royce, California, p. 156; Royce, Hope of the Great Community, pp. 26, 45-46.

52. Royce, Fugitive Essays, pp. 81, 94, 104. A conservatism based on the Roycean precepts of loyalty, community and provincialism might largely escape the stricture of critics like Louis B. Hartz that American conservatism is self-contradictory, i.e. that it has only a liberal tradition to conserve. I discuss this possibility in my article, "Josiah Royce and American Conservatism," Modern Age, XIII (Fall, 1969), 342-352.

53. Royce, Race Questions, pp. 74-75.

54. Ibid., p. 98.

55. Royce, Loyalty, pp. 242, 245, 248.

56. Royce, Problem of Christianity, p. 116.

57. Royce, Race Questions, p. 128.

58. Royce, Conception of God, pp. 331, 275, 337, 274-275.

59. Royce, Fugitive Essays, p. 128.

60. Josiah Royce, The Religious Aspect of Philosophy. A Critique of the Bases of Conduct and of Faith (New York: Harper & Brothers, 1958), p. 195. (Hereinafter cited as Royce, Religious Aspect.)

61. Royce, Hope of the Great Community, pp. 48-49.

62. Royce, Conception of God, p. 321; Royce, Fugitive Essays, p. 128; Royce, Modern Idealism, pp. 88-89.

63. Royce, Modern Idealism, pp. 68-69.

64. Buranelli, Royce, p. 55; Josiah Royce, Herbert Spencer. An Estimate and Review. Together with a Chapter of Personal Reminiscences by James Collier (New York: Fox, Duffield, 1904), pp. 115-116, 150. (Hereinafter cited as Royce, Herbert Spencer.)

65. Royce, Religious Aspect, p. 177.

66. Royce, Herbert Spencer, pp. 63-64.

67. Royce, World and the Individual, II, 330-331; I, 469.

68. Royce, Conception of God, p. 304.

69. Royce, Problem of Christianity, p. 85.

70. Royce, Loyalty, pp. vii, 114.

71. Royce, Loyalty, pp. 357-376; Royce, Race Questions, pp. 237-238, 244-245, 263-264.

72. Royce, *Loyalty*, pp. 130-131.

73. Royce, Problem of Christianity, p. 176.

74. Royce, Problem of Christianity, p. 42;
Royce, *Loyalty*, pp. 386, 377.

75. Royce, Problem of Christianity, p. 125;
Royce, Hope of the Great Community, p. 45; Royce,
Sources of Religious Insight, pp. 279-280.

76. Royce, William James, pp. 91-92; Royce,
Sources of Religious Insight, p. 73. "The mother
which is a republic, is a community, which is also a person,--and not merely an aggregate, and
not merely by metaphor a person. Precisely so
the individual patriot who leaves his home behind,
and, steadfastly serving, presses on in ardent
quest of the moment when his life can be fulfilled by his death for his country, is all the more
richly and deeply an individual, that he is also
a community of interpretation, whose life has its
unity in its restless search for death on behalf
of the great good cause,--its ever living Logos
in its fluent quest for the goal." Royce, Letters, p. 647. Royce to Mary Whiton Calkins,
March 20, 1916.

77. Royce, Problem of Christianity, pp. 162-
163.

78. Royce, Race Questions, pp. 248-251.

79. Royce, *Loyalty*, pp. 200-201.

80. Buranelli comments on the Hegelian element in California. Royce, pp. 34, 40.

81. Royce, Problem of Christianity, pp. 290,
339, 305.

82. Ibid., pp. 247-248, 253, 268, 382.

83. Ibid., p. 344; Royce, Letters, p. 246.

Royce to Mary Whiton Calkins, March 20, 1916.

84. Royce, Problem of Christianity, pp. 318-319, 339-341, 382-383.

85. Ibid., pp. 43, 50, 95.

86. Ibid., pp. 126-127.

87. Ibid., pp. 128-131.

88. Ibid., p. 134.

89. Ibid., p. 235.

90. Ibid., p. 269.

CHAPTER IV

WILLIAM JAMES: THE PERILOUS EDGE

Carl Becker's association of Enlightenment cosmology with that of the middle ages, set forth in The Heavenly City of the Eighteenth Century Philosophers, has been much challenged. But at least one of Becker's major observations seems as trenchant as ever. The eighteenth century is separated from the twentieth, he argued, by the Enlightenment sense of human life as part of a serious moral drama. This drama was played according to absolute rules of good and evil, and still customarily judged by an absolute God, however the philosophes may have altered the terms of traditional religion. But what of the nineteenth century? While many continued in disparate ways to embrace the absolutely defined cosmic drama, the century was marked by unmistakable signs of its breakdown. The philosophy of William James is symptomatic of this breakdown, while James himself is heroic in his effort to bridge the gap that opened between opposed understandings of the world. He attempted to conserve the idea of life as a significant moral drama while-- and by--destroying the absolute terms in which the drama had theretofore been played. He was as aware as Henry Adams that the drama was threatened by the twin horsemen of Necessity and Chaos. But the spectre behind these grim riders, for James,

181

was that of the damnable "Absolute" which threatened to render man an automaton and the universe
morally meaningless.

The Absolute, although James recognized it
in its scientific guise, had been in the society
of which he was a member preeminently a religious
concept, and he felt obliged to reject it on a
theological as well as philosophical level. But
James's own religious impulses were strong, and
he found solid terms for their expression in experience, risk, and moral decision. Above all,
he found a new arena for the exercise of ethical
and religious imperatives in the framework of his
pluralistic philosophy. Multiplicity, so fre-
quently the modern bane of faith, was thus to become its salvation and its medium.

i.

James's philosophy of pluralism was not offered merely as the antithesis of monism; it was
an attempt to validate an intermediate area of
existence, a region between the individual and
the hypothetical but denied Absolute, and also
between necessity and chaos--in either case, a
region in which freely chosen and morally significant action was possible. The immediate bel-
ligerence with which James attacked the monistic
notion of the Absolute, of course, reflected his
impatience with a number of nineteenth century
idols. His especial philosophic anathema was
Hegelian idealism with its offshoots and allies;
no more acceptable was the monistic interpretation given to evolutionary doctrine by Herbert
Spencer and his followers. Hegelianism and
Spencer's "synthetic" (or Fiske's "cosmic") philosophy seemed different expressions of a conception of the universe which denied individual
freedom, and therefore the moral meaning of life.
James's intense moralism was probably foremost
among the temperamental qualities which impelled

182

him to pluralism. When he went through a period
of severe emotional and intellectual crisis in
his late twenties, part of his distress was his
agonized sense that if prevailing monistic and
deterministic doctrines were true, individual
moral struggle had no meaning; moral choice did
not exist.

Temperamentally also, monism and its concomitant determinism were obnoxious because they
precluded genuine novelty and genuine struggle.
James was in certain respects very much a man of
his time. He believed in progress (although as a
possibility to be fought for rather than as an
inevitability), and he believed in the virtues
of struggle (although not in its barbaric military form). But if history is merely the unfolding of a preordained scheme, then progress, if
progress involves the overcoming of real obstacles and the attainment of a higher morality, becomes a sham; so too, there is in this case no
genuine novelty in the universe. Consequently,
the "struggle" of schematizers like Herbert Spencer seemed to James no more a real struggle than
a fixed boxing match, and the vaunted competition
of social Darwinian determinists, with its Utopian outcome, ultimately tame. James's scornful
criticism of Spencer in 1879 was therefore heavily ironic.

> If now I, a defective and imper-
> fectly evolved creature, full of the
> joy of battle and other survivals from
> a savage state, say to Mr. Spencer: "I
> know nothing of your highest life, or,
> knowing, despise it"; and if I add to my
> other riotous deeds the sneering at
> evolution and the writing of sarcasms
> on its eventual milk-and-water paradise,
> saying I prefer to go on like my ances-
> tors, and enjoy this delicious mess of
> fears and strivings, and agonies and
> exultations, of dramatic catastrophes
> and supernatural visions, of excesses,

183

> in short, in every direction, which
> make of human life the rich contradic-
> tory tissue of good and evil it now
> is, how shall Mr. Spencer reduce me to
> order or coerce me to bow the knee?[1]

Pluralism appeared to James to be the only satisfactory solution to the problem of free will and
moral meaning. Once assume that "the superhuman
consciousness, however vast it may be, has itself
an external environment, and consequently is finite,"[2] and the struggle between good and evil
became a real one, in which independent wills
might enlist.

It is most important, however, that James's
reaction against monism did not drive him to an
atomized view of the universe. In medieval terms,
as Ralph Barton Perry pointed out, James leaned
toward nominalism but never became a complete
nominalist. In making room for generals and uni-
versals, he retained a significant element of
realism in his philosophy. Perry perceived that
James was willing to admit a principle of unity
as long as the unity did not predetermine the
many. His universe was "not a block or an organism, but an all-navigable sea--a great neighborhood embracing lesser neighborhoods, in which accessibility is universal and intimacy propor-
tional to propinquity."[3] This view was in accord
with James's radical empiricism, which he believed
recognized the relations and conjunctions between
things more clearly than did "ordinary empiricism." Radical empiricism, as James understood
it, did "full justice to conjunctive relations,
without, however, treating them as rationalism
always tends to treat them, as being true in some
supernal way, as if the unity of things and their
variety belonged to different orders of truth and
vitality altogether."[4]

To be sure, James's philosophy, and especially his pragmatism, is often distinguished from

that of thinkers like John Dewey by its individualism. James, it is often pointed out, was more interested in the moral meaning of the individual life than in social engineering. The distinction has a rough validity, and whatever the intentions of James and Dewey, American pragmatism does seem to stand at a crossroads with them, individual and social primacy respectively diverging. The traditional American anti-institutionalism exemplified in disparate ways by Jacksonians and transcendentalists came naturally to him, while he embodied at the same time a modern revolt against giantism. "<u>Every</u> great institution is perforce a means of corruption," he remarked a propos of the Dreyfus case, "--whatever good it may also do. Only in the free personal relation is full ideality to be found."[5] Indeed, James expressed a view of life which on the surface seems radically atomistic:

> As for me, my bed is made: I am against bigness and greatness in all their forms, and with the invisible molecular forces that work from individual to individual, stealing in through the crannies of the world like so many soft rootlets, or like the capillary oozing of water, and yet rending the hardest monuments of man's pride, if you give them time. The bigger the unity you deal with the hollower, the more brutal, the more mendacious is the life displayed. So I am against all big organizations as such, national ones first and foremost; against all big successes and big results; and in favor of the eternal forces of truth which always work in the individual and immediately unsuccessful way, under-dogs always till history comes, after they are long dead and puts them on the top.[6]

Yet this is not the equivalent of Bancroft's

185

atomistic figure of the ocean as so many individual drops. The "invisible molecular moral forces" do, after all, work from individual to individual, thus forming links between them, and having, if not "big results," apparently results which transcend individuals. And there are "eternal forces of truth," though they work slowly and through individuals. James's comment, explicitly rejecting the mass organization and the mass solution, as clearly affirms the interconnectedness of life. James elsewhere remarked that ethically a pluralistic form of humanism took for him "a stronger hold on reality than any other philosophy I know of--it being essentially a social philosophy, a philosophy of 'co,' in which conjunctions do the work."7

A primary intent of James's pluralism, then, was to make room for a middle field of action between the atom and the mass. "Ordinary monistic idealism leaves everything intermediary out," James complained. "It recognizes only the extremes. . . . Isn't this brave universe made on a richer pattern, with room in it for a long hierarchy of beings?" Because nothing in it attained all-inclusiveness, the pluralistic world, James thought, was "more like a federal republic than like an empire or a kingdom." As federalism still made a nation, "our 'multiverse' still makes a 'universe'; for every part, tho it may not be in actual or immediate connexion, is nevertheless in some possible or mediated connexion, with every other part however remote, through the fact that each part hangs together with its very next neighbors in inextricable interfusion."8

To give moral sanction to intermediacy was a notable achievement for an American philosopher. However local in origin or acceptance, moral systems with which Americans were most apt to be familiar claimed the existence and sanction of an Absolute--none more emphatically, of course, than the Calvinist tradition. James as a philosopher of individual judgment and meaning might be said

to have been an ultra-Protestant--indeed, he envisioned pragmatism as constituting a sort of
Protestant Reformation in philosophy--but in denying any omnipotence he rejected the universe of
Calvin and Edwards. The sanction of intermediate
relationships and the suggestion that there was
room in the universe for a "long hierarchy of beings" were distinctly un-Protestant. James detested the Catholic Church as a big, authoritarian
institution, but in this respect his ideas seem
more congenial to Catholicism. At least he would
have destroyed that direct confrontation of the
individual and the absolute that was at the heart
of the Reformation.

To shift the moral struggle to intermediate
fields did not mean moral compromise, however;
here James was solidly within the predominant
American religious tradition. Although balance--
"the golden mean"--was essential to classical
morality, Christian morality was often that of
the extreme--an extreme of self-denial, for instance, or an extreme of love for the omnipotent
God. In practice, the margin of tolerance within
the medieval church tended to compromise the
ideal, but the Protestant conception of grace, at
its most uncompromising, made of virtue such a
precious quality as to be beyond man's own endeavor, and unattainable without the irresistible
act of God. Even in rejecting the predestinarian
extreme, James retained much of the Christian
absolutism; he evidently assumed the unqualified
existence of "good" itself as a standard to which
both God and man could rally, and one of the virtues of pluralism, he believed, was that it made
unnecessary any metaphysical compromise with
evil. The monistic God is necessarily implicated
in evil; the God of pluralism need not be responsible for it. Good and evil can stand forth clear
and distinct, forever incompatible and eternally
opposed, never reconciled as James thought they
must be in a monistic system. Probably in the
long run the effect of James's condemnation of
the Absolute, like the effect of his pragmatism,

was to depreciate absolutistic moral standards and lend support to relativism. But his intent was to show the eternal moral struggle as he thought it was--not the sham battle contrived by an alien and abstract Deity, but a life and death struggle on the middle level of existence where men meet other men, and the capillary forces work slowly between individuals to further or retard the good fight. Thus an intensely moral light was cast on this "all-navigable sea" between atom and hypothetical absolute.

James's likening of the pluralistic world to a federal republic seems the obvious allusion of an American philosopher, but here as elsewhere James represents one side of America against another side. Similarly, pragmatism, although often taken as the characteristic American philosophy, was only the revolt of a certain American practicality against an equally American abstractness--an abstractness which in James's view made his countrymen susceptible to the grand absolutes of German idealism and to the "synthetic" or "cosmic" philosophy of Spencer and Fiske, as well as to those of monotheistic religion. Absolute and abstraction were terms thoroughly American. Vast space and the lonely individual comprised a theme which fascinated American literature. Tocqueville noted that Americans could think only in terms very grand or very minute. On the other hand, the country was a federal republic, and purported to tolerate diversity within its borders, as in some respects it did. But monism did not deny diversity as long as the many were creatures of the one, and it remained doubtful that the American genius was truly a pluralistic one. James was an extraordinary combination of moral fervor and tolerance, and in bringing together qualities which were both American, but often at war with each other in America, he did justice to the heterogeneity which the national institutions were meant to contain, as well as to the legacy of the God of Judgment.

William James did offer a reformation in
American thought, but it was not one definable
by the term, "relativism," as that term is now
generally used. James's achievement was to redefine individualism. The American individual
had been identified primarily with precisely the
Absolute, that is to say by the possibility of
communion with the absolute God. In his inspired
righteousness, he was more or less set over a-
gainst society, although not necessarily as a
rebel. Lacking strong metaphysical sanction for
conjunctive relationships short of the transcendental, he might indeed flourish as an anarchist
or loner--none more brilliantly than Henry David
Thoreau. But the more usual course was to succumb in one fashion or another to the sway of
the mass. Individualism became too often mere
mean-spirited narrowness and avarice, all the
while taking its ruling ideas from public opinion.
It was even possible, in the manner of Bancroft,
to identify the voice of the people with the
voice of God, and thus destroy any ultimate dis-
crepancy between the cosmic and the social. Accepting such a presumption, one could treat with
the Absolute or the crowd with the same awe or
familiarity. Except as convenience, the social
dimension hardly existed; in the same way the
Protestant ministry existed as convenience, rather than as the essential intermediary of salvation.

James recognized the decreasing human significance of the anthropomorphic Absolute, and
proposed an individuality realizable through re-
lationship--realizable indeed through society,
in the root meaning of companionship. But this
by no means ruled out the divine; James admitted
divinity as an essentially social possibility. He
was willing to speculate about polytheism as fur-
nishing a warmer and more human cosmology than
monotheism, and about the hierarchy of beings that
there might be in the universe. A god worthy of
the name, he supposed, must be finite; he could
be a companion in the moral struggle; he could

189

not be an Absolute.

In contrast to others of his generation--
Henry Adams for notable example--James thus broke
with the intellectual need for unity--if not
wholeheartedly, at least with the greater part
of his mind and temperament. He brought the
diversifying and unifying principles into a new
sort of relation, yet without compromising the
moral integrity which had been attributed to the
Absolute. Threading a path between relativism
and rigidity, he attempted to find the element of
grace in the world of multiplicity.

James's pluralism thus recognized the breakup of the older Protestant-democratic cosmology
in a way that was both radical and conservative.
The destruction of the absolute extracted its very
core, and yet the essential elements of the system
were retained and strengthened--meaningful truth,
moral drama on a cosmic scale, and the reaching
out of the individual toward wider relationship
and consciousness. James made as well a notable
effort, although one not entirely successful, to
save the notion of divinity from the abstraction
of God as infinite, omniscient, and omnipotent.
His consistent effort, indeed, was to replace the
abstract whole of integral parts with voluntary
and contingent conjunction. Neither realist nor
nominalist, he found reality in the individual's
striving for relation, particularly a relation of
alliance in the moral struggle. James broke the
American primacy of the individual-absolute relationship, but he proposed a type of heterogeneous
relationship, the emblem and promise of which was
the federal system itself. John Calvin and James
Madison were at last to be reconciled.

It is in this context that the pragmatism
for which James is best known must be viewed. His
pragmatism was a far subtler philosophy than his
more concise definitions of it imply, and partly
in consequence the original concept has often been
grossly distorted. As he explained,

> true ideas are those that we can as-
> similate, validate, corroborate and
> verify. False ideas are those that
> we can not. That is the practical dif-
> ference it makes to us to have true
> ideas. . . .
>   This thesis is what I have to de-
> fend. The truth of an idea is not a
> stagnant property inherent in it.
> Truth happens to an idea. It becomes
> true, is made true by events.

Pragmatism, he elaborated, allows man to add to
reality, to create. "Man engenders truths upon"
the world.[9] James distinguished between the existential truth of pragmatism and the essential
truth of rationalism. "Existential truth,"he asserted, "is incidental to the actual competition
of opinions. Essential truth, the truth of the
intellectualists, the truth with no one thinking
it, is like the coat that fits tho no one has ever
tried it on, like the music that no ear has ever
listened to." It is most important, however, that
James did not deny the notion of absolute truth,
even while acknowledging the relativistic character of pragmatism.

> No relativist who ever actually walked
> the earth has denied the regulative
> character in his own thinking of the
> notion of absolute truth. What is
> challenged by relativists is the pre-
> tence on any one's part to have found
> for certain at any given moment what
> the shape of that truth is. Since the
> better absolutists agree in this, ad-
> mitting that the proposition "There is
> absolute truth" is the only absolute
> truth of which we can be sure,

further debate on the point seemed to him hardly
necessary. Absolute truth could therefore be accepted as "an ideal set of formulations towards
which all opinions may in the long run of experi-

191

ence be expected to converge."10

This postulation of absolute truth suggests
the degree to which James's own pragmatism differs
from "pragmatism" as now commonly understood. In
general usage, "pragmatism" has come to mean an
ultimately mindless opportunism, with no thought
beyond immediate gains. Even in James's day, as
he ruefully acknowledged, it suggested "sordid
practical interests," and was taken by critics
"to exclude logical ones." This, of course, was
far from James's meaning. "Pragmatism," he insisted, "so far from keeping her eyes bent on the
immediate practical foreground, as she is accused
of doing, dwells just as much upon the world's
remotest perspectives." If the "hypothesis of
God works satisfactorily in the widest sense of
the word, it is true. . .," for example.11

James was sensitive also about the allegedly
parochial character of his philosophy. With its
apparent emphasis on action and practicality,
pragmatism has impressed many as the quintessen-
tial American philosophy. James denied this characterization, at least in the simplistic form
usually offered. Rather than being primarily an
appeal to action, he pointed out, pragmatism
meant the working of ideas in the mental world,
with practical action secondary. He complained
that it was "usually described as a characteristically American movement, a sort of bobtailed
scheme of thought, excellently fitted for the man
on the street, who naturally hates theory and
wants cash returns immediately."12 It must be
admitted that James gave credence to such an interpretation by speaking of the "cash value" of
an idea. But he had in mind not a super-Ameri-
canism, but "an alteration in 'the seat of authority' that reminds one almost of the protestant
reformation. And, as to papal minds, protestantism has often seemed a mere mess of anarchy
and confusion," he admitted, "such, no doubt,
will pragmatism often seem to ultra-rationalist
minds in philosophy." But this philosophic
"protestantism," he was persuaded, would prosper

as had religious protestantism before it.[13]

Jamesian pragmatism, then, sought to reach
out toward the widest possible perspective, to
reach out to God Himself, perhaps just this side
of the Absolute. It sought to bring the most
distant horizons within the sphere of practical
concern, or, stated conversely, to extend experience as far as possible. Here too James's thought
is conjunctive: the individual reaches out toward
the social and the cosmic. This is far removed
from the vulgar pragmatism that truncates--or,
as James said, bobtails--experience, shortens perspective, and counts only immediate gain.

There is an American quality in James's original conception, though it is rather more profound
than the rationale of wheeler-dealers and political opportunists. James restates the old insistence, essential to the Protestant-democratic cosmology of a George Bancroft, on the communication
between the individual and the Absolute. In
James's "reformation," of course, there is no
Absolute, although perhaps a God, and the "seat
of authority" is removed from deity to practical
individual. This is a considerable reformation.
But it still requires a stretching toward the position that the Absolute would occupy, and James
gives pragmatic sanction for the conjunction of
the individual in his most immediate and practical
character with the widest conceivable spheres of
consciousness and meaning. Indeed, the intent of
pragmatism was to revitalize this cosmic outreach-
ing by insisting upon its practical effects. In
the same way the Puritans had been sure that reception of divine grace had a practical effect in
their lives. Far from being an uncomplicated
philosophical expression of practical Americanism,
Jamesian pragmatism was an extraordinary resolution of the American tension between the individual and cosmic perspectives.

As a corollary, James sought to make truth
more real by requiring it to pass the test of

practical consequence. Truth was a serious business; one could not gaze at it with detachment as on a blueprint, but rather carried the burden and bore the risk of having to validate it in a morally strenuous life. The intent was not to diminish truth, or to make it relative in itself, but to free it from preconceived and rigid contexts, and thus to make it more accessible. Through the pragmatic criterion of practical consequence, the ordinary individual was to regain the direct access to truth that had been basic to the Protestant scheme.

There is however another aspect to James's pragmatism. Here as elsewhere James was the champion of heterogeneity and diversity. This was one of the points which distinguished him from his forerunner in pragmatic thought, Charles S. Peirce. There was, Perry notes, an important difference in the final vision of the two men; "it is not merely that Peirce is more explicit in linking pragmatism to an ethical ideal, but also that there is an important difference in that ideal. For Peirce the good lies in coherence, order, coalescence, unity; for James in the individuality, variety, and satisfaction of concrete interests."14

Jamesian pragmatism was by its nature a versatile philosophy. James offered it "expressly as a mediator between tough-mindedness and tender-mindedness." It could, he thought, satisfy both temperaments. "It can remain religious like the rationalisms, but at the same time, like the empiricisms, it can preserve the richest intimacy with facts." The abstract rationalist, in James's view, erred in his aversion to concreteness; ordinary empiricism, on the other hand, was guilty of a "materialistic bias." "Pragmatism," however, "is willing to take anything, to follow either logic or the senses and to count the humblest and most personal experiences. She will count mystical experiences if they have practical consequences.

194

Beyond this, pragmatism was fitted to the middle, diversified range of experience between the absolutism of the concrete particular and the absolutism of the Absolute. Rejecting "sensationalistic atomism" as well as the Absolute, James here as elsewhere defended the concept of a "fluid, interpenetrating field of given existence."16 One result of this was to give latitude to his religious speculations. While remaining a staunch pluralist, he did not believe that human experience was the highest form of experience in the universe. "Between the two extremes of crude naturalism on the one hand and transcendental absolutism on the other," he suggested, "you may find that what I take the liberty of calling the pragmatistic or melioristic type of theism is exactly what you require."17 The point of the pragmatic reformation was indeed, as James said, to shift the seat of authority--to move truth, meaning, God into the middle region between nominalism and realism, the federal area of contingent conjunction, preserving in this way the ordinary individual's access to them. American practicality and the American reach toward the cosmic were brought together in a new way.

Did James succeed in occupying the philosophical middle ground? C. H. Grattan thought not:

> With his inveterate habit of setting up a middle course between pure anarchy and pure absolutism, he tried to enunciate a sort of representative democracy as a philosophical principle. His temperamental bias carried him over to the side of the anarchists, but he was unable finally to bomb the castles of the abstractionists. It was entirely natural that a self-scrutinizing individualist should be more impressed by the diversity of the world than the unity.

James's individualism, Grattan feared, had led

195

him "deeper and deeper into the mire of subjectivism."[18] If James did incline to the side of anarchy, however, his was an anarchism which, like Henry Adams' Conservative Christian Anarchism, sought to join with an object of worship.

ii.

Demanding a universe in which risk and struggle were real, and in which, paradoxically, good and evil were absolutes because there was no Absolute in which they could be subsumed and reconciled, James was obliged to find a course between extremes that, in their moral import, met: between monism and chaos. It is not too much to say that this was to demand a religious universe, which meant for James a cosmos not frozen in the image of God but open to the workings of possible superhuman forces with whom the individual could freely ally. Intellectually, his task was to make room for indeterminacy in the face of the monistic and deterministic disposition of so much of both the philosophy and the science of his day, and yet avoid fragmenting the world into unconnected and directionless pieces. James's Principles of Psychology was fundamental to this effort; as Gay Wilson Allen notes, it "restored purpose to the operations of mind and brain, and not only causal explanation, but moral purpose as well. This was to be the psychological foundation of his future philosophical doctrines of freedom and choice, of the influence of a man's emotions on his creative thinking and of volition on his character. . . ."[19]

As a psychologist James rejected the theory, advanced by Hodgson and Huxley, that man is a conscious automaton. This theory, as James understood it, stemmed from the extension of the notion of reflex action to the higher nerve centers. It denied that consciousness had any real efficacy; consciousness could not alter the responses of

196

man the automaton. James argued that the highest
forms of mental activity were the least determinate. "In short, a high brain may do many things,
and may do each of them at a very slight hint.
But its hair-trigger organization makes of it a
happy-go-lucky, hit-or-miss affair. It is as
likely to do the crazy as the sane thing at any
given moment. A low brain does few things, and in
doing them perfectly forfeits all other use." So
much could be said of the brain as a physical machine, but James believed that consciousness
could "load the dice." Consciousness provided
goals: "the words Use, Advantage, Interest, Good,
find no application in a world in which no consciousness exists." And to demonstrate the utility
of consciousness, in James's view, was to overthrow the automaton theory.[20] Admitting the im-
perfection of the science, he later concluded that
"to urge the automaton-theory upon us, as it is
now urged, on purely a priori and quasi-metaphys-
ical grounds, is an unwarrantable impertinence in
the present state of psychology."[21]

James pointed out in his Psychology that

> consciousness is at all times primarily
> a selecting agency. Whether we take it
> in the lowest sphere of sense, or in the
> highest of intellection, we find it al-
> ways doing one thing, choosing one of
> several of the materials so presented
> to its notice, emphasizing and accentu-
> ating that and suppressing as far as
> possible all the rest.[22]

The consciousness, or "soul," presented or created
nothing itself; it was "at the mercy of the material forces for all possibilities; but amongst
these possibilities she selects. . . ." James
thought it significant that consciousness was at
its height when a decision had to be made; "where
indecision is great, as before a dangerous leap,
consciousness is agonizingly intense." Indeed,
consciousness could be said to consist in the com-

197

parison of simultaneous possibilities, "the selection of some, and the suppression of the rest
by the reinforcing and inhibiting agency of Attention." Free will consisted, finally, in this
ability to concentrate attention. James was willing to admit that "the operation of free effort,
if it existed, could only be to hold some one
ideal object, or part of an object, a little longer or a little more intensely before the mind."[23]

This position was clearly tenuous as well as
tentative, and James acknowledged his belief that
"the question of free-will is insoluble on strictly psychologic grounds. After a certain amount
of effort or attention has been given to an idea,
it is manifestly impossible to tell whether either more or less of it might have been given or
not." Thrown back upon the uncertainties of
introspection on the one hand, and "a priori pos-
tulates and possibilities" on the other, one
could only choose to believe in determinism or in
a margin of freedom. James chose freedom, but he
made it clear that he did so on ethical rather
than on psychological grounds. Reflecting his
personal experience, James remarked that "freedom's first deed should be to affirm itself," but
admitted that "the utmost that a believer in
free-will can ever do will be to show that the
deterministic arguments are not coercive."[24]

This was enough on which to base a non-de-
terministic philosophy. James felt able to reject the automaton theory in favor of a conception of mental life that did justice to its complexity. "Man's chief difference from the brute,"
he exclaimed, "lies in the exuberant excess of
his subjective propensities; his preeminence
over them simply and solely in the number and in
the fantastic and unnecessary character of his
wants, physical, moral, aesthetic, and intellectual." Mind was, therefore, no mere machine
of stimulus and repose; "every actually existing
consciousness seems to itself at any rate to be
a fighter for ends, of which many, but for its
presence, would not be ends at all."[25] The re-

flex theory of mind, as accepted by James, committed us

> to regarding the mind as an essentially
> teleological mechanism. I mean by this
> that the conceiving or theorizing fac-
> ulty,--the mind's middle department,--
> functions exclusively for the sake of
> ends that do not exist at all in the
> world of impressions, but are set by
> our emotional and practical subjectiv-
> ity altogether. It is a transformer
> of the world of our impressions into
> a totally different world, the world
> of our conception; and the transforma-
> tion is effected in the interests of
> our volitional nature, and for no other
> purpose whatsoever.[25]

James's position left the way open for the
broadest spiritual speculations, though they
might be without the firm buttress of scientific
support. He confessed in his _Psychology_ that
"to posit a soul influenced in some mysterious
way by the brain-states and responding to them
by conscious affections of its own, seems to me
the line of least logical resistance, so far as
we yet have attained." For "our reasonings have
not established the non-existence of the Soul;
they have only proved its superfluity for scientific purposes." His temperamental disposition
was to widen the sphere of the individual psyche,
and to seek individual connections to larger
fields of consciousness. Thus he suggested the
existence of a "mother-sea" of consciousness,
perhaps a "collection of individual spirits,
each existing there in a completer and truer form
than in what filters through to this phenomenal
life." The brain might then be an organ for the
transmission rather than the production of
thought.[27] As elsewhere, James shows here a
characteristic, and very American, yearning for
the transcendental, balanced by a stubborn individualism. But he also again sought the middle
ground where individual psyche and "mother sea"

199

might meet.

James had come to his belief in indeterminacy
only after a severe struggle. His early scientific
studies had disposed him to accept the conception
of man as a "conscious automaton"; indeed, as
Perry notes, his "first idea was to adhere to this
view more strictly than many of its avowed pro-
ponents."[28] But he came to feel that this extreme determinism was too "crudely materialistic"
to be plausible, and, more important, morally ap-
palling by making good and evil meaningless.
This constituted the intellectual side of his
youthful crisis, when he pondered as to whether
he must accept the monistic, deterministic universe then in favor, with (as he saw it) its
negation of morality, or whether he could hazard
a belief in free-will. "To day," he recorded in
his Diary for February 1, 1870, "I about touched
bottom, and perceive plainly that I must face the
choice with open eyes: Shall I frankly throw the
moral business overboard, as one unsuited to my
innate aptitudes, or shall I follow it, and it
alone, making everything else merely stuff for
it?" Influenced by Charles Renouvier, he finally
decided that he could reject a strict determinism, and that his first act of free-will would
be to believe in free-will. His adopted position
was for him subjectively and ethically true, although he admitted that the question was psycho-
logically insoluble. "All that James could finally do with freedom, and perhaps all that anyone
can do," Paul Conkin points out, "was undermine
the determinist position and leave freedom as a
speculative position without any operational
guidelines for verification."[29]

James drew a significant distinction between fatalism and determinism, although he opposed both. For the fatalist, he explained, it
is impossible to breast the tide; to the determinist, even an independent effort to breast the
tide is inconceivable. Determinism "admits
something phenomenal called free effort, which

200

seems to breast the tide, but it claims this as a portion of the tide. . . . Fatalism, which conceives of effort clearly enough as an independent variable that might come from a fourth dimension, if it would come but that does not come, is a very dubious ally for determinism. It strongly imagines that very possibility which determinism denies."[30] James early interpreted fatalism as an ineluctably pessimistic outlook that held all striving to be in vain. He believed that it would "never reign supreme, for the impulse to take life strivingly is indestructible in the race." He found the taint of fatalism in much of the contemporary sociology. Herbert Spencer's denial of the possibility of individual initiative affecting human destiny seemed to him a "relapse into oriental fatalism."[31] Spencer's "fatalism" may seem now rather quaint, but not so the social scientific temper which disgusted James in 1890. "And I for my part, " he exclaimed, "cannot but consider the talk of the contemporary sociological school about averages and general laws and predetermined tendencies, with its obligatory undervalueing of the importance of individual differences, as the most pernicious and immoral of fatalisms."[32]

The more sophisticated foe, however, was determinism. James's attitude toward determinism reflected directly his pluralism, for he made it clear that for him "Determinism=monism," while conversely, as he wrote to Renouvier, "pluralism and indeterminism seem to be but two ways of stating the same thing."[33] The issue seemed basically clear. Determinism

> professes that those parts of the universe already laid down absolutely appoint and decree what the other parts shall be. . . . The whole is in each and every part, and welds it with the rest into an absolute unity, an iron block, in which there can be no equivocation or shadow of turning. . . .

201

Indeterminism, on the contrary,
says that the parts have a certain
amount of loose play on one another,
so that the laying down of one of them
does not necessarily determine what the
others shall be. . . . Indeterminism
thus denies the world to be one un-
bending unit of fact. It says there is
a certain ultimate pluralism in it;
and, so saying, it corroborates our
ordinary unsophisticated view of things.
To that view, actualities seem to float
in a wider sea of possibilities from
out of which they are chosen; and, some-
where, indeterminism says, such possibilities exist, and form a part of
truth.[34]

Determinism seemed to James to force one
either to pessimism or to subjectivism. This
was the "Dilemma of Determinism": ". . .if determinism is to escape pessimism, it must leave
off looking at the goods and ills of life in a
simple objective way, and regard them as materi-
als, indifferent in themselves, for the production of consciousness, scientific and ethical,
in us." Either one must succumb to the despair
which assumes that nothing can be changed, or one
says that objective reality does not matter. If
pessimism the more obviously went against James's
grain, so almost equally did pure subjectivism,
which seemed to him always to end in a corruption
of fatalism and ethical indifference. While extreme subjectivism might be dignifed as antinomianism in theology, or romanticism in literature,
"in practical life it is either a nerveless sen-
timentality or a sensualism without bounds."
James proposed an alternative to subjectivism:

The world must not be regarded as a
machine whose final purpose is the
making real of any outward good, but
rather as a contrivance for deepening
the theoretic consciousness of what

202

goodness and evil in their intrinsic
natures are. Not the doing either of
good or of evil is what nature cares
for, but the knowing of them. Life is
one long eating of the fruit of the
tree of <u>knowledge</u>. . . . According
to it, the world is neither an optimism nor a pessimism, but a gnosticism.[35]

This was a pluralist position. "The final
purpose of our creation," as James saw it, "seems
most plausibly to be the greatest possible enrichment of our ethical consciousness, through
the intensest play of contrasts and the widest
diversity of characters." While this obliged
some to be "vessels of wrath," and others to be
"vessels of honor," he found it preferable to a
subjectivism which "reduces all these outward
distinctions to a common denominator." As Perry
points out, James was less concerned in "The
Dilemma of Determinism" to reject determinism in
itself as to reject monistic determinism. "The
universe," he emphasized, "belongs to a plurality
of semi-independent forces, each one of which may
help or hinder, and be helped or hindered by, the
operations of the rest."[36]

James's defense of indeterminacy, although
unyielding, was properly qualified. While the
effect of his philosophy was to provide a margin
for individual freedom, he was for a time wary
of the word "freedom" itself, because of its
"eulogistic associations" and because some "soft
determinists" claimed that "freedom is only necessity understood." In "The Will to Believe" (18-
97), he insisted on chance rather than freedom.
"The stronghold of the deterministic sentiment,"
he thought, "is the antipathy to the idea of
chance." "Chance" seemed to him then a more
safely negative and relative term, telling us
nothing about what a thing might be in itself.
"All that its chance-character asserts about it
is that there is something in it really of its

own, something that is not the unconditional property of the whole."[37] At this fundamental level, the admission of chance seemed the most effective and honest way to crack open the block universe. From this position, he could advance to the defense of free-will.

Chance provided a margin in which free-will might operate; it indicated "not capriciousness or perversity, but a margin of _indetermination_ which might leave room for a decisive act of will." Influenced by Charles S. Peirce, James expounded a tychism which proclaimed "the spontaneity and unexpectedness of things."[38] However, James's tychism evolved; his earlier understanding of chance as "the sheer impact of the inexplicable, a happening out of the blue, gave way to the idea of 'novelty.'"[39] And novelty, he discovered with the help of Henri Bergson, was not incompatible with continuous growth. James explained near the end of his life:

> I think the center of my whole _Anschauung_, since years ago I read Renouvier, has been the belief that something is doing in the universe, and that _novelty_ is real. But so long as I was held by the intellectualist logic of identity, the only form I could give to novelty was tychistic, _i.e._, I thought that a world in which discrete elements were annihilated, and others created in their place, was the best descriptive account we could give of things; and if the elements were but minute enough, "scientific determinism" could be kept, as approximating the appearance sufficiently for practical error to be avoided in our dealings with nature's "laws." This sticks in the human crop --none of my students became good tychists! Nor am I one any longer, since Bergson's _synechism_ has shown me another way of saving novelty and keeping all the concrete facts of law-in-

204

change.[40]

James came then to share with Bergson the idea of a "really growing world," in which one could say that "two successive events both are and are not identical: the first develops into the second, the second emerges from the first. There is novelty, but it is a novelty which, when it comes, seems natural and reasonable, like the fulfillment of a tendency." They were both interested in rescuing tychism, James wrote Bergson in 1907. "But whereas I have hitherto found no better way of defending Tychism than by affirming the spontaneous addition of discrete elements of being (or their subtraction), thereby playing the game with intellectualist weapons, you set things straight at a single stroke by your fundamental conception of the continuously creative nature of reality." This new conception of reality increasingly occupied James during the last years of his life.[41]

He never demanded, however, that science accept the indeterminist position. It seemed to him to apply to a sphere outside of science; before indeterminism, "science simply stops." Ever wary of absolutist pretensions, he cautioned that science "must be constantly reminded that her purposes are not the only purposes, and that the order of uniform causation which she has use for, and is therefore right in postulating, may be enveloped in a wider order, on which she has no claims at all."[42] Yet James's point of view was too relational in nature--and he was still himself too much the scientist--to wish to call causation or continuity themselves into question. He acknowledged that free effort must operate between "genuine possibles," and thus sought to refute the argument used by John Fiske that if volitions are not determined, all is chance--that a man might, for example, jump from a window for no reason. The free-will position, he argued, involved no necessary break in continuity. The existence of different possible futures in no way made the past less continuous. "A train is the same train," he pointed out, "its passengers are the same passengers, its momentum is the same momentum, no matter which way the switch which fixes its direction is placed."[43]

Essential to James's indeterminacy was his temperamental and intellectual demand for a universe with risk. "Bravery and a willingness to risk all in the game with no certainty of reward is the most elementary summary of James's philosophy it is possible to give," C. H. Grattan observes.[44] "All that the human heart wants is its chance," James himself asserted. "It will willingly forego certainty in universal matters if only it can be allowed to feel that in them it has the same inalienable right to run risks, which no one dreams of refusing to it in the pettiest practical affairs." He contrasted this spirit of adventure with the Hindu and Buddhist ideals of Nirvana, which he believed symptomatic of a temper "afraid of more experience, afraid of life." He accounted it greatly to the credit of Christianity, on the other hand, that it recognized absolute uncertainty, to be overcome by faith. There was a strong "tendency in men of vigorous nature," he thought, "to enjoy a certain amount of uncertainty in their philosophic creed, just as risk lends a zest to worldly activity."[45]

James gave to his free-will position a basis in pragmatism, although he was careful to disentangle it from the knotty question of the imputability of good and evil: i.e. does merit or blame attach more truly to those with free-will, or to those without it? He thought the question futile:

> To make our human ethics revolve about the question of "merit" is a piteous unreality--God alone can know our merits, if we have any. The real ground for supposing free-will is indeed pragmatic, but it has nothing to do with this contemptible right to punish which has made such a noise in past discussions of the subject.

> Free-will pragmatically means
> novelties in the world, the right to
> expect that in its deepest elements as
> well as in its surface phenomena, the
> future may not identically repeat and
> imitate the past.

Free-will was therefore in essence a melioristic
doctrine, one which at least held out the possibility that things would be better. It was a
"cosmological theory of promise."[46] But James
finally demanded of free-will no more than "the
character of novelty in fresh activity situations."[47] This denied despair, and supported a
hard-won optimism.

Above all, James was a philosopher of choice.
He did not insist that the range of choice was
great, but he did uphold the ability of human beings to choose between alternatives. He was willing to sacrifice certainty and security to possibility and movement. His vision of life had
much the quality of an optimistic, receptive existentialism:

> We realize this life as something al-
> ways off its balance, something in
> transition, something that shoots out
> of a darkness through a dawn into a
> brightness that we feel to be dawn
> fulfilled. . . . In every crescendo
> of sensation, in every effort to recall,
> in every progress towards the satisfac-
> tion of desire, this succession of an
> emptiness and fulness that have refer-
> ence to each other and are one flesh
> is the essence of the phenomenon.[48]

Choice was central to James because it gave room
for the individual to move in the middle ground
between his own solitary sphere and an Absolute
which, if it existed, would freeze him eternally
as an atom in a perfect whole. Choice was the
movement of life.

207

Freedom is a multifarious concept devoid of meaning when not further defined. James was, comporting with his reputation, a philosopher of freedom, but his freedom was the strict function of a moralistic and pluralistic temperament. Clearly it was basic to him that genuine morality required moral choice; further, the very quality of freedom was for him imbued with moral purpose, and would have been virtually meaningless without it. Conservatives had once defined freedom in terms of its proper end: i.e. freedom consists in obedience to God, or freedom consists in doing what is right, and being prevented from doing that which is wrong. As a pluralist, James departed from such narrow prescriptions, but he maintained the traditional belief that freedom was properly directed toward a moral end. This was of course the assumption of his pragmatism. Like the Puritan orthodoxy, James steered a middle course between the monistic objectivity attempted for instance by Spencer, and the antinomian subjectivity which, without God, would have allowed each person to create his own moral universe. Unlike the Puritan, James defended freewill and rejected an Absolute, but the purpose of freedom was nevertheless to permit alignment, in whatever idiosyncratic way, with the forces of good assumed to be abroad in the cosmos.

James the pluralist showed a rare temperament, that of a man who can genuinely think in terms of diversity, envisioning manifold passages across the "all-navigable sea" of the universe, without lapsing into a vacuous relativism or pantheism. Pluralism was more than the demotion of God, which was itself, James made clear, perhaps no more drastic than that from Absolute to mastermind with ninety-nine chances out of a hundred to win the cosmic game. The distinction between Absolute and non-Absolute was itself the crucial one, since it implied a degree of independent action and judgment in any lesser will. Without an absolute, there were special purposes, diversities, eccentricities, however leagued with

larger principles. For Bancroft, in a spiritual
sense, there could be but one way to serve divinity, by heeding the inner voice of "reason." For
James, the ways to ally with divinity were many.
But James's pluralism has a radical quality not
so much because of the range of choices envisioned
--he did not slough off entirely a New England and
American provincialism--but because of its uncompromising insistence on final disjunction in the
universe. As for the Puritan the last awful reality was the very quality of God's sovereignty
over eternity, for the pluralist it was the reverse: the negative absolutism of unqualified
uncertainty, risk without recompense, contingency
without ultimate reconciliation. James discovered
in 1870 that he must look contingency full in the
face, and he made it the foundation of his
thought.

James's pluralism is relational in nature.
Multiplicity carries not for him, as it does for
Henry Adams, the overtones of chaos; rather, the
ultimate disjunction of things makes possible
their genuine relationship. Things locked together in a monism are ultimately not related,
but parts of the same whole. Relationship, in the
Jamesian view, has always more or less of the
element of contingency, in that it is not an absolute connection, but depends upon variable
factors. The variable may be a voluntary alliance, or it may be only the tacit agreement to
regard an incident of congruence--blood relationship, for example--as relating the one to the
other. If estranged brothers could in earnest
have "nothing to do with each other," their relationship would be reduced to a biological convention.[49] James argues not the mechanical connectiveness of the Newtonian model of the universe, nor one of the varieties of organic connectiveness, but a federative connectiveness, with
relation partial and contingent, as had been the
case with the ante bellum American political
federation.

Pluralism and the concomitant imperative of

moral association constituted James's version of
George Bancroft's Protestant-democratic cosmology.
In one sense it lessened the distance between man
and God. God was less than absolute; the individual was required morally to be more than individual. Unable to rely on Bancroft's "reason," he
must reach out for comrades-in-arms in the struggle against evil. Yet in another sense, God was
less accessible: His nature and very existence
were problematical, and the same loss of an infal-
lible principle of "reason" cut off direct communication with Him. The traditional cosmos had
been, in a sense, God-centered, and man had felt
at home in it, no doubt because he understood God
in his own image. Yet with the principle that
"man is the measure of all things" truly installed, he seemed to himself a stranger in this cosmos, as he had no self-image to encompass it, and
the burden of measuring all things was too great.
To Henry Adams the inescapable conclusion was a
world of both chaos and necessity, but James was
constitutionally averse to the idea of such absolute qualities in furious retreat from the
everyday reality of struggle and hazard. He
needed no desperate recourse to a symbolic Virgin
to juxtapose for a fragile moment moral liberty
and moral order; he proposed instead a federal
cosmos, conjunction contingent and never absolute, and the possibility of joining forces in a
battle that availed not everything, but much.
James could imagine the intermediate, neither
atom nor Absolute, as Adams finally could not.
This made James in a way less Protestant, and less
American if Tocqueville was correct that Americans
thought in only grand or minute terms. Yet James
advanced also from perceptibly American assumptions.

It was not merely James's pragmatism which
made him a distinctively American thinker, although as William G. McLoughlin suggests, pragmatism ran more deeply in the national consciousness than has been commonly supposed. McLoughlin
points out that American pragmatism has had a

"pietist-perfectionist tone." Drawing upon the pietistic assumption that the individual is the best judge of moral truth, its value has been to sanction innovative methods in the task of perfecting society.[50] Certainly there is enough of the pietist in James to correct the impression of him as a "cash value" philosopher, but he believed only in the possibility of social amelioration, and not in that of social perfection. He was in this more modest than many who were pragmatic idealists in the American mold. Nor does his preference for freedom mark him as archetypal American, considering the strength of the determinist tradition in American thought, from Calvinism to behaviorism. Indeed, none of the fundamental philosophical problems with which James was concerned could be branded as exclusively American. But James's way of dealing with the problem of disjunction and conjunction did have a profoundly American quality. For that matter America, where social atomism worked itself out to the fullest on the one hand, and transcendentalism and popular idealisms flourished on the other, was virtually a coliseum for the renewal of the ancient battle of the nominalists and the realists. It was not accidental that Henry Adams struggled so earnestly with the medieval debate in Mont-Saint Michel and Chartres. James, however, dealt more successfully with its modern and American counterpart.

James sympathized with the eccentric, with the outlawed, with that proscribed by one presumptuous monism or another. He saw a special value in the proscribed, as Adams's Virgin found those worthy of mercy whom rigorous justice would condemn. Yet it was an American trait to suppose that the underdog might be not merely acceptable, but might pass judgment himself, as Huckleberry Finn, unfit for civilized society, and willing to be damned by its standards, unwittingly passed judgment upon it. James from his own perspective perceived the lustrous inner light of the eccentric. It was a pietistic union of stubborn individual judgment with a particular idealism, theistic or not. "The solid meaning of life is always the same eternal thing," said James, "--the marriage, namely of some unhabitual ideal, however special, with some fidelity, courage, and endurance; with some man's or woman's pains.[51]

Equally with that of individual specialness, James invoked the principle of conjunction; his, he emphasized, was a philosophy of "co." Thus he developed his idea of the universe as a sort of federal republic. The term was metaphorical, and yet not entirely so. A federal universe would retain both the quality of interconnectedness and that of indeterminacy. It would be a whole in the sense of a sea that all could sail, without any wind or tide controlling all. To make a cosmology of federalism was inherently no more frivolous than to reason an Absolute from the example of kingly power, or to deduce nominalism from anomie. It was by no means inconsistent with the ordinary experience of life crowded with the strands of relatedness, but so often breaking off in disjunction and chaos. Perhaps after all the alternatives were less stark than those posed by Adams; the cosmos might be big enough to contain both order and disorder. And federalism, although not an exact term for such a cosmos, was a convenient American one.

No less American, of course, was the emphasis on striving, although we see it here not so much as that bootless chase of the felicity which Tocqueville believed always escaped the American, but as the moral impulse to league oneself with the forces of good. This striving-relational system expressed perhaps more deeply the American social genius than did the cosmology of Bancroft. For all that the latter taught that the voice of the people is the voice of God, there was still something in the relation of God to individual of a king to his foot-soldier; indeed, to orthodoxy, any other sort of relationship would be absurd. But James's cosmology was one of voluntary and fluid associations, of mobility, of the authentic novelty which, in his view, no deterministic

212

system could admit. At the least, the pluralist offered a reformation in the American sense of the providential which reflected the character of American experience.

iii.

Religious terms apply naturally to James, not alone on account of his own eccentrically religious temperament. Aside from his formal study of religious psychology, The Varieties of Religious Experience, the major terms of his thought--pluralism, pragmatism, and radical empiricism--were designed in their fullest applications for a world of religious experience and of moral struggle transcending the human. The heterodoxy of his religious speculations, like that of his father, does not greatly obscure the Protestant roots of his thought. Henry James, Sr., a Swedenborgian, maintained man's freedom of choice and carried "liberal ideas. . .as far as possible into an idealized anarchism." Yet he retained the marks of his Calvinist heritage in his firm insistence on the reality of evil, and in his belief that the individual was sustained only by the power of God. His son in turn abandoned the idealist and monistic elements in his father's belief, and in his pluralism travelled even farther from orthodoxy.[52] His moral strenuosity was eminently at home in the Puritan tradition, however, and the Protestant concept of the saving religious experience seems fundamental to his thought. "When Luther, in his immense manly way, swept off by a stroke of his hand the very notion of a debit and credit account kept with individuals by the Almighty," James thought, "he stretched the soul's imagination and saved theology from puerility."[53] Grace, the Protestant sense of the "unmerited love or favor of God," was an urgent and personal problem for James in his younger days, Allen notes. While rejecting the "antinomian" tendency of his fa-

213

ther,[54] he retained a sense of moral and emotional experience and of alliance with broader realms of consciousness which owed much to this notion of grace.

James had of course no sympathy with orthodox Calvinism as such. "A God who gives so little scope to love, a predestination which takes from endeavor all its zest with all its fruit," he remarked in 1881, "are irrational conceptions, because they say to our most cherished powers,There is no object for you."[55] But there was a continuity "from Edwards to Emerson," Perry Miller pointed out, in the pietistic yearning for direct communication with God, and James, while rejecting transcendentalism in its monistic character, found much of the kindred spirit in its exemplar. Speaking at the Emerson Centenary in Concord in 1903, he paid tribute to a "real seer":

> The matchless eloquence with which Emerson proclaimed the sovereignty of the living individual electrified and emancipated his generation, and this bugle-blast will doubtless be regarded by future critics as the soul of his message. The present man is the aboriginal reality, the Institution is derivative, and the past man is irrelevant and obliterate for present issues.
>
> *   *   *
>
> The same indefeasible right to be exactly what one is, provided one only be authentic, spreads itself, in Emerson's way of thinking, from persons to things and to times and places.[56]

The connection between sovereign individual and divine Absolute, however, seemed to James no longer to work, and his pluralism was designed in part to make God, like the qualities of good and evil, a distinct and uncompromised entity. Religion must be saved from abstraction. James pointed out that the God of popular Christianity had always been part of a pluralistic system; He

214

was practically regarded as a power separate from the Devil and from ordinary souls, whatever His theoretical omnipotence. He could "hardly conceive of anything more different from the Absolute than the God, say, of David or Isaiah."[57] There was in popular religion, he believed, a sound impulse to view God as cosmic chieftain; "for morality life is a war, and the service of the highest is a sort of cosmic patriotism which also calls for volunteers." In such a Miltonic battle, "the only God worthy of the name must be finite. . . ."[58]

This did not mean that James felt it necessary to make God merely another actor in the cosmic drama. God might, he speculated, leave room for alternatives and possibilities, and yet in the end be able to guide the universe in the paths that He desired, combatting adversary forces like an expert chess player against novices. The vital point was that there must be a standard to which to rally in a real moral struggle.

> The ideal is only a part of this world. Make the world a pluralism, and you forthwith have an object of worship. Make it a unit, on the other hand, and worship and abhorrence are equally one-sided and equally legitimate reactions. Indifferentism is the true condition of such a world, and turn the matter how you will, I don't see how any philosophy of the Absolute can ever escape from that capricious alternation of mysticism and satanism in the treatment of its great Idol, which history has always shown. Reverence is an accidental personal mood in such a philosophy, and has naught to do with the essentials of the system. At least, so it seems to me; and in view of that, I prefer to stick in the wooden finitude of an ultimate pluralism, because that at least

gives me something definite to worship
and fight for.[59]

In similar vein, James professed perplexity as
to why, from the time of Plato and Aristotle,
philosophers have scorned the particular, although
the most "adorable" things were "all concretes
and singulars." It seemed to him that "the traditional universal-worship can only be called a
bit of perverse sentimentalism, a philosophic
'idol of the cave.'"[60]

In keeping with the conjunctive and relational character of James's thought, these "concretes
and singulars" were not wholly detached from one
another, but aware of higher levels of affinity.
"And just as we are co-conscious with our own mo-
mentary margin," he speculated, "may not we our-
selves form the margin of some more really central
self in things which is co-conscious with the
whole of us? May not you and I be confluent in
a higher consciousness, and confluently active
there, tho we now know it not?" This was an idea
that particularly engaged his religious sensibilities. He believed that religious experiences
"point with reasonable probability to the continuity of our consciousness with a wider spiritual
environment from which the ordinary prudential
man (who is the only man that scientific psychology, so called, takes cognizance of) is shut
off."[61]

This is a more sophisticated universe than
James's two-dimensional chess game analogy would
imply. His basic complaint against late nineteenth century science was that it was radically
reductionist, and in his Varieties of Religious
Experience, he did not conceal his satisfaction
that the experiences described "plainly show the
universe to be a more many-sided affair than any
sect, even the scientific sect, allows for. . . .
And why, after all, may not the world be so complex as to consist of many interpenetrating
spheres of reality. . .?" There were, he was

216

persuaded, "many worlds of consciousness," with meaning for, and possible connection with, our own. The function of religion in this multi-dimensional cosmos was precisely the connective one of reaching across the boundaries of ordinary consciousness; one could not, he thought, avoid the conclusion "that in religion we have a department of human nature with unusually close relations to the transmarginal or subliminal region."[62]

This impulse toward wider regions of experience seems the best way to view James's religious sensibility. In more conventional terms, he proposed a theism which would stand midway between agnosticism and gnosticism. "With agnosticism," he explained, "it goes so far as to confess that we cannot know how Being made itself or us. With gnosticism, it goes so far as to insist that we can know Being's character when made, and how it asks us to behave." James acknowledged that he could not feel volitionally at home with either materialism or agnosticism. Theism radically transformed the cosmic situation. "At a single stroke, it changes the dead blank it of the world into a living Thou, with whom the whole man may have dealings."[63]

Beyond this tentative theism, James embraced no theology. Indeed, he disdained theological systems as secondary superimpositions on religious experience, and believed that the best path to religious truth was empirical, despite, "by some strange misunderstanding," the more usual association of empiricism with irreligion.[64] With his usual pluralistic tolerance, James was willing to risk a certain amount of superstition in order not to preclude any possibly valid sort of religious experience.

James's God was evidently a pragmatic God, and made Himself known pragmatically. "To co-operate with his creation by the best and rightest response seems all he wants of us," James

suggested. "In such cooperation with his purposes, not in any chimerical speculative conquest
of him, not in any theoretic drinking of him up,
must lie the real meaning of our destiny." In a
pluralistic universe, moreover, there was no reason why God Himself might not draw strength from
the faithfulness of human beings. James argued
that a

> thoroughly "pragmatic" view of religion
> has usually been taken as a matter of
> course by common men. They have inter-
> polated divine miracles into the field
> of nature, they have built a heaven out
> beyond the grave. It is only transcen-
> dentalist metaphysicians who think that,
> without adding any concrete details to
> Nature, or subtracting any, but by
> simply calling it the expression of
> absolute spirit, you make it more di-
> vine just as it stands. I believe
> pragmatic religion to be the deeper
> way. It gives it body as well as soul,
> it makes it claim, as everything real
> must claim, some characteristic realm
> of fact as its very own.[65]

Religious faith, like other kinds of faith,
received sanction from "The Will to Believe,"
James arguing in this most famous of his essays
that "our passional nature not only lawfully may,
but must, decide an option between propositions,
whenever it is a genuine option that cannot by
its nature be decided on intellectual grounds. .
. ."[66] The necessity of faith was one with the
necessity of taking risks. One could not live,
indeed, without faith. And like Brooks and Henry
Adams, James was profoundly conscious of the
actual and observable power of specific religious
faith. "Every sort of energy and endurance, of
courage and capacity for handling life's evils,"
he pointed out, "is set free in those who have
religious faith. For this reason the strenuous
type of character will on the battlefield of human

history always outwear the easy-going type, and religion will drive irreligion to the wall."[67] Virtually evangelical in tone, the statement was entirely characteristic of James's fundamentally religious sense of life.

As elsewhere in James's thought, there was in his speculations on religion an extraordinary feeling for both the intensity and the diversity of experience. It is almost inevitable either to sacrifice intensity to pluralism, or pluralism to intensity, but James managed to preserve a simultaneous sense of both. He had a pietistic understanding of feeling as "the deeper source of religion"--deeper than theological formulations--and of the inspired obduracy of true faith. "In its acuter stages every religion must be a homeless Arab of the desert," he noted. "The church knows this well enough, with its everlasting inner struggle of the acute religion of the few against the chronic religion of the many, indurated into an obstructiveness worse than that which irreligion opposes to the movings of the Spirit." (He appropriately cited Jonathan Edwards in defense of this observation.) Yet without losing his empathy with religious intensity, he could revel in "the enormous diversities which the spiritual lives of different men exhibit," and give his own interpretation to an often ignored Biblical proposition: "in our Father's house are many mansions, and each of us must discover for himself the kind of religion and the amount of saintship which best comports with what he believes to be his powers and feels to be his truest mission and vocation."[68] This pluralistic pietism lies at the heart of William James, and it suggested a path which a nation burdened and illuminated by its pietism and its pluralism might take.

The existentialist aspect which has in recent years been especially remarked upon in James's thought gives support to this view of him. The starting point is his fundamental individualism,

219

and concomitant distrust of institutions, American attitudes which he sometimes expressed in a characteristically American way. "The breath of the nostrils of all these big institutions is crime. . .," he remarked with reference to the Dreyfus affair. "Every great institution is perforce a means of corruption--whatever good it may also do. Only in the free personal relation is full ideality to be found."[69]

James was not, of course, a philosophical anarchist, any more than he was a genuine nominalist. He recognized the value of society and its institutions, but it was a value emphatically dependent upon their usefulness to individuals, which constituted the only living world.[70] Individuality was sacred, because each individual possessed his own unique truth: "neither the whole of truth nor the whole of good is revealed to any single observer, although each observer gains a partial superiority of insight from the peculiar position in which he stands. Even prisons and sickrooms have their special revelations."[71] Institutions were good insofar as they nurtured these individual perspectives and eccentricities. His attitude was well summarized in his tribute to Thomas Davidson in 1905:

> The memory of Davidson will always strengthen my faith in personal freedom and its spontaneities, and make me less unqualifiedly respectful than ever of "Civilization," with its herding and branding, licensing and degree-giving, authorizing and appointing, and in general regulating and administering by system the lives of human beings. Surely the individual, the person in the singular number, is the more fundamental phenomenon, and the social institution, of whatever grade, is but secondary and ministerial. Many as are the interests which social systems satisfy, always unsatisfied interests

220

remain over, and among them are interests to which system, as such, does
violence whenever it lays its hand upon
us. The best Commonwealth will always
be the one that most cherishes the men
who represent the residual interests,
the one that leaves the largest scope
to their peculiarities.[72]

James recognized in late nineteenth century
science the same absolutist pretensions to which
he objected in theology or in overweening political institutions. "In my essay ["The Will to
Believe"] ," he wrote in 1904, "the evil shape
was a vision of 'Science' in the form of abstraction, priggishness and sawdust, lording it over
all."[73] His own background was scientific; what
he objected to was not science but scientific
claims to all-sufficiency. This seemed to him a
fatal narrowing of vision, and he warned that if
the "religion of exclusive scientificism" should
ever succeed in destroying alternative ways of
understanding among a people, "that nation, that
race, will just as surely go to ruin, and fall a
prey to their more richly constituted neighbors,
as the beasts of the field, as a whole, have fallen
a prey to man."[74] Contemplating the fruits of
scientific reductionism, James struck an unusual
note of pessimism. For a century and a half, he
observed, "the progress of science has seemed to
mean the enlargement of the material universe and
the diminution of man's importance. The result
is what one may call the growth of naturalistic
or positivistic feeling. . . . The romantic
spontaneity and courage are gone, the vision is
materialistic and depressing."[75] He was all the
more anxious therefore to preserve a plurality
of perspectives and to keep all possibilities
open, as evidenced particularly by his friendly
interest in eccentric religious and psychical
phenomena.

James's indeterminism, hostility to scientific reductionism, and emphasis on individual

truth, choice, and moral responsibility, all give
support to the characterization of him as a proto-
existentialist. His personal crisis of 1870,
during which he came to confront the precariousness and contingency of his own existence, has certainly an existentialist tone. He never lost his
sense that

> the sanest and best of us are of one
> clay with lunatics and prison inmates,
> and death finally runs the robustest
> of us down. And whenever we feel this,
> such a sense of the vanity and provi-
> sionality of our voluntary career comes
> over us that all our morality appears
> but as a plaster hiding a sore it can
> never cure, and all our well-doing as
> the hollowest substitute for that well-
> being that our lives ought to be ground-
> ed in, but, alas! are not.[76]

James's context here was a discussion of religion,
and he added that it was at this point that religion came to the rescue. But he never believed
that religion could absorb evil; this was his
quarrel with monistic idealism. His medical experience had left him with too vivid an impression
of the worst of human experience, of insane melan-
cholia, for example, with its "desperation absolute and complete, the whole universe coagulating
about the sufferer into a material of overwhelming horror, surrounding him without opening or
end," to doubt absolute evil. There was a perspective, indeed, in which he could see in this
dark vision the lineaments of life itself. There
was a profound truth, he remarked, in the insistence of the Schopenhauer school on moral progress
as an illusion. "The more brutal forms of evil
that go are replaced by others more subtle and
more poisonous. Our moral horizon moves with us
as we move, and never do we draw nearer to the
far-off line where the black waves and the azure
meet." Not the final conquest of evil, but the
enrichment of ethical consciousness, was left as

the final purpose of our creation."[77]

The existentialist element in James's thought was to be sure much qualified, not least by the assumption that there could be such a thing as a final purpose of creation. It was strongly tinged with an American optimism. Although a permanent reality, despair as a mood was transitory: "This life is worth living, we can say, since it is what we make it, from the moral point of view; and we are determined to make it from that point of view, so far as we have anything to do with it, a success." As always, there was in this a moral emphasis; he had no patience with the mere celebration of life for the sake of life, which he discerned with some annoyance in his friend Oliver Wendell Holmes, Jr. He viewed duty and discipline as the concomitants of spontaneity. As Perry puts it, "he could finally accept no spontaneity save that of the enthusiastic will already pledged to righteousness"[78]--an attitude well-rooted in American Protestant pietism. Above all, James retained a heroic and dramatic sense of life, as conscious of evil as the twentieth century existentialist temper, but with a more vivid contrast of darkness and light:

> The world thus finds in the heroic man its worthy match and mate; and the effort which he is able to put forth to hold himself erect and keep his heart unshaken is the direct measure of his worth and function in the game of human life. He can stand this Universe. He can meet it and keep up his faith in it in presence of those same features which lay his weaker brethren low. He can still find a zest in it, not by "ostrich-like forgetfulness," but by pure inward willingness to face the world with those deterrent objects there. And hereby he becomes one of the masters and the lords of life. He must be counted with henceforth; he

> forms a part of human destiny. Neither
> in the theoretic nor in the practical
> sphere do we care for, or go for help
> to, those who have no head for risks,
> or sense of living on the perilous
> edge.[79]

The "perilous edge" was an appropriate image
for an American thinker. It had an easy association with the frontier, and with those lonely
explorers and pioneers, without institutions or
tradition for support, which folklore deemed the
country's best representatives.[80] If the master
values of the frontier were enshrined in formal
thought as the frontier vanished, it would be a
pattern familiar to the history of thought. Contemporaneously Frederick Jackson Turner's "frontier thesis" appeared in American historiography;
contemporaneously too the loudest paeans were
being raised to competitive risk as businessmen
moved toward "combination. . .in restraint of
trade." Underneath the official reliance on
Providence, there had been in the encounter with
the wilderness (which might be deified as Nature
but which was Nothingness from the standpoint of
civilization) a native streak of the existentialist. The entrepreneur lived on his own perilous
edge, and the risk in which he dealt did not invariably respond to the Invisible Hand. Looking
toward the past, there was much in James of the
moral entrepreneur, risktaker, and rugged individualist, at a time when the type was increasingly overshadowed by the social engineer and his
socializing of morality, which cut out the old
partnership of God and the individual. Looking
toward the future, there was much in him of the
existentialist, and he provided a formal expression to the sense of life as contingency that the
twentieth century could understand.

There is a tension in James's thought, however, which mirrors a similar tension in the
American experience. Pluralism meant the strenuosity of the genuine unfixed fight on the moral

frontier, and a God of moral battles to Whom one could freely rally; pluralism thus conceived tended still to polarize experience between the sharply distinguished qualities of good and evil. Yet pluralism meant also diversity, tolerance, the "varieties of religious experience." In this conception, the old religious idea of grace was pluralized, and consisted in the individual's true aspiration toward and grasp of ever-wider areas of consciousness. This suggested no steep edges at all, but the cosmos as "all-navigable sea," if not a unit, at least accessible to whatever reaches one could attain--a federal universe. Similarly, it had long been uncertain whether the deeper national meaning was to be found in the expansive urge of geographical and economic frontiers, or in the religiously endowed notion of the fraternal union, the harmony of diverse states and sections and peoples.

Both pluralisms answered the American counterpoint which pleaded for the outlaw, the man untamed by convention, while yearning for a message from the heart of the universe. The pluralism of the perilous edge contemplated the extraordinary man on the periphery of experience, yet at the center of the ethical struggle. The pluralism of the all-navigable sea sought to bring the eccentric and the outlaw within the folds of legitimate human experience, and found the proper field of aspiration in conjunction and connectedness. The two visions were not then totally incompatible; they organized in different ways a profound feeling for openness in the morally instructed individual aspiration, for the lonely and painful struggle toward "some habitual ideal, however special." A proper federalism would find no contradiction in the centrifugal pull of the varieties of experience and the accessibility of each to all, limited only though inevitably by the individual perspective. Such an experiential federalism remained of course as remote from reality as Plato's Republic. Pragmatism as the clearest expression of this openness

225

became in popular usage too often a reductionism which truncated experience at the point at which it should have begun, reducing the range of possibilities to the immediately expedient. The first American steps of the unparalleled cosmic adventure of the late twentieth century remained ambiguous in the minds of many; was the journey to the moon the narrow triumph of technology or the beginning of an inconceivable widening of human experience? James offered Americans a pluralism cast of their own historic traits, of their preoccupation with individual striving and their sensitivity, at best, to the moral imperative, of their pietistic hunger for grace and their too often grudging allowance for diversity.

iv.

Unlike Bancroft, Fiske, the Adamses, and even Royce, William James was not an historian. He did profoundly influence historical theory and practice, as Cushing Strout emphasizes. In particular, he seemed to furnish formal grounds for interpreting the past in the light of the needs of the present. Although this approach was apt to misapply his philosophy, his larger ideas retained their significance for history. "If James's Pragmatism can be seen as an effort to give a historical account to the process of knowing," Strout points out, "his Pluralism was also deeply responsive to the centrality of history in human experience." Unlike the Absolute, finite beings whether human or divine are necessarily involved in the historical process.[81] Time itself had no use in a universe where all phenomena were subsumed by an Absolute, James believed, for in such a case there could be no genuine novelty.

In the early part of his career, before his decision to believe in free-will, James was much disturbed by the social implications of the prevailing materialistic schools of thought. Ac-

226

knowledging his developing commitment to empiricism, he expressed his anxiety in a letter to Oliver Wendell Holmes, Jr., then a close friend:

> If the end of all is to be that we must take our sensations as simply given or as preserved by natural selection for us, and interpret this rich and delicate overgrowth of ideas, moral, artistic, religious and social, as a mere mask, a tissue spun in happy hours by creative individuals and adopted by other men in the interests of their sensations, --how long is it going to be well for us not to "let on" all we know to the public? How long are we to indulge the "people" in their theological and other vagaries so long as such vagaries seem to us more beneficial on the whole than otherwise?

He went on to ask whether, if the path of "sensationalism" were to be followed,"we" ought

> to begin to smite the old, hip and thigh, and get, if possible, a little enthusiasm associated with our doctrines? If God is dead or at least irrelevant, ditto everything pertaining to the "Beyond." If happiness is our Good, ought we not try to foment a passionate and bold will to attain that happiness among the multitudes? Can we not conduct off upon our purposes from the old moralities and theologies a beam which will invest us with some of the proud absoluteness which made them so venerable, by reaching the doctrine that Man is his own Providence, and every individual a real God to his race, greater or lesser in proportion to his gifts and the way he uses them?[83]

The suggested solution was far removed from James's later pluralism, as receptive to religious as to scientific truths, but it affords some insight into a mind for whom the "old moralities and theologies" still held a powerful attraction. The attraction was insufficient for him either intellectually or temperamentally to remain their prisoner, but his subsequent work was devoted largely to the project of directing a "beam" from them to illuminate the world in which they were supplanted. In one sense it was ironic that he should cite the "proud absoluteness" of the old doctrines as the quality which must be appropriated from them, as he later viewed their absolutism as their one attribute that must be destroyed. Yet the phrase implied also a quality of irreducible self-assurance, of a willingness to steer constantly by whatever star in the cosmos seemed to offer the truest course, which amounted in itself to an absolute. James did not so much "damn the absolute" as fix it in this relation between the traveler and his chosen way. The claims to absolute truth of scientific no less than religious systems were broken down in order to confer an absolute value on this individual act of choice.

This sovereignty of the unique individual vision, which was to replace that of the Calvinist God, and which James attributed even to the sickroom and the prison cell, would become familiar enough in the twentieth century. But for James it meant neither anomie nor moral anarchy, and certainly not the absurdity of the universe. The personal vision was rather a medium in which the multiplicity of existence could assume the shape of meaning. This required the sort of openness to disparate modes of experience that permitted James to act, in the Roycean sense, as interpreter between religious and scientific perceptions of truth, and between the older idealist and monistic perspectives, and the incipient existentialist thinking of his own time. In grasping the significance of relations as well as of individuals, James's radical empiricism

228

comprehended the most usable elements of both schools.

Yet just as for George Bancroft the religious assumption of individual access to divine truth was essential to his progressive and democratic scheme of history, so the coherence of James's vision depends to a great extent on an essentially religious sense of the individual reaching out toward ever wider modes of consciousness. The "pluralistic universe" was one which, if not safe for religion, at least remained open to religious truth. The reality of moral choice, and the legitimacy of personal experience of the super-human, were the minimal terms which William James required from the western religious tradition.

Footnotes

1. [William James], "Herbert Spencer's Data of Ethics," The Nation, XXIX (September 11, 1879), 179. Julius Seelye Bixler thought that pluralism lacked intrinsic interest for James, and amounted chiefly in his philosophy simply to a rejection of monism. Religion in the Philosophy of William James (Boston: Marshall Jones Company, 1926), pp. 47-49. (Hereinafter cited as Bixler, Religion in the Philosophy of William James.) However, as I think this passage indicates, James did delight in the variousness of life for its own sake, and his pluralism was partly an expression of such positive feelings.

2. William James, "Pluralism and Religion," The Hibbert Journal, VI (July, 1908), 725.

3. Ralph Barton Perry, The Thought and Character of William James as Revealed in Unpublished Correspondence and Notes, together with His Published Writings, 2 volumes (Boston: Little, Brown, and Company, 1935), II, 407, 590-591. (Hereinafter cited as Perry, Thought and Character.) "Freedom and unity," John K. Roth maintains, "are the values that James wishes most to protect and to extend. . . ." Freedom and the Moral Life: The Ethics of William James (Philadelphia: The Westminister Press, 1969), p. 62. Roth seems to me to overemphasize the attraction of unity to so emphatic a pluralist. This is not to say that the attraction was absent, however. Bixler for example called attention to conflicting religious impulses in James: the one active and aggressive, requiring a pluralistic universe; the other a more passive desire for peace and assurance, monistic in tendency. Bixler, Religion in the Philosophy of William James, pp. 2-3.

4. William James, Essays in Radical Empiricism (New York: Longmans, Green and Co., 1958), p. 44. (Hereinafter cited as James, Radical

Empiricism.) "The truly empirical mind," as Perry understands James, "is not the mind which yields to habit or passively accepts its own history as a revelation of existence, but the mind which imagines curious possibilities and gives nature every chance to reveal itself in unfamiliar ways." But further, "it is necessary that the order of existence itself be experienced. An empiricism which reduces experience to items, no one of which can ever be an experience of the very order in which they occur, is a confession of failure. Nor will it suffice to experience relations as merely so many more items. Terms must be experienced in their very acts or states of relatedness." Thought and Character. I, 558, 564. John Wild more succinctly explains that James holds "that our lived experience comes to us originally as related and organized. We know its relational aspects by direct acquaintance as well as conceptually, just as we know its substantive parts." The Radical Empiricism of William James (Garden City, N. Y.: Doubleday, 1969), p. 61. (Hereinafter cited as Wild, Radical Empiricism.)

5. Henry James [son of William], ed., The Letters of William James, 2 volumes (Boston: The Atlantic Monthly Press, 1920), II, 101. James to William M. Salter, September 11, 1899. (Hereinafter cited as James, Letters.)

6. Ibid., II, 90. James to Mrs. Henry Whitman, June 7, 1899.

7. James, Radical Empiricism, p. 194. "Neither James nor [Charles] Renouvier was interested in a pluralism of unrelated entities,--a many without unity,--but it was of first importance to them that the unity should not predetermine the many." Perry, Thought and Character, I, 659.

8. William James, A Pluralistic Universe (New York: Longmans, Green and Co., 1958, pp. 174-175, 321-322, 326. (Hereinafter cited as James, Pluralistic Universe.) Perry notes that

James was attracted by G. T. Fechner's conception of the universe as "a series of overlapping souls from God down through the earth-soul to man, and from man to the unobservable psychic states that lie below the threshold of his consciousness." Thought and Character, II, 587.

9. William James, Pragmatism: a New Name for Some Old Ways of Thinking. Popular Lectures on Philosophy by William James (New York: Longmans, Green and Co., 1921), pp. 201, 257. (Hereinafter cited as James, Pragmatism.)

10. William James, The Meaning of Truth, a Sequel to "Pragmatism" (New York: Longmans, Green, and Co. 1914), pp. 205, 265-267. (Hereinafter cited as James, Meaning of Truth.)

11. Perry, Thought and Character, II, 542. James to Charles A. Strong, August 4, 1907; James, Pragmatism, pp. 122, 299. "James, like Thoreau, was more interested in well-being than in well-doing, trusting to intuition as a revelation of reality. He never lost his awareness of the mystery and believed pragmatism to be a method whereby the values of the old supernaturalism could be preserved." Ralph Henry Gabriel, The Course of American Democratic Thought. Second edition (New York: Ronald Press, 1956), p. 348. (Hereinafter cited as Gabriel, American Democratic Thought.)

12. James, Meaning of Truth, pp. 184-186.

13. James, Pragmatism, p. 123.

14. Perry, Thought and Character, II, 411.

15. James, Pragmatism, pp. 269, 33, 72, 80.

16. Perry, Thought and Character, I, 461.

17. James, Pragmatism, pp. 299-301.

18. C. Hartley Grattan, The Three Jameses: a Family of Minds. Henry James, Sr., William James, Henry James. With an introduction by Oscar Cargill (New York: New York University Press, 1962), pp. 195-196. (Hereinafter cited as Grattan, Three Jameses.)

19. Gay Wilson Allen, William James: a Biography (New York: Viking Press, 1967), p. 226. (Hereinafter cited as Allen, William James.)

20. William James, "Are We Automata?" Mind, IV (January, 1879), 1-6. (Hereinafter cited as James, "Are We Automata?")

21. William James, The Principles of Psychology, 2 volumes (New York: Dover Publications, 1950), I, 138. (Hereinafter cited as James, Psychology.)

22. Ibid., I, 139.

23. Ibid., I, 142; II, 576, 584; James, "Are We Automata?" 13. John Wild points out that James broke with the traditional conception of freedom of the will, "which held that the mind was determined by its objects, but that the special faculty of will has a limited freedom of action. For James, on the other hand, there is no such isolated active freedom. The first source of our actual freedom is rather mental. . . . By focusing his attention on certain broad patterns of meaning, the person may then reform and combine them in new ways." Wild, Radical Empiricism, p. 262.

24. James, Psychology, II, 571-574.

25. William James, "Reflex Action and Theism," Unitarian Review and Religious Magazine, XVI (November, 1881), 405-406. (Hereinafter cited as James, "Reflex Action"); James, Psychology, I, 141.

26. James, "Reflex Action," 394-395.

27. James, Psychology, I, 181, 350; Perry, Thought and Character, II, 136-137; William James, Human Immortality: Two Supposed Objections to the Doctrine (Boston: Houghton Mifflin Company, 1898), pp. 21-22 and passim.

28. Perry, Thought and Character, I, 615; II, 25-26. James to Charles A. Strong, October 21, 1889. "With Professor Perry we must discriminate an early positivistic phase of James's idea of evolution. In this phase James pitted himself against his anti-Darwinian teacher of zoology, the famous Louis Agassiz. Next, under the influence of Chauncey Wright and Charles Peirce, James began to criticize Spencer's mechanical evolutionism, but still clung to Darwin's theory of spontaneous variations despite Peirce's metaphysical criticisms. Finally we have the metaphysical phase of James's later years, when he espoused Peirce's radical tychism: the extension of spontaneous chance to the whole of nature and its laws." Philip P. Wiener, Evolution and the Founders of Pragmatism. With a foreword by John Dewey (Cambridge: Harvard University Press, 1949), p. 100. (Hereinafter cited as Wiener, Founders of Pragmatism.)

29. Allen, William James, p. 164; Paul K. Conkin, Puritans and Pragmatists: Eight Eminent American Thinkers (New York: Dodd, Mead & Company, 1968), p. 309. (Hereinafter cited as Conkin, Puritans and Pragmatists.

30. James, Psychology, II, 574.

31. William James, "German Pessimism," The Nation, XXI (October 7, 1875), 234; William James, "Rationality, Activity, and Faith," Princeton Review, X (1882), 69, 77. (Hereinafter cited as James, "Rationality, Activity, and Faith.")

32. William James, The Will to Believe and

Other Essays in Popular Philosophy (Cambridge: Longmans Green and Co., 1905), pp. 261-262. (Hereinafter cited as James, Will to Believe.

33. James, Letters, I, 238. James to G. H. Howison, February 5, 1885; Perry, Thought and Character, I, 686. James to Charles Renouvier, December 6, 1882.

34. James, Will to Believe, p. 151.

35. Ibid., pp. 165-166, 170-171.

36. Ibid., pp. 169, 175; Perry, Thought and Character, II, 212.

37. James, Will to Believe, pp. 149, 153-154.

38. Perry, Thought and Character, II, 663.

39. Ibid., II, 411-412.

40. Ibid., II, 656. James to James Ward, June 27, 1909.

41. Ibid., II, 664; James, Letters, II, 292. James to Henri Bergson, June 13, 1907. "Both men," Perry notes of James and Bergson, "have the same sense of the copiousness of reality, and of the pathetic thinness of the concepts with which the human mind endeavors to represent it." Thought and Character, II, 603.

42. James, Psychology, II, 576.

43. Ibid., II, 576-577; James, Meaning of Truth, p. 251.

44. Grattan, Three Jameses, p. 158.

45. James, "Rationality, Activity, and Faith," 70-71, 86; James, Pragmatism, p. 292.

46. James, _Pragmatism_, pp. 118-119.

47. Perry, _Thought and Character_, II, 640, quoting James. "The world as James now depicts it is a scene of perpetual transition, in which the parts, instead of merely succeeding, inherit one another and usher one another in," Perry notes. "No event expires until after another has already begun, so that there is always a zone of commingled dawn and twilight through which the one leads over into another. But while each object is thus woven into the fabric of reality, its threads extend only for a limited distance, so that it is only indirectly connected with remoter regions." _Ibid_., II, 590.

48. James, _Pluralistic Universe_, p. 283.

49. John E. Smith observes that James's idea of the "conjunctive relation" can mean either "continuity" or "being with." _Themes in American Philosophy: Purpose, Experience, and Community_ (New York: Harper, 1970), p. 34.

50. William G. McLoughlin, "Pietism and the American Character," _American Quarterly_, XVII (Summer, 1965), 185 and _passim_.

51. William James, _Talks to Teachers on Psychology: and to Students on Some of Life's Ideals_ (London: Longmans, Green, and Co., 1908), p. 299. (Hereinafter cited as James, _Talks_.)

52. Dwight W. Hoover, _Henry James, Sr. and the Religion of Community_ (Grand Rapids, Mich.: William B. Eerdmans Publishing Co., 1969), pp. 74, 138, 71. William A. Clebsch, who stresses the "humanistic," man-centered element in the religious thought of both Jameses, goes so far as to say that William James took the content, but not the form, of his father's religion. _American Religious Thought: a History_ (Chicago: University of Chicago Press, 1973), pp. 134-135. (Hereinafter cited as Clebsch, _American Religious_

<u>Thought</u>.) Bixler earlier remarked that James appeared to have "more rather than less sympathy for his father's views as he grew older," particularly with regard to mysticism. In Bixler's view, which I think should balance the recent emphasis on James's humanism, "nearly all the paths in James's thought led to a conception of the Deity. . . . That God exists is thus the testimony of many different elements in James's philosophy." Bixler, <u>Religion in the Philosophy of William James</u>, pp. 196, 122.

53. William James, <u>The Varieties of Religious Experience: a Study in Human Nature. Being the Gifford Lectures on Natural Religion Delivered at Edinburgh in 1901-1902</u> (New York: Modern Library, 1902), p. 340. (Hereinafter cited as James, <u>Varieties</u>.)

54. Allen, <u>William James</u>, pp. 147-148. "Schiller's doctrine of 'grace' [in his essay on "Grace and Dignity," ca. 1868] touched William's psychological sore spot: 'My old trouble and the root of antinomianism in general seems to be a dissatisfaction with anything less than grace.' Of course Schiller was thinking of 'grace' as an aesthetic effect of supple and coordinated animal movement, but William applied it in the theological sense, that is, unmerited love or favor of God." Allen adds that Henry James, Sr. took the "antinomian" view that all wickedness stemmed from Man's assertion of his independent will; William, of course, could not finally accept this. <u>Ibid</u>., pp. 147-148. Indeed, Conkin suggests William James's opposite affinities: "Like the Arminians of old, he wanted some supernatural agency in man, some exemption from both physical and moral necessity. Only then could our desires have cosmic significance." <u>Puritans and Pragmatists</u>, p. 307. Perry describes a religious quality in his subject: "To James the ultimate vision is intuitive, while to Dewey it is discursive. Or, while James <u>is</u> percipient, artistic, and religious, Dewey elaborates ideas <u>about</u> perception, art, and religion. With James the essence of life and ex-

237

perience can be grasped only in the living and the experiencing, and this conviction springs from the abundance and vividness of personal living and experience; whereas with Dewey the essence of things emerges only upon reflection. . ." *Thought and Character*, II, 515.

55. James, *Will to Believe*, p. 126.

56. William James, *Memories and Studies* (New York: Longmans, Green, and Co., 1912), pp. 25-26, 29. (Hereinafter cited as James, *Memories and Studies*.)

57. James, *Pluralistic Universe*, pp. 110-111.

58. James, *Varieties*, pp. 45-46; James, *Pluralistic Universe*, p. 125.

59. Perry, *Thought and Character*, I, 772. James to George H. Howison, February 5, 1885.

60. James, *Psychology*, I, 479-480.

61. James, *Pluralistic Universe*, pp. 290, 310. "We may be in the universe as dogs and cats are in our libraries, seeing the books and hearing the conversation, but having no inkling of the meaning of it all. . . ." *Ibid.*, p. 309.

62. James, *Varieties*, pp. 120, 509, 473.

63. James, *Will to Believe*, p. 142; James, "Reflex Action," 402. Certain writers have emphasized the humanistic or "man-centered" quality of James's concern with religion: e.g. Clebsch, *American Religious Thought*, pp. 169-172; Patrick Kiaran Dooley, *Pragmatism as Humanism: The Philosophy of William James* (Chicago: Nelson-Hall, 1974), pp. 82-93. It might be more accurate to locate the center of James's religious concern not in the human being himself, but in his very act of reaching out for "dealings" with a wider consciousness or stronger volition--a "living Thou"--within the universe.

64. James, _Pluralistic Universe_, p. 314.

65. James, _Will to Believe_, pp. 141, 61; James, _Varieties_, pp. 508-509.

66. James, _Will to Believe_, p. 11.

67. James, "Rationality, Activity, and Faith," 73-74; James, _Will to Believe_, p. 213.

68. James, _Varieties_, pp. 422, 112, 107, 368. "Mysticism is commonly monistic," Perry observes, "and supernaturalism is commonly dogmatic; but James proposes a radical departure: a pluralistic mysticism, and an experimental supernaturalism." _Thought and Character_, II, 334. James defined his own religious stance: "My personal position is simple. I have no living sense of commerce with a God. I envy those who have, for I know that the addition of such a sense would help me greatly. The Divine, for my active life, is limited to impersonal and abstract concepts, which, as ideals, interest and determine me, but do so faintly in comparison with what a feeling of God might effect, if I had one. This, to be sure, is largely a matter of intensity, but a shade of intensity may make one's whole centre of moral energy shift. Now, although I am so devoid of _Gottesbewusstsein_ in the directer and stronger sense, there is _something in me_ which _makes response_ when I hear utterances from that quarter made by others. I recognize the deeper Voice. Something tells me:-- 'thither lies truth'--and I am sure it is not old theistic prejudices of infancy. Those in my case were Christian, but I have grown so out of Christianity that entanglement therewith on the part of a mystical element has to be abstracted from and overcome, before I can listen. Call this, if you like, my mystical _germ_. It is a very common germ. It creates the rank and file of believers." _Ibid._, II, 350-351. James to James H. Leuba, April 17, 1904. Wiener points out that "the variety and complexity of nature which Wright called 'cosmic weather' and Peirce 'tychism,' became for

James the metaphysical ground of the theory of an open universe and individual moral freedom." *Founders of Pragmatism*, p. 101.

69. James, *Letters*, II, 100-101. James to William M. Salter, September 11, 1899. William Barrett has discussed the existentialist element in James. *Irrational Man: a Study in Existential Philosophy* (New York: Doubleday, 1962), pp. 18-19. Allen maintains that by 1870 James had begun to work out "a kind of crude existentialist philosophy. . . ." *William James*, p. 167. Cushing Strout observes that James seems very close to existentialism in his ethical position, but without its "tragic despair." "The Unfinished Arch: William James and the Idea of History," *American Quarterly*, XIII (Winter, 1961), 507. (Hereinafter cited as Strout, "Unfinished Arch.") Andrew Reck believes that "a return to James's thought today may serve to bridge the gulf which, in the affairs of the intellect, at present divides Europe from America, correcting in Europe the excesses of existentialism and in America the excesses of scientism." *Introduction to William James: an Essay and Selected Texts* (Bloomington: Indiana University Press, 1967), pp. 85-86. John Wild perhaps most carefully locates James, not only in the existentialist tradition, but also in the more existential wing of modern phenomenology: ". . .in assigning the central position to this world," he notes, "James's position is similar to that of recent phenomenologists who have rejected Husserl's transcendental reduction, and have developed an existential rather than a transcendental phenomenology." Wild, *Radical Empiricism*, p. 401.

70. James, *Varieties*, p. 492: "Individuality is founded in feeling; and the recesses of feeling, the darker, blinder strata of character, are the only places in the world in which we catch real fact in the making, and directly perceive how events happen and how work is actually done. Compared with this world of living individualized

feelings, the world of generalized objects which the intellect contemplates is without solidity or life."

71. James, _Talks_, p. 264.

72. James, _Memories and Studies_, pp. 102-103.

73. James, _Letters_, II, 208. James to L. T. Hobhouse, August 12, 1904. Wiener suggests that James sought "in private experience the certainties and ideals no longer attainable by scientific method." _Founders of Pragmatism_, pp. 124-125.

74. James, _Will to Believe_, p. 132.

75. James, _Pragmatism_, p. 16. "The God whom science recognizes must be a God of universal laws exclusively, a God who does a wholesale, not a retail business," James thought. "He cannot accommodate his processes to the convenience of individuals." _Varieties_, pp. 483-485.

76. James, _Varieties_, p. 47.

77. James, _Varieties_, pp. 158-159; James, _Will to Believe_, p. 169. Cf. James, _Letters_, I, 245: "For life is evil. Two souls are in my breast; I see the better, and in the very act of seeing it I do the worse." James to Shadworth H. Hodgson, December 30, 1885.

78. James, _Will to Believe_, p. 61; Perry, _Thought and Character_, II, 250-251, 259.

79. James, _Psychology_, II, 578-579.

80. Josiah Royce cited the "robust faith" of James: "It is the spirit of the frontiersman, of the gold seeker, or the home builder, transferred to the metaphysical and to the religious realm. There is our far-off home, our long-lost spiritual fortune. Experience alone can guide us towards the place where these things are; hence you indeed need experience. You can only win your

241

way on the frontier in case you are willing to live there. Be, therefore, concrete, be fearless, be experimental. But, above all, let not your abstract conceptions, even if you call them scientific conceptions, pretend to set any limits to the richness of spiritual grace, to the glories of spiritual possession, that, in case you are duly favored, your personal experience may reveal to you." William James and Other Essays on the Philosophy of Life (New York: The Macmillan Company, 1912), pp. 22-23, (Hereinafter cited as Royce, William James.) Gabriel believes that James "made his most important choice when he drew back from Royce's sophisticated collectivism to a primitive individualism which was reminiscent of the American frontier of an earlier period." American Democratic Thought, p. 336.

81. Strout, "Unfinished Arch," 508-511.

82. Royce, William James, pp. 17, 19-20.

83. Perry, Thought and Character, I, 516-517. James to Oliver Wendell Holmes, Jr., May 18, 1868.

CHAPTER FIVE

THE ADAMSES: THE HIVE AND THE OCEAN

Unity and multiplicity, order and freedom: these enduring problems of human life and thought were cast in unusually sharp relief in nineteenth century America. The national motto, e pluribus unum, appeared then to signify not so much the almost facile act of federation between new states, but immensely difficult ordeals involving the relationships of sections, classes, nationalities, and races. On a deeper level, both heredity and environment seemed to enmesh the United States in a series of paradoxes. The country was heir to Protestant Christianity, and Protestantism carried as an inmost message a freedom from institutions, the liberty of the individual to treat with his God as he would. Yet in His most vital American manifestation the Protestant God had been also a Calvinist God, Whose will admitted of no moral interposition. Furthermore America was (or appeared to Europeans) a great tabula rasa; free of the obscure hieroglyphics of tradition, what new paeans to God and man might not Americans inscribe? But by the end of the nineteenth century it seemed to some, including Henry Adams, that the vacuity of the continent meant only that there were fewer impediments to the sweep of universal forces. As the winds bore

across the Great Plains without hindrance, so,
it was apprehended, might a relatively tradition-
less society offer little shelter, which is to
say little sphere of freedom, from whatever laws
of nature or society there might be. Bancroft's
democratic man had been free in order to obey
God; without God he was free only to become the
prisoner of impersonal and unsympathetic necessity. As if by condition of its appearance in
a finite world, freedom in one way or another
turned back against itself.

God had been, of course, the more satisfactory resolution of the problem, the sole principle capable satisfactorily of reconciling the
one and the many, order and liberty. For God
was not merely a representation of unity, even
for Protestants; He meant also plenitude and
diversity, however ordered by the divine will.
The Christian God remained ineluctably anthropomorphic, even for those like John Fiske, who
tried to purge Him of this quality. To be sure,
whenever theology pushed the question to its
logical limits, the assumption of divine omnipotence threatened to preclude creaturely freedom
altogether. Jonathan Edwards had labored mightily
to define a "freedom of the will" compatible with
predestination. Yet to the more ordinarily intelligent and godly understanding of the early
nineteenth century, the sense of God as superhuman
rather than inhuman permitted a certain very human
and very godly ambiguity, or mystery, at the juncture of mortal and divine volitions. Freedom in
the divine scheme could never be chaos, because
it was ordered by God; yet "Providence" was something far different from and greater than the sum
of blindly running physical forces. With no conscious contradiction, George Bancroft could describe the divinely ordained progress in the enlargement of human freedom; John Fiske, moderniz-
ing the teleology with Herbert Spencer's master
formula, could describe the fixed but liberating
progress from incoherent homogeneity to coherent
heterogeneity. But with Brooks and Henry Adams,

the reconciling God was lost, although the brothers yearned to reconstitute Him, and the opposite parts of the providential cosmos flew off from the center.

The Adamses have remained a riddle in the history of American thought. Henry especially, has been obscured by the stereotypes which casual critics have invoked: the patrician confounded by industrial civilization, the self-pitier, the failure who wrote his failure into the universe. At the other extreme, he has been hailed as a seer, a sort of Nostradamus of the twentieth century. He has also received an exegesis of a quantity, and often of a quality, that would do credit to a subtle father of the church. His explicators have found radically different meanings in Adams's work, but they have illuminated the manifold facets of a complex man. To a lesser extent, Brooks Adams has exercised a similar attraction. In keeping with our theme, the present essay will treat with the Adamses as members of a religious tradition.

i.

Brooks Adams, the younger of the brothers, stands out in sharper relief. Less enigmatic than Henry, he is adjudged by some to have been the more incisive. Perry Miller thought that Brooks Adams ". . .now looms as an intellect which, with all its perversity, read the lesson of modern civilization as profoundly as any in his time, or, for that matter in our own."[1] Lovell Thompson found in Adams' The Law of Civization and Decay an unparalleled insight into modern life. "In less than 300 pages," Thompson exclaimed, "it sets forth one outlook upon history that Henry later avoided at much greater length in 'Mont Saint Michel and Chartres'; that Spengler much later ornamented and obscured in some 900 pages, and which Toynbee has taken several volumes in some measure to substantiate."

Thompson attempted to place Adams in a New England
"satanic tradition" with Hawthorne and Melville;
like The Scarlet Letter and Moby Dick, he thought,
The Law of Civilization and Decay harbored "rebellion against the ways of God." For "in giving
history a system and in denying to it an objective, Brooks. . .signed something of a compact
with the devil." The price of Adams' bleakly
clear vision of history, this was to say, was the
sacrifice of "moral" or purpose. Thompson concluded by citing the elder brother's appraisal.
"'Your book,' wrote Henry to Brooks, 'is a Bible
of Chaos.' That may be, but it is a majestic and
ordered chaos, and he who reads it cannot deny
in it a deep infernal justice."[2]

An "ordered chaos"--the oxymoron suggests
a paradox in the Adamses' vision of history, as
well as a significant progression in American
thought: George Bancroft's need to make a system
of freedom had given way to Brooks Adams' need
to make a system of chaos. Freedom had indeed
become chaos just as Providence had become the
coldly impersonal operation of physical laws. The
universe which with Bancroft had been imbued with
Providential purpose, in which man was deeply involved, and which, in large measure, he could divine, was now drained of such teleology. The new
scheme was at once determined and chaotic--an ordered chaos in this sense. It was determined in
that man was utterly the victim of forces beyond
his control, even his own actions being passive
responses to these forces; it was chaotic in that
it lacked meaning; atoms ran blindly to ends of
no human significance, perhaps of no significance
at all. It is the spectre of this determinism
of chaos--or chaos of determinism--which coils
at the center of the Adams vision of history. It
is indeed almost a Satanic parody of the earlier
nineteenth century vision of freedom within the
scheme of God, which, according to Brooks, had
been part of the faith of his grandfather, John
Quincy Adams.

Adams' bleakly modern pessimism was the

product of a sometimes painful progression of thought. A rather conventional patrician liberal in his early career, he analyzed away human freedom until it reached the vanishing point. In the preface to his masterwork, The Law of Civilization and Decay, he noted " . . .the exceedingly small part played by conscious thought in moulding the fate of men. At the moment of action the human being almost invariably obeys an instinct, like an animal; only after action has ceased does he reflect."3 In his later thought, Adams elaborated the hypothesis that man is absolutely determined, not only collectively, as with Bancroft, but also individually. There is a belligerent, self-conscious tough-mindedness in Adams' repetitive characterizations of complex historical processes-- the growth of European trade, for example--as "automatic." Needless to say, the hero was not a decisive factor in history: "When the temple of Corinth arose, Mesopotamia was already sinking, and Darius, when he succeeded Belshazzar, could no more withstand his destiny than a log can withstand the torrent of the Mississippi."4 In 1919, in his introduction to his brother's essays in The Degradation of the Democratic Dogma, he summarized the philosophy to which his experience had brought him.

> Like Henry, I inherited a belief in the great democratic dogma, as I inherited my pew in the church at Quincy, but. . .in my early middle life I fell into difficulties which only good fortune prevented from turning out as tragically for me, as did the election of 1828 for my ancestor. In this crisis of my fate I learned, as a lawyer and a student of history and of economics, to look on man, in the light of the evidence of unnumbered centuries, as a pure automaton, who is moved along the paths of least resistance by forces over which he has no control. In short, I reverted to the pure Calvinistic philosophy. As I perceived that the strongest of human pas-

sions are fear and greed, I inferred
that so much and no more might be expected from any automaton so actuated.[5]

This passage is revealing. Most obviously,
it exemplifies the strong tendency in the Adamses
to identify their personal and family fortunes not
only with the state of the nation but with the
state of the universe, a trait which has caused
some readers of the Adamses to suppose, quite mis-
takenly in my opinion, that their cosmic pessimism
was nothing more than a private complain writ
large. As in Brooks Adams' account his grandfather had been severely shaken in his faith in a
benevolent God by his defeat at the hand of Andrew
Jackson in 1828, so evidently Brooks projected
private grievances, exacerbated by the Panic of
1893, on the universe. Yet personal experience
can open the way to valid general perceptions,
and however hyperbolic and idiosyncratic Brooks
Adams' perception of the world, it was hardly divorced from reality, as many in the late nineteenth and the twentieth century came to understand reality.

More generally and characteristically American
than the peculiarly proprietorial Adams patriotism
is the identification of democracy with a particular metaphysical scheme, the sort of identification so clearly effected by George Bancroft. Democracy might logically be accommodated to any
number of cosmologies; it is, presumably, a mode
of government and not a metaphysical statement.
But the "democratic dogma," which Adams casually
counterpoised to his later disillusioned beliefs,
was precisely such a statement, assuming the existence of freely willing men whose behavior en
masse, at least, was nevertheless regulated by
Providence. Adams' self-conscious assertion that
in rejecting the democratic dogma he had "reverted
to the pure Calvinistic philosophy" was no less
metaphysical in tone, although it says more about
his perception of Calvinism than about the actual
direction of his thought. Calvinism was deterministic, but it never regarded man as an automaton.

248

If man could not save himself by his own efforts, he was still morally responsible for his sin. Man was free in the only meaningful sense, said Jonathan Edwards, when he was free to act upon the dictates of his will. And, of course, there was a personal God, Whose excellence and beauty Calvinists perceived in His creation. Adams' cosmos was a cosmos stripped of both God and man, as they had been traditionally conceived. "Man," remarked Adams, "is not and can never be a free agent. He is an instrument charged with energy by nature, or, as our ancestors would have said, by God."6 This was at best a perverse and perverted Calvinism, not merely because of the substitution of impersonal nature for the ancestral God, but because of its reduction of man to passive "instrument."

"Instrument," at least, implies a user; it implies purpose, teleology, order. Yet Adams denied all of this. "Each day I live," he wrote in 1919, "I am less able to withstand the suspicion that the universe, far from being an expression of law originating in a single primary cause, is a chaos which admits of reaching no equilibrium, and with which man is doomed eternally and hopelessly to contend."7 This was a starkly modern universe:

> If we insignificant atoms look abroad upon the immensity about us, we may perceive a measureless space whose void is at intervals partly filled by a scattered torrent of matter streaming furiously, and, so far as our unaided reason permits us to judge, aimlessly, from out of an inconceivable past toward an equally inconceivable future. What matter is, whither it is going, and what object its headlong flight may serve, we know not, nor could we, perhaps, comprehend, were we told. . . . The point. . .in this which immediately concerns us is that our bodies are doubtless a form of matter, and thus are subject to all the stimulants and to all the limitations of that chaotic mass

which we may not unreasonably conclude
to be the substance of which material
nature consists. For, on the evidence
palpable to our senses, though perhaps
not to the eye of faith, we should seem
to be justified in inferring that order,
as order is understood by our intelligence, does not reign in the material
universe, but rather chaos; and this
supposition is supported by the fact
that no man has as yet been able to
conceive, far less to formulate, any
theory by which the apparent diversity
about us may be resolved into a harmonious progression from a first cause
to a final effect, or from a beginning
to an end.[8]

It is significant, however, that in 1915 Adams
tucked two qualifications into this passage which
maintained the Cartesian admission of another
world than that of extension: we are unable to
perceive order in the material universe; further,
there is left open the possibility that the "eye
of faith" might perceive such order. Earlier,
the qualifications might have been sarcastic, but
the direction of Adams' thought at this time in
his life suggests that they did represent the hope
of escape from the world of furiously streaming
matter and the resolution of its anarchic "diversity."

One impulse behind the theorizing of both
Brooks and Henry Adams was to push the determinis-
tic-chaotic conception of the universe along to
its destruction. They forced it to the limits of
absurdity in the hope, which is sometimes quite
explicit, of hastening its antithesis, of quick-
ening the turn in the historical cycle which would
bring a new vision of ordered freedom. Thus
Brooks's historical determinism, an amalgam of
economic laws and social Darwinism, was at once a
"Satanic" parody of the Providential scheme of
historians like Bancroft, and an at times grotesque exaggeration of fashionable ideas. Cliche

supported hyperbole. "Masses take the form of corporations," he declared in The New Empire, "and the men who rise to the control of these corporations rise because they are fittest. The process is natural selection." "Nature is consistent," he added later in the same work. "The fit survive, the discarded perish." The tyranny of the marketplace was the key to history, and permitted Adams to explain complex events with breathtaking simplicity:

> In March, 1897, Pittsburg [sic] achieved supremacy in steel, and in an instant Europe felt herself poised above an abyss. As though moved by a common impulse, Russia, Germany, and England precipitated themselves upon the shore of the Yellow Sea, grasping at the positions which had been conquered by Japan, and for the same reason.[9]

It cannot well be argued that Adams' intent here was parodic; no doubt he honestly believed in the mechanistic determinism that underlay such interpretations. But that his belief was reluctant or perverse seems apparent from his emotional commitment to the martial and imaginative man in The Law of Civilization and Decay, his corresponding and aristocratic contempt for the capitalist type, and his own eventual gravitation toward religious faith. Determinism yielded ample returns in terms of explanation, but Adams seemed sometimes to embrace it as if to exorcise it with his ferocious acceptance.

Darwinism and economic determinism easily lent themselves to Adams' uses, scientific or social hypothesis being ever the plaything of one cosmic perspective or another. John Fiske, espousing similar laws of social behavior, used them to support a theory of universal evolutionary progress which was the negation of chaos. Adams believed in progress in the sense of centralization and consolidation ("because the administration of the largest mass is cheapest"),[10] but this

251

was hardly a vision of the New Jerusalem. Both
men of course used the convenient insights of
nineteenth century economic and biological determinism to elaborate their respective visions
of the cosmos--in Fiske's case a vision of benevolent order, in Adams' case one purportedly of
meaningless chaos.

During the pre-Panic years in which he had
written The Emancipation of Massachusetts, Brooks
Adams' determinism had had an optimistic and
liberal cast. As for Fiske, evolution was then
for him a liberating process. The Emancipation
was memorably iconoclastic in its anti-philio-
pietistic denunciation of the seventeenth century
Puritan "theocracy," a reign, in Adams' view, of
priestly superstition. His historical interpretation resembled that of Bancroft and Fiske, although he fashioned a sharp distinction between
an oppressive clergy and an instinctively liberty-
seeking people. Of the latter, he explained that

> what they did in reality was to sur-
> render their new commonwealth to their
> priests. Yet they were a race in whose
> bone and blood the spirit of free
> thought was bred; the impulse which had
> goaded them to reject the Roman dogmas
> was quick within them still, and revolt
> against the ecclesiastical yoke was cer-
> tain. The clergy upon their side trod
> their appointed path with the precision
> of machines, and, constrained by an in-
> exorable destiny, they took that posi-
> tion of antagonism to liberal thought
> which has become typical of their order.
> And the struggles and the agony by which
> this poor and isolated community freed
> itself from its gloomy bondage, the
> means by which it secularized its edu-
> cation and its government, won for it-
> self the blessing of free thought and
> speech, and matured a system of consti-
> tutional liberty which has been the
> foundation of the American Union, rise

252

in dignity to one of the supreme efforts of mankind.[11]

Unlike Bancroft and the later Fiske, Adams did
not in The Emancipation view religion as an ark
of universal truth. The partisan of science as
opposed to theology, he observed that "the two
methods are irreconcilable, and spring from the
great primary instincts which are called conservatism and liberality."[12] Yet there remained with
Adams at this time the familiar American sense of
historical order, of human freedom broadening
down through the ages in accord with "destiny,"
if not with the plan of Providence.

His "reversion to Calvinism" persuaded Adams
that the will of man could avail him nothing a-
gainst the facts of material existence. No ideal
or abstraction could be reached, he noted, "because, as Paul pointed out in the Epistle to the
Romans, the interposition of the flesh makes impossible the fulfillment of the law." Therefore,
"in this conflict between mind and matter, on
the whole, matter has decisively prevailed. . . .
Perfect order, perfect obedience, and perfect
peace are incompatible with the flesh."[13] Adams
could resemble a modern Jonathan Edwards, as
Ernest Samuels suggests, in his jeremiads against
the economically damned.[14] But for Adams there
had ceased to be the possibility of Grace; Chaos,
not God, was enthroned.

Brooks Adams did retain, however, something
of the emotional yearning for religion which was
more conspicuous in his brother Henry. Arthur F.
Beringause notes that both in The Emancipation of
Massachusetts and in The Law of Civilization and
Decay, Adams maintained an ambivalent attitude
toward religion, "at whose base was intense dis-
gust with life and all its ways." Like Henry,
Brooks was quite aware of the historical force
of supernatural belief, and was capable of feeling
the force himself, as he stood in ecstasy in a
Gothic cathedral.[15] Toward the end of his life,

253

indeed, Adams arose in his family's church at Quincy to make a public confession of faith.

> The form of Brooks' confession would have surprised his forbears, yet it merely denounced the appeal on moral questions to private judgment as leading to "an emasculate church, a renunciation of the old canons of duty, and an impotent administration of justice." Neither science nor philosophy had offered explanations or substitutes, and, renouncing the agnosticism of his youth, he accepted the ecclesiastical tradition. "Lord, I believe, help thou my unbelief."[16]

Religion was exceedingly attractive as a principle of cosmic order, yet like Henry, Brooks found it impossible to accede to rationally. Much of the desperate, hyperbolic character of the brothers' systematizing of history derives from the disparity. It was not however simply a case of emotion demanding what reason could not provide; rational system itself, as the Adamses understood it, ultimately demanded God. At times, sentiment seemed able to provide Him (or more appropriately with Henry's Virgin, Her), but this was as yearning only, and incapable of being sustained otherwise through an intellectual system. The Adamses' system required God, but their Heaven was empty.

In partial compensation, it would seem, Brooks Adams constructed an ideal of society which appropriated some of the attributes of the traditional Providence. The universe might be a chaos, the individual an automaton; but society was an organism, albeit one functioning mechanically. The universe and the individual cancelled each other out; neither a cosmic chaos nor an automatic individual was worth the philosopher's sustained attention. Only in society was there a principle of vitality; if not ultimately free from the laws of existence, society at least was—or should be—a rational order over against mindless chaos and automatism. Order was of paramount importance; Adams began his book, The Theory of Social Revolutions, with the proposition: "Civilization, I apprehend, is nearly synonymous with order." Only an organic conception of society could satisfy this need for order, and one that in Adams' version was almost more than metaphor:

> Human society is a complete living organism, with circulation, heart, and members. The heart lies at the seat of international commercial exchanges, the circulation flows through the arteries of trade, and the members usually show more or less vitality in proportion to their direct relations with the heart.

Or with a slightly different application: "Human society is a living organism working mechanically, like any other organism. It has members, a circulation, a nervous system, and a sort of skin or envelope, consisting of its laws and institutions."[17]

Adams emphasized so strongly the organic, orderly society, disciplined rather than libertarian, necessarily expansive if it were to succeed, and imbued with the martial virtues, that he has been described as proto-fascist in his later years.[18] But although Adams' ultra-Progressive political thought did contain elements which admit of this description, and are no doubt symptomatic of broader ideas and attitudes which helped to engender western fascism, the tendency in his case seems primarily to reflect intellectually a cosmic order writ small, a contraction of that splendid universal system once perceived by Edwards, still credited by Bancroft, and glimpsed by Fiske, into the confines of the national state viewed as the only effective unity of organization and meaning.

The complexion of Adams' thought makes it impossible, indeed, to categorize him by any conventional political label. Adams the Progressive saw the need for social authority over lawless capitalists; Adams the conservative saw the need for domestic tranquility as opposed to social revolution; Adams the martial nationalist preached the necessity of self sacrifice. There was an element missing, however; Adams the erstwhile liberal came to see little meaning in individual liberties. His insistence on the automatism of individuals precluded his social vision from embodying the old principle of ordered freedom. From the individual or cosmic perspective, society could at best represent an ordered chaos; it made sense only on its own terms. Thus the traditional institutions which had sought to adjust the individual to the mass, multiplicity to unity, appeared now to be socially harmful. Democracy was an encumbrance, and Adams drew an invidious distinction between deliberative and administrative governments. "Of the inefficient, or deliberative type," he thought, "we stand easily foremost. Such social organisms as ours are those most open to attack and least capable of defense; they have little faculty for unified thought and less for unified action."[19] An independent judiciary was intolerable to social movement, federalism an absurdity. As perverse as such ideas would seem to most Americans (despite his attempted enrollment of George Washington as the archetypal American "collectivist"), Adams' social thought did contain the attenuated idea of a cosmic harmony. True, ". . .man must in some way contrive to reach a social relation with his kind in which the mass can co-operate, more or less effectually, against the individual." Yet this, for Adams, was only to recognize reality, for "unless the individual can be mastered and denied liberty of combat, even an approximation to order, justice, mercy, peace, or any of the ideals is impossible."[20]

The sense of the need for order, in particular, is the most nearly constant element in Adams' political thought. His apparent tergiversations were in one way superficial.

256

> In The Emancipation he praised liberal-
> ism, but was really a conservative de-
> siring to maintain the status quo by
> means of law; in 1903 he praises con-
> servatism, but is really a radical de-
> termining to institute a new form of
> governmental dictatorship. Yet Adams
> has not changed. He still reveres
> authority. What has varied is the
> method he considers most effective to
> establish the rule of an all-powerful
> central administration.[21]

Order, with its concomitant principle of authority, had once been conceivable within the framework
of the "democratic dogma." This was a plan of
ordered freedom, presupposing a benevolent and
overruling Providence, and depending ultimately
on a Protestant belief in a direct relation between God and the individual which minimized the
need for worldly authority. Up to a point the
idea was susceptible of plausible secular permu-
tations, including the economic liberal's faith
in the "invisible hand" and the unchurched political liberal's vague reliance on popular virtue. All flourished, however, when it seemed
natural to assume the environing support of a
harmonious and friendly cosmos.

For some, the failure of the old religious
and quasi-religious formulas would be liberating.
Brooks Adams suggests the reverse effect. It
would be difficult to say whether his mundane or
cosmic disappointments were the more disturbing
factor in his personal outlook; the two in any
event cannot be entirely separated. He explicitly
joined politics and metaphysics in the "democratic
dogma," and for him they stood or fell as part of
a whole. Obliged, as he believed, to adapt his
politics to a universe in which no ultimate order
could be seen, he considered it necessary to constitute artificially as much of this order as
could be within society itself. A social order
that was once the product of the individual's

257

obedience to God would thus have to be arbitrarily
contrived and maintained. Society of itself would
have to bear the weight of authority that had for-
merly been entrusted to an accessible Providence.

The idea of freedom was the casualty of this
translation of cosmos into social order. The existentialist conception of the individual condemn-
ed to be free in a universe without inherent meaning would have been entirely alien to Adams; without Providence, the universe could only be a chaos
and the individual an automaton. The only hope
was to make, in society, an ordered chaos. This
was an act of interpretation no less radical than
it was conservative, these terms being simply relative to the standpoint from which it is regarded.
Its perverse quality derived from its inversion
of Adams' own original values, for on this level
Adams did change. The disappointed liberal became
savage in his insistence on human helplessness.
The man who in The Law of Civilization and Decay
implicitly championed the martial and imaginative
"Man of Fear" against the capitalistic "Man of
Greed" proposed to harness military might to the
securing of trade routes and the conquest of the
economic resources of Asia. Democratic order was
transmogrified into an order approaching the fa-
scistic. The Roycean act of interpretation here
took the form of moral suicide.

If Adams' vision of modern social order was
a bleak and diminished one, it reflected his sense
of what had been lost. He perceived, with possibly greater clarity than any of his countrymen, the
collapse of that system of reason, religion, science and politics which he called the "democratic
dogma," and which in any of its facets he now
thought must end in chaos. The Adams family ad-
mirably exemplified the collapse of faith. John
Quincy Adams was a starting point, and in the
Sixth President Brooks saw much of his own disillusionment.

Granted that there is a benign and
omnipotent Creator of the world who

watches over the fate of men, [John
Quincy] Adams' sincere conviction was
that such a being thinks according to
certain fixed laws, which we call scientific laws; that these laws may be
discovered by human intelligence and
when discovered, adapted, and practised
they must lead men certainly to an approach to perfection, and more especially to the elimination of war and
slavery.[22]

As far as it goes, this was essentially the understanding of George Bancroft. It ultimately failed, Brooks Adams concluded, because it could not
solve the problem of the one and the many. His
grandfather, he thought, had in particular fallen
victim to the cardinal fallacy of modern democracy: that the selfish instinct of competition
could be made to harmonize with "the moral principle that all should labor for the common good."
Democracy, wrote the "reverted Calvinist," could
not in the long run surmount servitude to "the
flesh." Expanding knowledge merely undid the
cosmic underpinnings of the democratic faith, and
John Quincy Adams ". . .found to his horror that
he, who had worshipped education and science, had
unwittingly ministered to the demon." Nevertheless, John Quincy had made a final trip to Cin-
cinnati to help dedicate an observatory, and
Brooks found a terrible irony in the surmise that
the rigors of the journey had hastened the old
man's death. His grandfather, he believed, "always adored order and loathed the very idea of
chaos. Yet he died for astronomy, the science of
chaos. Such is human effort and prescience."[23]

Brooks Adams' real achievement was to show
the failure of the nineteenth century providential
cosmos in its starkest terms. The failure left a
strangely bloodless universe, which seemed to be
confirmed scientifically by the Michelson-Morley
experiment of 1887, leading to the abandonment of
the hypothesis of "luminiferous ether" and its

concomitant of "absolute motion." There was apparently no universal circulation, such as Emerson had described, to feed the individual with the grace of the whole. The components of the providential scheme were left to their peculiar atrophies: the individual to become an automaton, the physical universe a chaos, and society a machine-like organism. Adams grimly pursued the logic of all of these developments, in the apparent yearning to get beyond them to some sort of religious faith, which had itself been reduced to an emotional and aesthetic craving. The "democratic dogma" fell with Providence. Democracy, as Adams conceived of it, was above all a way of reconciling the one and the many, freedom and order, competition and the general welfare. In its providential frame, ideal democracy held not only the many to the one, but the one to the many. That is to say, God was both a unifying and a diversifying principle. The orthodox conception of a divinely appointed and universal whole implied not only unity, but the parts which had to be brought into unity. The absence of Providence meant not only chaos, but a dead uniformity of rushing particles of matter. There were other interpretations of the demise of Providence, but the Adamses in theirs persevered to the end of a well-travelled but dwindling American trail.

ii.

Brooks Adams is the starting point for the study of Henry. The brothers influenced each other profoundly, and it is often difficult to tell where the thought of one leaves off and that of the other begins. But the younger brother presented in stark outline themes more fully elaborated by the elder. Both felt the collapse of the earlier American sense of Providence; both perceived necessity and chaos conjoined at the center of the modern consciousness; both longed for a renewal of the grace which once had suffused multifarious creation with purpose and order. No more bold and original than that of Brooks, the work of Henry Adams was richer in its sense of irony and paradox, and these qualities gave it finally the larger vision.[24]

Henry Adams' experiments in the application of laws of physical science to history were most clearly in the vein of his younger brother. Use of the Second Law of Thermodynamics to prove the degradation of civilization, and similar ventures, were elaborations of the historical determinism espoused by Brooks. As stated by Henry in "The Tendency of History":

> Any science assumes a necessary sequence of cause and effect, a force resulting in motion which cannot be other than what it is. Any science of history must be absolute, like other sciences, and must fix with mathematical certainty the path which human society has got to follow.[25]

Despite the element of jeu d'esprit in Adams' use of science, it evidently represented a serious intellectual endeavor for him.[26] Science furnished him with more than allegory and prophecy, although the uses of entropy which he found in the Second Law no doubt afforded personal satisfactions. Adams could turn the tables on those, like Fiske, who believed that biological evolution taught human progress. Physics, said Adams, taught degradation. "As a Puritan heir of Saint Augustine," Ernest Samuels comments, "he exhausted his ingenuity in deriding insect man. Entropy enacted the myth of Genesis as the cosmic fall of man. From the fated original sin of becoming human to the ultimate sin of socialism the path had been inexorably marked out."[27]

Yet Adams aspired to a larger role than that of Jeremiah. The impulse at work was that of a cosmologist; if not to construct, Adams hoped to point the way toward, a comprehensive system that would contain the movement of atoms as well as the vagaries of man. He was explicitly working toward the repair of the breach opened by the Cartesian dualism of mind and matter:

> . . .Descartes offered a compromise, and in that respect differed from Kelvin. Descartes proposed to free man from material bondage, provided he might mechanize all other vital energies. Society rose in arms to protect the dog, and so defeated the scheme, leaving the world to go on asserting the two contradictory principles in the same breath, down to the present day, to the undiminished embarassment of Universities, and with little perceptible change in the situation, except that the Universities of today hesitate to assert with confidence the old conviction of spiritual authority, showing in this respect a distinct decline in energy; while technical instruction has reached,--or seems on the verge of reaching,--the point where it must insist on the universal application of its thermodynamic law.
> Since compromise of principle seems to be out of the question, there remains only the resource of direct conflict. Each party is thrown back on the horns of a dilemma,--the same old dilemma of St. Augustine and Descartes,--the deadlock of free will.[28]

But Adams, in this phase of his thought, was willing firmly to grasp one of the horns of the dilemma, sacrificing free-will to necessity, and the multiplicity which free-will implies, to universally operative law. So far, he attained only the mock Calvinist anti-Providence of his younger brother.

Such a cosmos as this might be justified if it were truly productive of unity. Unity, elusive

as it was, was the fixed goal of Henry Adams'
thought, as order was that of Brooks. "The idea
of unity," he was convinced, "survives the idea
of God or of Universe; it is innate and intuitive."[29] By 1910 he had glimpsed the chance of a
new unity. "Nothing in the history of philosophy," he observed, "is more distinctly marked
than the effort of physics and metaphysics, since
1890, to approach each other. . . . The chaos is
more chaotic than ever, but the effort to make
the laws of Energetik cover all, is perhaps the
only very vigorous intellectual activity now in
evidence."[30]

Adams' last serious work was directed toward
just this effort. The scientific fallacies committed by Adams in his essays, "The Rule of Phase
Applied to History," and "A Letter to American
Teachers of History," have been exhaustively
pointed out, especially by William H. Jordy.[31]
There is no denying that for these essays to have
accomplished their purpose of making "the laws of
Energetik cover all," their science would have had
to have been much better. But the point of present interest is Adams' conception of his own role.
He could be coy about this. ". . .I like metaphysics and I like physics," he wrote in 1909,
"--but I don't much care to reconcile them, though
I enjoy making them fight."[32] Nevertheless, much
of his best thought and writing was directed precisely toward the unity of physics and metaphysics. Far more indicative of Adams' real point
of view was his self-description of 1902, in a
letter to his brother Brooks. Explaining his ab-
sorption with a certain train of thought, he remarked, "I owe it only to my having always had a
weakness for science mixed with metaphysics. I
am a dilution of Lord Kelvin and St. Thomas Aquinas. . . ."[33] Henry Wasser concludes similarly
that "Adams was completely modern in his recognition that science had become divorced from philosophy, and his constant effort was to reunite
them."[34]

Adams' synthesizing looks particularly forced

and grotesque from the present standpoint, when
the breach between science and what remains of
metaphysics has grown even wider. But as an effort to repair the breach, it was well within the
intellectual tradition with which we have been
dealing. George Bancroft, or John Quincy Adams,
or Jonathan Edwards, might have described himself
in a similar casual fashion, as a dilution of Sir
Isaac Newton and John Calvin. Edwards did not
hesitate to mix the principles of gravitation, as
well as those of the Lockean sensationalist psychology, with problems of divine omnipotence and
individual salvation; Bancroft perceived in history the providentially directed movement of social atoms in the mass. But Henry Adams shifted
the affinities of democracy. Traditionally conjoined with freedom and progress (or, more recently, with evolution), democracy was now associated
with necessity and devolution. Drained of teleology, Adams' determinism was qualitatively different from that of Bancroft, tending as it did
toward entropy and chaos rather than toward a
widening of ordered freedom. Between Providence
and the Second Law of Thermodynamics, there is
not much in common. Adams sought to preserve the
democratic dogma as a cosmology, but it was entirely degraded by the sacrifice of teleology;
in fact, it was turned inside-out.

As an historian, Adams espoused the determinism which came naturally enough to many of his
colleagues; from the professional standpoint he
could be damned only for reductio ad absurdum, and
in some cases serious deficiency of method. He
came to view history as a synthesizing system, the
only discipline broad enough to co-ordinate lines
of thought and force, and suggested that university education be centered on history as the study
of mental evolution. Such a study, he was convinced, could be unified within a "general formula."35 His well known comment on Jefferson, Madison, and Monroe makes clear an animating principle of his History of the United States.

. . .they appear like mere grasshoppers

kicking and gesticulating on the middle
of the Mississippi River. There is no
possibility of reconciling their theories with their acts, of their extraordinary foreign policy with dignity.
They were carried along on a stream
which floated them, after a fashion,
without much regard to themselves.

This I take to be the result that
students of history generally reach in
regard to modern times. The element
of individuality is the free-will dogma
of the science, if it is a science. My
own conclusion is that history is simply
social development along the lines of
weakest resistance, and that in most
cases the line of weakest resistance is
found as unconsciously by society as by
water.36

This determinism, however, does not negate democracy, although it negates the "democratic dogma."
Rather, as Adams emphasized, democracy offered the
clearest confirmation of historical determinism.
He was satisfied, he wrote to Francis Parkman in
1884, ". . .that the purely mechanical development of the human mind in society must appear in
a great democracy so clearly, for want of disturbing elements, that in another generation psychology, physiology, and history will join in proving
man to have as fixed and necessary development as
that of a tree; and almost as unconscious."37

Adams' democracy mocks that of Bancroft. For
both, the outstanding quality of democracy was
that it offered little resistance to the movement
of cosmic forces, but the historians differed dramatically on the meaning of this condition. Like
Bancroft, Adams used the metaphor of the ocean,
but to a contrasting effect:

A child could find his way in a river
valley. . .but science alone could sound
the depths of the ocean, measure its
currents, foretell its storms, or fix

265

its relations to the system of Nature. In a democratic ocean science could see something ultimate. Man could go no further. The atom might move, but the general equilibrium could not change.[38]

Bancroft had used the ocean as an optimistic, transcendental metaphor: the ocean as the ever-productive field for the play of individual and popular thought, inspired by God, yet active rather than passive. With Adams, passivity is all. The democratic ocean represented the dead level of energy from which no progress is possible. Democracy had ceased to be the rational and progressive, and had become the mechanical and entropic.

As did Bancroft, Adams harnessed the ocean metaphor to a sense of social atomism, even conceding his own diminution to fit the figure. "I have never been at any time of life more than ten years ahead of the majority," he wrote in 1902, "and I have been always an atom in the mass. What I am, the mass is sure to become; and in allowing fifty years for it, probably I allow twice too much."[39] This theme of social atomism recurs in Adams' later writings. The breakdown of "old-fashioned liberalism"--"the collapse of our nineteenth century J. S. Mill, Manchester, Chicago formulas"--and the prospective "social disintegration" seemed to him more than ever to leave the individual an atom in a mass, moved by forces beyond his control.[40] Adams wrote in characteristic sardonic fashion to his brother Brooks in 1903:

> When you have leisure from the Greeks and Persians you can study the dynamic theory of gases. There you can repose your mind on nature, and build up your laws on a Crooke's tube. The only question of serious interest to the world is the atom. What is the atom? Is there an atom? I hold, as a working hypothesis, that an atom is a man. His conduct is singularly alike in each

case. Hydrogen is uncommonly Greek.
How hydrogenic the American may be, I
do not venture to decide, but he is now
preparing for a general election, and
you will probably find your hydrogenic
qualities called into play. You and
your brother Charles will both be quite
sure that Clerk-Maxwell's demon who runs
the second law of Thermo-dynamics ought
to be made President.41

George Bancroft also had conceived of the American
as an atom in the social mass--this to him was the
essence of what Adams now thought of as "old-fashioned liberalism"--but for Bancroft it had been
God, not Clerk-Maxwell's demon, who presided over
the movement of atoms. Once again, the providential had become the demonic.

The comparison of Bancroft and Adams suggests
that the democratic dogma was a Janus-faced cosmology, the fragile optimistic facet of which
crumbled under the impact of nineteenth century
change to reveal its opposite. It suggests further that the Bancroftian vision was illuminated
by the brief convergence of religious and secular
lines of thought, which convergence could be neither maintained nor recaptured. The sense of
ordered freedom was replaced by the sense of determined chaos. The virtue of democracy in one
generation was that it was porous to the ways of
Providence; in the later generation it simply offered little shelter from the blind play of natural forces. The metaphors show the ambivalence.
One man's mighty potentiality of force, the ocean
was another man's dead level of energy. Bancroft
understood American society as an expanding quantity of restless, darting molecules; Adams perceived that these "hydrogenic qualities" only
served the end of entropy.

Adams himself remained long uncertain about
the meaning of democracy, and it is doubtful that
he ever entirely abandoned the democratic dogma.
In his History of the United States he still took

267

a balanced view. As the United States "offered less field for the development of individuality" than some more traditional societies, he pointed out, the "chief function of American society must be "to raise the average standard of popular intelligence and well being. . . ." The final success of this experiment in uplift seemed still in doubt. "The inertia of several hundred million people, all formed in a similar social mould," he feared, "was as likely to stifle energy as to stimulate evolution."[42] The History was less indicative of his personal pessimism than his earlier anonymous novel Democracy, but not until later would he be ready to harness despair to the Second Law of Thermodynamics.

The "degradation of the democratic dogma," as the Adamses understood it, demonstrates the vulnerability of the Protestant underpinnings of the system. Doing away with priestly mediation as a requisite of salvation, Protestants put an immense strain on the relation between the sinner and God, the individual and the cosmic. One possessed the universe or one was cut off from it. No purgatory mediated between fullness and emptiness. For the sake of spiritual purity, Luther had gambled on "faith alone" as the saving relation between man and omnipotence. Similarly, Bancroft's Protestant-democratic cosmology depended on the access to divine truth of the intuitive "reason" of the individual. No aristocracy, no hierarchy, could mediate between the people and the higher truths to which their civilization aspired. As grace is withdrawn, or comes to seem illusory, and Providence "fades out into the pale irony of the void,"[43] the people assume to the disillusioned the aspect of formless and passive masses. The doctrine of progress is inverted; the democratic cosmology is Satanized; the Adamses act out their own version of the death of God. What remained?

What remained was the more interesting part
of the thought of Henry Adams. Adams crystalized
the mechanistic determinism of the nineteenth century into a brittle shell, and found that it
could not contain the universe. Temperamentally,
he was never more than ambivalent about science,
his vehicle of determinism. He was very much a
modern man in his qualms; at least since the Civil
War he had harbored a cataclysmic vision of runaway science, which he restated to his brother in
1902:

> I apprehend for the next hundred
> years an ultimate, colossal, cosmic
> collapse; but not on any of our old
> lines. My belief is that science is
> to wreck us, and that we are like mon-
> keys monkeying with a loaded shell;
> we don't in the least know or care
> where our practically infinite energies
> come from or will bring us to.[44]

Deeper than such familiar fears as these, however,
was Adams's pained realization that science failed
to do what it had promised: to provide intellectual unity.

Feeling the loss of the traditional Christian
unity, Adams hoped to replace it with a scientific
unity. To accomplish this, he was willing to sacrifice teleology to a purposeless determinism. No
doubt his overriding concern for unity reflected
the latent idealism which critics have discerned
in Adams, as well as a more general concern of
nineteenth century thinkers; Fiske and other evolutionary philosophers, for instance, were vitally
concerned to establish the sequence between unity
and multiplicity, or homogeneity and heterogeneity.[45] Yet there seems no reason to deny Brooks
Adams' explanation; behind all such intellectual
puzzles was the spectre of the "degradation of

the democratic dogma," the failure of the providential cosmology.

The particular failure of science, the one component of the democratic dogma around which it seemed a new order might be constructed, therefore appeared to offer the final disillusionment. "Did I tell you how deeply I was touched--in my own sense--," Adams wrote in 1908, "by Lord Kelvin's dying confession,--that he had totally failed to understand anything? I, who refuse to face that admission, am delighted to have somebody do it for me by proxy."[46] There is little doubt that "George Strong" in Adams' novel _Esther_ spoke for the author in his remark, "mystery for mystery science beats religion hollow." The scientific mystery failed to unify, for "in plain words, Chaos was the law of nature; Order was the dream of man."[47] Determinism crumbled finally into chaos; indeed, as Adams suggested in his _Education_, ". . .the scientific synthesis commonly called Unity was the scientific analysis commonly called Multiplicity. The two things were the same, all forms being shifting phases of motion."[48] Yet the convergence of unity and multiplicity was itself to suggest a way out.

For it was a harmony of the one and the many which Adams sought to recapture, not merely a thirteenth century unity. This becomes clear in his paean to the Thomistic system of thought:

> Compared with it, all modern systems are complex and chaotic, crowded with self-contradictions, anomalies, impracticable functions and outworn inheritances; but beyond all their practical shortcomings is their fragmentary character. An economic civilization troubles itself about the universe much as a hive of honey-bees troubles about the ocean, only as a region to be avoided. The hive of Saint Thomas sheltered God and man, mind and matter, the uni-

verse and the atom, the one and the
multiple, within the walls an harmonious
home.[49]

Adams reflects the apparent fading out, in the
nineteenth century, of the possibility of genuine
philosophic cosmology. Fiske's "Cosmic Philosophy" had been symptomatic: in its insistence on
unifying phenomena within a bag woven of New England values and Spencerian formulae, it had
stretched religion and philosophy to the breaking
point. Like William James, Adams perceived the
collapse of cosmology, but unlike James he was
not content for it to collapse. He attempted two
ways of restoring cosmology: by subsuming all
within a system of mechanistic determinism, and
by proposing, very tentatively, a system reconsti-
tuted around certain fragments of human values
salvaged from the wreckage of modern civilization
--a virgin's doll-house in place of the "hive of
Saint Thomas."

        The hive itself, of course, no longer suf-
ficed. The Thomistic system was symbolized for
Adams by the precarious Gothic architecture, of
which he observed at the close of <u>Mont-Saint-
Michel and Chartres</u>, "the delight of its aspirations is flung up to the sky. The pathos of its
self-distrust and anguish of doubt is buried as
its last secret." Aquinas had tried to do what
Adams concluded was finally impossible on intellectual lines: to steer between a realism tending
to pantheism and a nominalism tending toward chaos, to balance between divine omnipotence and a
measure of <u>liberum arbitrium</u> or "free choice."
Given the function of God as first cause, it appeared to Adams that man's "apparent freedom was
an illusion arising from the extreme delicacy of
the machine. . .," the motive power in human action as in the growth of a vegetable being finally that of God. Aquinas at best left man ambiguous, ". . .a two-sided being, free or unfree,
responsible or irresponsible, an energy or a victim of energy, moved by choice or moved by com-
pulsion, as the interests of society seemed for

the moment to need." Yet in a sense, man had
greater freedom of action than God:

> While man moved about his relatively
> spacious prison with a certain degree
> of ease, God,being everywhere, could
> not move. In one respect, at least,
> man's freedom seemed to be not rela-
> tive but absolute, for his thought
> was an energy paying no regard to space
> or time or order or object or sense;
> but God's thought was his act and will
> at once; speaking correctly, God could
> not think; He is.

In Thomas's church, Adams added, ". . .man's
free will was the aspiration to God. . . ."[50]
These comments reflect, first, a sense of freedom
as being a purely human and subjective quality,
and secondly, an attribution of freedom to a kind
of grace: ideas which Adams had already attached
to his figure of the Virgin.

The Dynamo and the Virgin, if not Adams'
"ultimate symbols," were his most trenchant.[51]
Both were natural products of Adams' turn-of-the-
century milieu: the electric dynamo, as recalled
by Adams from the Great Exposition of 1900, as
vivid an expression of modern technological force
as was then possible, the Virgin Mary suggested
obviously by the medieval revival and "Catholic
Renaissance" of the late nineteenth century. The
cult of the Middle Ages animated the Pre-Raphaelite movement which influenced the Adams circle.
Adams' artistic friend John La Farge, for instance, "liked nothing better than discussing the
relation of Catholic theology to the art of the
church and was especially interested in the influence of the Virgin."[52] Brooks Adams had pre-
ceded his brother in joining the "intellectual
counter-revolution" against modern values, although he was something of a double agent.

The Dynamo and the Virgin have remained co-
gent symbols, representing, as they seem to, a

timeless opposition. They can be understood, of
course, in many ways and on various levels, representing the thirteenth versus the twentieth century, religion versus technology, unity versus
multiplicity, human compassion versus mechanical
efficiency, spontaneity versus blind determinism,
and so on indefinitely. Neither the significance
nor the bitterness of the opposition has dimmed
in the twentieth century; the Virgin and the Dynamo speak clearly, and almost without need of
explanation, to a generation familiar with vastly
more elaborate technological systems, as well as
with a far more widespread intellectual revulsion
against them, than obtained in Adams' day.

We are still driven to ask what lies behind
the layers of symbolism; what is the truth that
Adams wished to embody in the Virgin? Unable to
accept rationally the orthodoxy with which she was
traditionally associated, he permitted himself
directly only the assertion that her cult "was
very childlike, very foolish, very beautiful, and
very true--as art, at least. . . ."[53] Despite
the last diffident qualification, Adams never
claimed that art could save. If Mary represented
a more fundamental truth, it was manifested in a
leap of faith--the aspiration of humanity, in a
unique access of freedom, to transcend itself
through religious expression. In this sense, the
Virgin is possibly the clearest representation in
American writing of the bond between the idea of
freedom and the religious principle. In Mont-
Saint-Michel and Chartres, she appears as the sole
principle of freedom in a universe of divine and
masculine logic, and, Adams suggests, as the sole
credible intercessor for sinners.

> Mary was their only hope. She alone
> represented Love. The Trinity were, or
> was, One, and could by the nature of
> its essence, administer justice alone.
> Only childlike illusion could expect a
> personal favour from Christ. Turn the
> dogma as one would, to this it must
> logically come. Call the three God-

273

heads by what names one liked, still
they must remain One; must administer
one justice; must admit only one law.
In that law, no human weakness or error
could exist; by its essence it was infinite, eternal, immutable. There was
no crack and no cranny in the system,
through which human frailty could hope
for escape. One was forced from corner
to corner by a remorseless logic until
one fell helpless at Mary's feet.

Mary was, in sum, "the only court in equity capable of overruling strict law."54

Adams' Virgin is a paradox. Historically
she represents a time when purportedly western
Christendom united in her adoration. As the at-
tracting force of the love of people of all classes and many lands, she represents unity. She is
a focus of sympathy and belief that the modern
world has lost. And yet she represents at the
same time what was outside the law, what was dis-
unity, as Adams made quite clear. Medieval man,
as Adams understood him, had longed for such a
principle. "The individual rebelled against restraint; society wanted to do what it pleased;
all disliked the laws which Church and State were
trying to fasten on them." They yearned for a
power above the law, or what passed for law in
an unfair world. The Trinity did not suffice.
"God could not be Love. God was Justice, Order,
Unity, Perfection; He could not be human and imperfect, nor could the Son or the Holy Ghost be
other than the Father. The Mother alone was human, imperfect, and could love; she alone was
Favour, Duality, Diversity." By default, if for
no other reason, Mary must embody the qualities
which the masculine machinery of the cosmos left
out. "If the Trinity was in its essence Unity,
the Mother alone could represent whatever was not
Unity; whatever was irregular, exceptional, outlawed; and this was the whole human race." The
path of logic led Adams to an utter and pessimis-

274

tic determinism; the passionate eloquence with
which he described the Virgin shows how profoundly
he wished to reject this logic:

> Mary concentrated in herself the whole
> rebellion of man against fate; the whole
> protest against divine law; the whole
> contempt for human laws as its outcome;
> the whole unutterable fury of human na-
> ture beating itself against the walls of
> its prison-house, and suddenly seized by
> a hope that in the Virgin man had found
> a door of escape. She was above the
> law; she took feminine pleasure in turn-
> ing hell into an ornament; she delighted
> in trampling on every social distinction
> in this world and the next. She knew
> that the universe was as unintelligible
> to her, on any theory of morals, as it
> was to her worshippers, and she felt,
> like them, no sure conviction that it
> was any more intelligible to the Creator
> of it. To her, every suppliant was a
> universe in itself, to be judged apart,
> on his own merits, by his love for
> her.[55]

How is the paradox of unity which is also
the negation of unity to be resolved? On one
plane, Adams suggested, a genuine unity must be
tolerant of diversity. This was why the Second
Law of Thermodynamics could not finally be a principle of unity: it reduced all to entropy, same-
ness, and chaos. None of the scientific deter-
minisms did any better; by reducing phenomena to
their own narrow terms, they excluded as much as
they included. "If," on the other hand, "a Unity
exists, in which and toward which all energies
centre, it must explain and include Duality, Diversity, Infinity--Sex!"[56] Unity implied tolerance, and hence implied freedom; otherwise unity
could not truly possess or encompass the totality
of things.

Consequently Adams depicts "twentieth century

multiplicity" in monochrome--all tends toward a
drab sameness--while he delights in the many col-
ors of "thirteenth century unity." "The windows
of Chartres," he points out, "have no sequence,
and their charm is in variety, in individuality,
and sometimes even in downright hostility to each
other, reflecting the picturesque society that
gave them." The Gothic cathedral itself seemed
to Adams the most eloquent representation of "multiplicity in unity" ever conceived. In this tra-
dition-bound society of the Middle Ages, evidently, was a "greed for novelty" that the vastly ac-
celerated pace of the modern world could not
match: "Our age has lost much of its ear for
poetry, as it has its eye for colour and line,
and its taste for war and worship, wine and wom-
en."[57]

Not even the Virgin could make the world a
harmony, however. To be sure, <u>Mont-Saint-Michel
and Chartres</u> leaves an idealized impression of
the Middle Ages, but that is because Adams was
describing an architectural construct: the Gothic
cathedral and what it represented of a people's
longing to believe. He knew the reality of evil,
and did not suppose that any providential or
transcendental plan could absorb it. Describing
the death of his sister in his <u>Education</u>, Adams
had dwelt on the apparent sensual pleasure with
which nature trafficked in pain, concluding that
the idea that any personal deity was responsible
was blasphemous.[58] Multiplicity, as Adams used
the term, meant not variety or diversity, but a
catalogue of chaos which no principle of divinity
could reduce to moral order, and he did not suppose that the Middle Ages were an exception:

> The student of the Latin Quarter was
> then harder to convince than now that
> God was Infinite Love and His world a
> perfect harmony, when perfect love and
> harmony showed them, even in the Latin
> Quarter, and still more in revealed
> truth, a picture of suffering, sorrow,
> and death; plague, pestilence, and

> famine; inundations, droughts, and
> frosts; catastrophes world-wide and
> accidents in corners; cruelty, per-
> versity, stupidity, uncertainty, insan-
> ity; virtue begetting vice; vice work-
> ing for good; happiness without sense,
> selfishness without gain, misery with-
> out cause, and horrors undefined.[59]

"Unity," then, was not a control manifested
outward from the center; it was an attraction--
a convergence of human feelings. But these feelings are freely directed; the Virgin is the focus
of spontaneity, and Adams clearly associated freedom with her paradoxical unity that escapes unity,
order which embraces disorder. Unity and multiplicity join in the receptive woman, and by her
grace bring a remission from the inexorable workings of the cosmos--or so the sinner hopes. Adams then restates the principle which he ascribes
to Thomas Aquinas: that man's free will is the
aspiration to God. If freedom exists, the modern
"angelic doctor" (so-called by his friends) appears to say, it is a human quality, and lies in
the aspiration to transcend oneself and one's situation, an aspiration that reaches toward convergence with the countless other aspirations in
similar travail.

The Virgin is related to her antithesis, the
Dynamo, in that both are manifestations of force,
the attractive power of Mary being as real as the
electricity generated by the great modern machinery. In a way also, however, both are manifestations of divinity. Adams' personal response to
the dynamo is well-known: "Before the end, one
began to pray to it; inherited instinct taught
the natural expression of man before silent and
infinite force."[60] The Dynamo is a last attenuation of the providential cosmology of an earlier
generation, Providence become the mere determinism
of the machine. The "reason" that was essential
to Bancroft's Providence, for instance, becomes
the strictly technical rationalism so familiar to
the twentieth century; the difference is that be-

tween infinite intelligence and an electronic system. Nevertheless, as Ernest Samuels points out, Adams entertained a virtually religious notion of force as the stuff of a sort of "scientific pantheism. Force is the new deity, all pervasive, omnipresent, omnipotent, multiple, and mysterious."61 Although often mistaken in his appraisal of forces, man, Adams was sure, was never mistaken in "the value he set on the whole, which he symbolized as unity and worshipped as God."62 But the Dynamo was God stripped of grace, of the very anthropomorphic qualities which had made a unity of man and the cosmos. If Brooks Adams had reverted to Calvinism, as he claimed, it was to the Calvinism of the Dynamo; grace (God's freely given and unmerited love and favor) had taken refuge with the Virgin. The resort to Catholic imagery simply underscored the bankruptcy, for Henry Adams, of the Protestant system of freedom-under-God defined by George Bancroft.

As a symbol, the Dynamo was naturally the converse of the Virgin in the puzzle of Unity and Multiplicity. The Dynamo represented the dispersion of force: force flowing outward to be lost in space and time, like the primordial explosion now believed to have been the birth of the universe. The Dynamo was energy lost--entropy, finally. Adams reiterates his sometimes despairing conclusion that all the logical system that man can distill from nature, that the scientific or philosophic principle of determinism itself, is tantamount to chaos. In the world of the Dynamo, men are driven by forces beyond their control toward ends, if any, which are not theirs; and this constitutes neither freedom nor order. No longer aspiring freely to the center of life, they are driven outward from the center, and vitality fades.

One response to the tyranny of the dynamo lay in the familiar civilized recourse to the primitive. Henry Adams was never more of a modern man than when he sought to recapture a lost

wholeness in pre-modern settings. His figure of
Mary did itself clearly embody elements of primitivism. The Virgin was the quintessence of feminine force, and in a civilization shaped primarily
according to masculine values, women represented
something older than civilization, and more basic.
Adams explicitly identified the Virgin with Venus
and other expressions of the female sexual and
generative force. Woman's was a profounder, intuitive wisdom that mocked and circumvented masculine logic. Adams found this quality not only
in the Virgin of Chartres but in friends like
Elizabeth Cameron, his fictional heroines Madeline
Lee and Esther, and in his ill-fated wife. Feminine sexuality never ceased to rebuke the Dynamo's world. And Adams was able to conclude as a
general law of his Education that ". . .no woman
had ever driven him wrong; no man had ever driven
him right."63

The opposition expressed in sexual terms was
paralleled by the division in Adams' own life
which is a theme of the Education. From the beginning, life was double, represented by summer
vacations in Quincy on the one hand, and winter
school days in Boston on the other. "Town was restraint, law, unity. Country, only seven miles
away, was liberty, diversity, outlawry, the endless delight of mere sense impressions given by
nature for nothing, and breathed by boys without
knowing it." The notable identification of diversity with outlawry, which carried over to the
Virgin herself, was strengthened by Adams' en-
counters with the South. The moral horror of
slavery, the raggedness of the slave states,did
not lessen the seductiveness of southern life--
". . .the freedom, openness, swagger of nature
and man. . . ." There was something in him that
responded, more than his "quarter taint of Maryland blood," to the "intermixture of delicate
grace and passionate depravity that marked the
Maryland May."64

Adams was not immune either to the attraction of the Noble Savage, especially when femi-

279

nine. He sojourned in Tahiti in 1891, and wrote a history of the island from the accounts given him by his native hostess. Adams was impressed by the part that women had played in Tahitian history; "the fight about a woman," he noted, "is the starting-point of all popular revolutions and poetry. . ." Like so many travellers to the South Seas, he found an idyllic quality to the islanders' life, but lamented the inroads of civilized knowledge and disease. From Samoa, Adams wrote home happily of the unselfconsciousness of the people, of the naked dignity and innocence of the Polynesian women, of "languor that is not languid, voluptuousness that is not voluptuous; a poem without poetry." The naturalness of the qualities, Adams seemed to say, ran deeper than the self-conscious categories of civilization. "People who wear clothes," he summed it up, "can't dance."[65]

Adams was not ready to abandon civilization, however, as much as he detested its contemporary phase. His Virgin, while appealing to some of the deepest of human emotions, was a figure set in western civilization. Her function was intelligible only in the western cosmology. She was the kinder vestige of the Christian idea of Providence, who reconciled unity and multiplicity, freedom and order. In her, Providence had undergone a sort of existentialist shrinkage. She could not embrace the cosmos as God Almighty had done; she possessed no secret of its meaning, and indeed, as Adams states, was skeptical that it had one. She could only serve as an attractive force for those who chose to venerate her, in the faith that she could make bearable the evils of the world. Mary was the emblem not of anti-civilization, but of a civilization less abstract than that of the Dynamo, and more deeply rooted in humanity itself.

The riddle contained in the symbols of the Virgin and the Dynamo was expressed also in Adams' espousal of "Conservative Christian Anarchism." To an extent, this was a <u>jeu d'esprit</u> that showed Adams' love of paradox for its own sake. Thus he suggested a Conservative Christian Anarchist Party, the two members of which (Adams and George Cabot Lodge) would be obliged to contradict each other for the sake of a dialectic. Unlike the "amiable doctrines of Kropotkin," Adams pointed out, in which anarchy was only a means to order and unity, his would be a thoroughgoing anarchism.

> Adams proclaimed that in the last synthesis, order and anarchy were one, but that the unity was chaos. As anarchist, conservative and Christian, he had no motive or duty but to attain the end; and to hasten it, he was bound to accelerate progress; to concentrate energy; to accumulate power, to multiply and intensify forces; to reduce friction, increase velocity and magnify momentum, partly because this was the mechanical law of the universe as science explained it; but partly also in order to get done with the present which artists and some others complained of; and finally--and chiefly--because a rigorous philosophy required it, in order to penetrate the beyond, and satisfy man's destiny by reaching the largest synthesis in its ultimate contradiction.[66]

Who knows? Perhaps, there is the suggestion, the acceleration of progress would bring a new cycle of Brooks Adams' Age of Fear, and artist, priest, and soldier would have less of which to complain.

It is possible also to see in the Conservative Christian Anarchist figure, as J. C. Levenson suggests, the acceptance of humane and Christian values in "a world in which religion and society no longer provided sanctions for individual conduct." Adams observed in Mont-Saint-Michel and Chartres that "absolute liberty is absence of restraint; therefore, the ideally free individual is responsible only to himself. This principle is the philosophical foundation of anarchism, and,

281

for anything that science has yet proved, may be the philosophical foundation of the universe. . . ."67 Adams' use of the terms "anarchism" and "anarchy" was typically freighted with hyperbole, referring often to what would ordinarily be called liberty. Perhaps in the age of the Dynamo, anarchy was the only type of freedom conceivable. Adams described himself to John Hay in 1900 "as one who belongs wholly to the past, and whose traditional sympathies are with all the forces that resist concentration and love what used to be called liberty but has now become anarchy, or resistance to civilisation. . . ."68

In proclaiming that "order and anarchy were one," Adams reasserted the paradox of the Virgin, who reconciled unity with freedom. And the unity was chaos, in the sense that the Virgin represented an intellectual outlawry, and forgave that which omniscience could not embrace. Adams the Conservative Christian Anarchist remained both the intellectual, yearning for "the largest synthesis in its ultimate contradiction," and the supplicant of the Virgin, hoping to get done with a present uncongenial to her. Capturing the conflicts in Adams' own nature, the term was his best self-description. It was as well an attempt at a sort of intellectual heroism. He perceived this quality, for instance, in Michelangelo, "the artistic chief of the conservative Christian anarchists, . . . [who] . . . plunged art into despair and crime."69 He saw this heroism as the dramatic motive in the works of his young friend, George Cabot Lodge.

> It was that of Schopenhauer, of Buddhism, of Oriental thought every where,-- the idea of Will, making the universe, but existing only as subject. The Will is God; it is nature; it is all that is; but it is knowable only as ourselves. Thus the sole tragic action of humanity is the Ego,--the Me,--always maddened by the necessity of self-sacrifice, and, of course, by destroying the attachments

which are most vital, in order to attain. The idea is a part of the most
primitive stock of religious and philosophical motives, worked out in many
forms, as Prometheus, as Herakles, as
Christ, as Buddha,--to mention only the
most familiar,--but, in our modern conception of life, impossible to realize
except as a form of insanity. All
saviors were anarchists, but Christian
anarchists, tortured by the self-con-
tradictions of their role. All were
insane, because their problem was self-
contradictory, and because, in order to
raise the universe in oneself to its
highest power, its negative powers must
be paralyzed or destroyed. In reality,
nothing was destroyed; only the Will--
or what we now call Energy--was freed
and perfected.[70]

There is in this heroic view of the "Christian anarchist" something essential of the American Protestant. Despairing of clerical mediation,
the Protestant must rely on the possibility that
his will converges with that of God. The individual must thus realize the universe--"make" the
universe in this sense--himself, perforce subjectively, as no objective scheme could conceivably
join him to the infinite. Further, the Protestant
plan, in ripping grace from its social context,
may be said to destroy "the attachments which
are most vital, in order to attain." Did not
Michael Wigglesworth revel in the complacency with
which the Elect view wife or husband damned at the
"Day of Doom"? There is a heroic dimension in
this. Of course Adams goes a long step further,
in doubting a Providence with Whose will the individual's can merge; in the absence of an intelligible Providence, the will deifies itself. The
effort to join heaven and earth becomes a rebellion against both, as the Virgin in her subtle
and womanly fashion rebels against the oppres-
sion of God and man, embodying the whole human
protest against unjust fate. The Christian anar-

chist effort "to raise the universe in oneself to
its highest power" does then indeed meet with
contradiction.

What then of the Protestant nation which believes itself to have a special commission to ele-
vate the human condition? Such was the rationale
of American democracy, as described by Adams in
his History of the United States. Quite shrewdly,
Adams perceived the national roots of his figure.
"In America," he observed, "all were conservative
Christian anarchists; the faith was national, racial, geographic. The true American had never
seen such supreme virtue in any of the innumerable
shades between social anarchy and social order as
to mark it for exclusively human and his own."[71]
The American, as described by Bancroft and others, was ultimately an anarchist, at least to the
extent of secular authority. Skeptical of social
order, wary of all institutions, he was nevertheless confident that his personal will, if he followed his inmost voice of "reason" or conscience,
coincided with the divine order. This, after all,
was the Protestant lesson. And this was the way
of a peculiar American symbiosis of liberalism and
conservatism: primarily, however the principle
was twisted and perverted, it was the divine order, unmixed with the authority of man over man,
which was to be upheld, not an "artificial" social
order. But if the divine order were to come a-
part, what would happen to the conservative American anarchist?

Adams held up to the nascent twentieth century a cosmology and an anti-cosmology. The one
represented the present, and its emblem was the
Dynamo. It exploded the notion of Providence,
with its religious resolution of the problem of
the one and the many; it perceived energy driven
outward, away from the center, to end in entropy.
Unity with it meant determinism; freedom meant
chaos. This cosmology had the appeal of power,
and Adams appears the Calvinist servant of omnipotence in his impulse to pray to the Dynamo as an
expression of infinite force. The Second Law of

Thermodynamics spun out this aspect of the providential cosmology to its last bleak attenuation.
But Adams perceived the hollowness of such a cosmos, even as he understood its grip on the modern
world. The vision of enfolded chaos and determinism prefigured Paul Tillich's description of
nonbeing in the modern consciousness, with its
double face of annihilating narrowness and annihilating openness. It neatly bisected the sense
of meaninglessness which nags contemporary life.

If the Dynamo was the shell of Providence,
the Virgin was the quick. She was also a vestige,
and all the more because her time was past--and,
possibly, yet to come. She addresses herself to
a twentieth century longing for subjective inter-
cession, with its peculiar disposition to conjure
the future with remnants of the past, its worship
of primitivism and revolution. Adams spoke here
too in the guise of a Calvinist, but addressing
himself to the Calvinist concern for rescue in a
shipwrecked world:

> My idea is that the world outside--the
> so-called modern world--can only per-
> vert and degrade the conceptions of the
> primitive instinct of art and feeling,
> and that our only chance is to accept
> the limited number of survivors--the
> one-in-a-thousand of born artists and
> poets--and to intensify the energy of
> feeling within that radiant centre. In
> other words, I am a creature of our poor
> old Calvinistic, St. Augustinian fa-
> thers, and am not afraid to carry out my
> logic to the rigorous end of regarding
> our present society, its ideals and pur-
> poses, as dregs and fragments of some
> primitive, essential instinct now nearly
> lost.[72]

Mary is the patroness of these dregs and fragments, retaining her force as an outlaw, unin-
volved in the collapse of the logical universe,

yet also as harmony, drawing to herself the free veneration of her people.

As the older cosmology faded, America had come to mean mobility, expansion, and the multiplication of physical force. With the catholic Virgin she seemed to have little to do. Although her sexual and human qualities represented an energy which had exercised "vastly more attraction over the human mind than all the steam engines and dynamos ever dreamed of. . .yet this energy was unknown to the American mind. An American Virgin," Adams feared, "would never dare command; an American Venus would never dare exist."[73] If Adams was correct, and if this source of energy were not to be altogether foregone, the American would have to become a Conservative Christian Anarchist on a new plane. From reliance on Providence to maintain the social order, he would have to find his way to an order that was not providentially prescribed, but which consisted in voluntary allegiance to that which the Virgin symbolized, and which partook of the ancient religious notion of grace. He would have to regain a sense of cosmology, but it would be an imploded cosmology, no longer attempting to embrace the heavens and the earth, but internalized and loyal. Then conceivably the primordial outlawry of an expatriate people would converge with the Puritan longing for the divine marrow of human experience, and possibilities which were profoundly American would at last be realized.

iv.

"What could become of such a child of the seventeenth and eighteenth centuries," Henry Adams asked of himself in his Education, "when he should wake up to find himself required to play the game of the twentieth?"[74] This is the sort of game required of Everyman, as whom Adams occasionally posed, even when the pace of history is slower than during the last several centuries. He who

survives his childhood must make his life in a
world not quite the same as that in which he was
born, if only because it has ceased to be a
child's world. He must find a way of interpreting
this life in order to come to terms with perpetual
exile.

But Everyman is also, as Carl Becker put it,
his own historian, and is obliged on some level to
comprehend those changes in his world which transcend the personal. The obligation was enormously
heightened in Adams' case, not only by his historical sensitivity but by his peculiar nativity. Indelibly "branded" by his genealogy, it was natural
for an Adams to identify his fortunes with those
of his country. America was commonly understood
as representing a break with the past, even by
those, like George Bancroft, who could show that
all human history had prepared for this break.
Ironically, as Adams reached his intellectual maturity, it appeared that the future was breaking
with America. If America was defined by what his
brother Brooks called the "democratic dogma,"
postulating a system of ordered freedom and providentially ordained progress, then America was to
be left in a limbo of lost hopes between the discarded burden of European tradition and the dead
weight of materialistic determinism. America,
and Adams, were caught in the shift from the cosmos of the "dogma" to the anti-cosmos of blind
necessity. In a world where all men and all ages
are transitional, Adams and his time were more
transitional than most.

Adams was as conscious of historical movement as any latter day expositor of "future
shock." "The movement from unity into multiplicity, between 1200 and 1900," he wrote, "was un-
broken in sequence, and rapid in acceleration."
Indeed, in retrospect from the early twentieth
century, "he wondered whether, on the whole, the
boy of 1854 stood nearer to the thought of 1904,
or to that of the year 1."[75] In the chapter of
his Education entitled "A Law of Acceleration,"
he invoked the image of a comet increasing in

velocity as it wheeled around the sun, to represent the course of modern society. In 1909, in "The Rule of Phase Applied to History," he suggested that history could be understood as a series of phases, governed by religious, mechanical, electrical, and ethereal energy, successively, each phase the square root of the preceding in years of duration. The sequence would run out, and thought reach the limit of its possibilities, in the 1920's, or allowing for error by 2025.[76]

Critics have never agreed how seriously or literally to regard the "Rule of Phase," or Adams' complementary effort in "A Letter to American Teachers of History" to apply to human energies the Second Law of Thermodynamics. But there is no denying the intensity with which he pursued the goal of making sense of history, which he was convinced that none of the traditional methods did. "The old formulas had failed," he perceived, "and a new one had to be made, but after all, the object was not extravagant or eccentric. One sought only a spool on which to wind the thread of history without breaking it."[77] Intended probably as less than anti-democratic dogma, and as more than joke or allegory, these essays of Adams' old age punctuated his long effort intellectually to master the gross phenomena of change.

Progressive and evolutionary models of change, such as those put forward by Bancroft and Fiske, were naturally precluded by Adams' disillusionment; they were among the old formulas which had failed. Theories of the inexorable and linear advancement of humanity, they did not stand logically disproven; they simply failed to answer to existential reality. Adams' remark that "the progress of evolution from President Washington to President Grant, was alone evidence enough to upset Darwin,"[78] was facetious, but not entirely so. It well illustrates the disposition to identify political and universal categories, which was the hallmark of so much nineteenth century thought. John Quincy Adams' faith in God had been

severely shaken by his defeat at the hands of
Andrew Jackson, according to his grandson Brooks;
indeed he had never "reconcile[d] himself to the
destiny which this betrayal by God entailed on
the world."[79] Whether this was an accurate interpretation of the old man's feelings or a projec-
tion of his grandson's, there is no doubt that
the shabby spectacle of American politics in the
post-Civil War period contributed to Henry Adams'
cosmic gloom.

This universalizing of the political was
often conscious and deliberate, but of course it
had a root too in the normal human tendency to
read one's mood into the universe. The suicide
of Adams' wife and the Panic of 1893 which threatened the family fortune were personal reasons
enough for pessimism, which as the end of the century approached brought his prolonged private
trumpeting of the collapse of civilization. "I
am myself more than ever at odds with my time,"
ran an extreme but representative outburst in
1893.

> I detest it, and everything that be-
> longs to it, and live only in the wish
> to see the end of it, with all its in-
> fernal Jewry. I want to put every money
> lender to death, and to sink Lombard
> Street and Wall Street under the ocean.
> Then, perhaps, men of our kind might
> have some chance of being honorably
> killed in battle and eaten by our ene-
> mies. I want to go to India, and be a
> Brahmin, and worship a monkey.[80]

Here, except for the wit of his gallows humor,
Adams became Everyman's own worst historian, scur-
rilous and desperate in his rage at time and
change.

Doom had more intelligent uses, to adapt Gerrit H. Roelof's phrase. One could move rationally
in the direction that logical necessity marked
out, Adams acknowledged[81]--although this was an

approach more typical of Brooks. A more attractive solution lay in the cyclical interpretation of history. The younger brother had provided a model in The Law of Civilization and Decay, that "somewhat grotesque world poem, or symphony in blue & gray," as Oliver Wendell Holmes, Jr. called it.[82]

In Brooks' historical scheme, thought, as a manifestation of energy, had two archetypal phases, Fear and Greed. The velocity of a social movement was proportionate to its energy and mass; its centralization was proportionate to its velocity. In the earlier stages of concentration, fear was the channel through which mental energy found its readiest outlet. This was consequently the age of imagination, with religious, military, and artistic types in the ascendancy. Fear of the seen produced the warrior, fear of the unseen the priest, and the artist celebrated the triumphs of both.[83]

Surplus wealth, in more advanced stages of concentration, came to predominate over productive energy. Capital became autocratic as "imagination fades, and the emotional, the martial, and the artistic types of manhood decay." In the new age of greed two extreme economic types were bred, the usurer and the "peasant whose nervous system is best adapted to thrive on scanty nutriment." At length greed could go no further, and either a stationary period supervened, as with Byzantium, or disintegration set in, as with the western Roman empire; the civilized population perished, and survivors could only await the infusion of barbarian blood. Using this formula, Adams traced western history from the decay of Rome to the zenith of imagination in the Middle Ages, to the avarice of the new economic man personified by Henry VIII, and finally to the advent of the Rothschilds and great concentrations of wealth. The current fear-greed cycle in world history, Adams estimated, spanned the years between 310 A.D. and 1900.[84]

Adams characteristically used history as a
bullwhip with which to chastise the capitalists
whose machinations had imperiled his family's com-
fort, and whose values appalled its sense of fit-
ness. But behind the creaking mechanism of economic determinism, as Charles A. Beard apprehended, was an eccentrically perceptive psychological
interpretation of history,[85] which even skeptical
readers like Holmes found immediately compelling.
Fear and greed, at least, were qualities as familiar to the Middle Ages as they were in the late
nineteenth century. Brooks Adams broke through
the interpretation of history as linear progress,
according to which modernity was in flight from
the past. Even while juxtaposing the medieval age
of fear with the modern age of greed, he appealed
to those modern sentiments which would at once
empathize with his Middle Ages. Furthermore the
cyclical scheme, suggesting the possibility of a
new age of fear, seemed to lend these sentiments
a more than nostalgic value.

The historical cycle had obvious appeal for
Henry Adams. It contributed to his Conservative
Christian Anarchism the principle that the speedy
overthrow of the existing order was the best way
toward the restoration of those emotional and
imaginative values which it suppressed. (This
was entirely a theoretical remedy; Adams actually
shrank from the collapse that he viewed as inevitable.) Ultimately, though, he lacked faith in
a favorable turn of the cycle. His last formal
expressions of historical theory inverted the
idea of progress as incorporated in the "democratic dogma." For progress in a cosmos of ordered
liberty he substituted entropy in an anti-cosmos
of determined chaos. This left the past as inaccessible as ever.

Despite their differences, The Law of Civilization and Decay and "A Letter to American
Teachers of History" were united by their profound
melancholy, reflecting the loss of the sense of an
hospitable and perceptibly dramatic cosmos. The

291

loss naturally darkened the Adamses' interpretations of history. Cyclical "repetition emptied of its religious content necessarily leads to a pessimistic vision of existence," Mircea Eliade points out.

> When it is no longer a vehicle for reintegrating a primordial situation, and hence for recovering the mysterious presence of the gods, that is, when it is desacralized, cyclic time becomes terrifying; it is seen as a circle forever turning on itself, repeating itself to infinity.

Modern "historicistic and existentialist" philosophies make time terrifying in their own way, Eliade adds. "Definitively desacralized, time presents itself as a precarious and evanescent duration, leading irremediably to death."[86]

Henry Adams surmounted this estrangement from time only tentatively through the media of his polarizing symbols. Those which most capture the imagination, the Virgin and the Dynamo, are effective not only because of their radical incompatibility, but because they are united as manifestations of energy, a concept as comprehensible applied to medieval religious emotion as to the generation of electricity. It is this ambivalence of being opposites and yet of being the same that permits the symbols to relate the thirteenth and twentieth centuries.

Yet the interpretive quality of the Dynamo and the Virgin is due not only to their being based in specific historical periods, but in their transcending those periods. As Robert Mane notes, Adams explicitly associated the logical God of Thomas Aquinas with the Dynamo, finding in the "prime motor" (translated thus, instead of as the more usual "prime mover") no source of free will.[87] The Virgin was associated with the primeval qualities of sexuality and fecundity which

he found alike in Diana of the Ephesians and in
the contemporary Samoan, potentially indeed even
in civilized woman. Any hope for the future, any
prospect of an "outburst of the emotional classes"
against economic man, such as Brooks Adams allowed
himself occasionally to entertain,[88] would be in
the name of the Virgin. For Henry, such hope was
fleeting and fragmentary, although he ended his
Education with the thought that if he were allowed
to return to earth in 1938, his centenary, he
might find, "for the first time since man began
his education among the carnivores. . .a world
that sensitive and timid natures could regard
without a shudder."[89] This grace note of optimism
became far more ironic than Adams could have meant
it to be, in light of the events of 1938, but it
shows Adams still capable of resolving his contempt for the present into hope as well as memory.
The Virgin could stand for both.

Attaining in his own way Royce's "community
of interpretation"[90] binding past to present and
future, the historian succeeded most as mythmaker.
For certainly his Dynamo and Virgin were figures
more of myth than of either strict history or of
genuine religion. As attenuations of the masculine logic and the feminine sympathy which Adams
found in the old religion, they provided as much
a mythic unity of human experience as they did a
hyperbolic division of it. Adams' favored figure
of Mary, in particular, was not a personage known
to Catholic orthodoxy, medieval or modern. But
she served as an ideal figure of last resort for
the Age of the Dynamo, representing equally the
harmony with Creation toward which those who were
loyal to her struggled, and the outlawry of humanity in a universe incomprehensible to it--
both cosmos and anti-cosmos. Finally she transcended both, for she embodied the highest qualities accessible to humanity, heedless of all the
metaphysical schemes that angelic doctors, medieval or modern, might devise.

293

Footnotes

1. Brooks Adams, The Emancipation of Massachusetts. The Dream and the Reality. Second edition with a new introduction by Perry Miller (Boston: Houghton Mifflin, 1962), p. viii. (Hereinafter cited as Adams, Emancipation of Massachusetts.)

2. Lovell Thompson, "'Bible of Chaos,'" The Saturday Review of Literature, XXVI (June 19, 1943), 30.

3. Brooks Adams, The Law of Civilization and Decay. An Essay on History. With an introduction by Charles A. Beard (New York: Alfred A. Knopf, 1951), p. 58. (Hereinafter cited as Adams, Civilization and Decay.) "Loving paradox, Adams has a host of seeming contradictions unravel with his theories. In the age of fear, the reader understands, man is martial. In the age of greed, when man has succeeded in amassing great wealth, humanity is poor and exhausted. While in the age of imagination knowledge is restrained by the clergy, in the age of economy science proceeds to open new insights to the imagination. Woman is a chattel, yet admired and respected, in the era of decentralization; she is an equal, yet rejected and despised, in the era of centralization. Art, the highest expression of the human mind, flourishes when man is organized in a relatively barbarous society, but deteriorates when man is organized in a highly civilized and centralized society. Perhaps the strangest paradox of all is the periodic change in human character while nature attempts to keep man unchanged through the medium of hereditary instinct. Perhaps the greatest paradox of all is that human society, constantly in motion, continuously seeking outlets for its energy, ends in a stagnation from which the only escape is a route through change that leads inevitably to stagnation." Arthur F. Beringause, Brooks Adams: a Biography (New York: Alfred A. Knopf, 1955),

pp. 122-123. (Hereinafter cited as Beringause, Brooks Adams.)

4. Brooks Adams, The New Empire (New York: Macmillan, 1903), p. 32. (Hereinafter cited as Adams, New Empire.)

5. Henry Adams, The Degradation of the Democratic Dogma. With an introduction by Brooks Adams (New York: Peter Smith, 1949), pp. vii-viii. (Hereinafter cited as Adams, Democratic Dogma.) Thornton Anderson notes that Adams "was never strictly logical in his theory of automatism. . . .he coupled it at times with a rigid determinism and at other times with a process by which men and societies made mistakes in estimating the path of least resistance." Brooks Adams: Constructive Conservative (Ithaca: Cornell University Press, 1951), p. 199.

6. Brooks Adams, "Can War Be Done Away With?" Publications of the American Sociological Society, X (1915), 120. (Hereinafter cited as Adams, "Can War Be Done Away With?")

7. Adams, Emancipation of Massachusetts, p. 5.

8. Adams, "Can War Be Done Away With?" 104-105.

9. Adams, New Empire, p. 191.

10. Brooks Adams, America's Economic Supremacy (New York: Macmillan, 1900), p. 78. (Hereinafter cited as Adams, America's Economic Supremacy.) Beringause calls attention to the influence on Adams of Fiske's ideas of scientific history. Despite Adams' disagreement with William James on basic points, Beringause adds, Adams was also influenced by James's conception of "mind or consciousness as nothing more than the flowing function by which man adjusts to environment. This view James had undoubtedly seen discussed in Her-

295

bert Spencer's <u>Principles of Psychology</u> (1855), where mind was described as an 'adjustment of internal to external conditions,' a type of human adaptation to environment. Thus both James and Spencer reinforced Henry Adams's belief that the role of habit and instinct is of transcending importance in human affairs." <u>Brooks Adams</u>, pp. 78, 81.

11. Adams, <u>Emancipation of Massachusetts</u>, p. 213.

12. <u>Ibid.</u>, p. 408.

13. Adams, "Can War Be Done Away With?" 104, 107.

14. Ernest Samuels, <u>Henry Adams: The Major Phase</u> (Cambridge: Belknap, 1964), p. 117. (Hereinafter cited as Samuels, <u>Adams: Major Phase</u>.

15. Beringause, <u>Brooks Adams</u>, pp. 123, 145.

16. Worthington Chauncey Ford, "Memoir of Brooks Adams," <u>Proceedings of the Massachusetts Historical Society</u>, XI (May, 1927), 357-358.

17. Brooks Adams, <u>The Theory of Social Revolutions</u> (New York: The Macmillan Company, 1913), pp. 1, 6-7. (Hereinafter cited as Adams, <u>Social Revolutions</u>); Adams, <u>America's Economic Supremacy</u>, p. 142.

18. Beringause, <u>Brooks Adams</u>, pp. 346, 371-374.

19. Adams, "Can War Be Done Away With?" 123.

20. <u>Ibid.</u>, pp. 105-106.

21. Beringause, <u>Brooks Adams</u>, p. 253.

22. Adams, <u>Democratic Dogma</u>, p. 30.

23. <u>Ibid.</u>, pp. 78-79, 85-86, 122.

24. Samuels says of The Law of Civilization and Decay that "its effect upon Henry was electric, bringing to an end the period of intellectual torpor and irresolution, and it helped launch him upon the greatest effort of his thought. It brought his anarchic disgusts into focus, gave him a scapegoat, identified the enemy, and supplied him with a scientific rationale for rejecting contemporary civilization. Here was the scientific basis for modern pessimism." Adams: Major Phase, p. 127.

25. Adams, Democratic Dogma, p. 127.

26. Worthington Chauncey Ford, ed., Letters of Henry Adams, 2 volumes (Boston and New York: Houghton Mifflin, 1930-1938), II, 531, 533. Adams to Elizabeth Cameron, January 24, 1910; Adams to Brooks Adams, January 30, 1910. (Hereinafter cited as Ford, Letters of Henry Adams); Samuels, Adams: Major Phase, pp. 437-438.

27. Samuels, Adams: Major Phase, p. 485. Yvor Winters placed Adams in "the Ockhamist tradition; and as for the Mathers, so for him, the significance could not reside within the event but must reside back of it. He would scarcely have put it this way, and he might have denied the paternity of Ockham; but he belonged to a moral tradition which had taken its morality wholly on faith for so long that it had lost the particular kind of intelligence and perception necessary to read the universe for what it is; and had developed instead a passion to read the universe for what it means, as a system of divine shorthand or hieroglyphic, as a statement of ultimate intentions." "The Anatomy of Nonsense," In Defense of Reason (Denver: Alan Swallow, 1947), p. 391.

28. Adams, Democratic Dogma, p. 232.

29. Ibid., p. 242.

30. Ibid., pp. 196-197.

31. William H. Jordy, Henry Adams: Scientific Historian (New Haven: Yale University Press, 1951). Jordy notes for example "the central fallacy of the Letter: [that] the steady decline in the amount of energy available for the future use of both biological evolution and history automatically implied a steady decline in the end products created by the depletion of the energy reservoir" (p. 207).

32. Ford, Letters of Henry Adams, II, 524. Adams to Margaret Chanler, September 9, 1909.

33. Ibid., II, 392. Adams to Brooks Adams, August 10, 1902. Michael Colacurcio, however, points out the dissimilarity of Adams and Aquinas: "Adams, the seeker of unity, sought always to simplify his conception of the universe (he got it down, eventually, to the single concept of force). St. Thomas on the other hand, trusting in the existence of Transcendental Unity (though as Adams observes his philosophy did not begin by assuming it), never hesitated to multiply distinctions when necessary. St. Thomas is ineradicably a dualist, Adams a monist." "The Dynamo and the Angelic Doctor: The Bias of Henry Adams' Medievalism," American Quarterly, XVII (Winter, 1965), 702. (Hereinafter cited as Colacurcio, "Dynamo and the Angelic Doctor.")

34. Henry Wasser, The Scientific Thought of Henry Adams (Thessalonike: N. Nicolaides, 1956), p. 3. (Hereinafter cited as Wasser, Scientific Thought.)

35. Harold Dean Cater, ed. Henry Adams and His Friends. A Collection of His Unpublished Letters (Boston: Houghton Mifflin, 1947), pp. 783-784. Adams to unknown recipient, January 1, 1909. (Hereinafter cited as Cater, Adams and His Friends.)

36. Ibid., p. 126. Adams to Samuel J. Tilden, January 24, 1883.

37. Ibid., p. 134. Adams to Francis Parkman, December 21, 1884.

38. Henry Adams, History of the United States of America During the Jefferson and Madison Administrations, 9 volumes (New York: Antiquarian Press, 1962), IX, 225. (Hereinafter cited as Adams, History of the United States.) There is an extended discussion of Adams' use of water imagery in Melvin Lyon, Symbol and Idea in Henry Adams (Lincoln: University of Nebraska Press, 1970), pp. 191-224. (Hereinafter cited as Lyon, Symbol and Idea.)

39. Ford, Letters of Henry Adams, II, 386. Adams to Elizabeth Cameron, April 13, 1902.

40. Ibid., II, 123. Adams to Cecil A. S. Rice, February 12, 1897.

41. Cater, Adams and His Friends, p. 545. Adams to Brooks Adams, May 2, 1903.

42. Adams, History of the United States, IX, 237, 241.

43. The phrase belongs to Oliver Wendell Holmes, Jr., "The Soldier's Faith," The Holmes Reader, ed .Julius J. Marke (New York: Oceana, 1955), p. 149.

44. Ford, Letters of Henry Adams, II, 391-392. Adams to Brooks Adams, August 10, 1902. "You may think all this nonsense, but I tell you these are great times," Henry Adams wrote to his brother Charles Francis Jr. during the Civil War. "Man has mounted science, and is now run away with. I firmly believe that before many centuries more, science will be the master of man. The engines she will have invented will be beyond his strength to control. Some day science may have the existence of mankind in its power, and the human race commit suicide by blowing up the world. Not only shall we be able to cruize in space, but I see no reason why some future generation should-

n't walk off like a beetle with the world on its back, or give it another rotary motion so that every zone should receive in turn its due portion of heat and light. . . ." Worthington Chauncey Ford, ed., A Cycle of Adams Letters, 1861-1865, 2 volumes (London: Constable and Company, Ltd., 1921), I, 135. April 11, 1862. In later life, and, "from the side of feeling, instinct, art, romantic aspiration," Samuel holds, "Adams unequivocally leagued himself with the counterrevolution against materialistic science." Adams: Major Phase, p. 308.

45. Wasser, Scientific Thought, p. 14. In Adams' "dynamic theory of history," John Stephen Martin points out, "Teleology was sacrificed to preserve necessity." Martin views Adams as bringing together two traditions. "One was the older New England idealistic dialectic, stressing ontology by assuming two elements which made spirit primary without neglecting nature, and which had a real existence only in their opposition." The second drew upon Scotch realism and Berkeleyan idealism, and "found the problem of knowledge to be resolved in phenomenalism." "Henry Adams's 'Dynamic Theory of History' and the New England Dialectic of Necessity" (unpublished Master's thesis, University of Georgia, 1961), pp. 108, 120. The influence of Spencer and Fiske on Henry Adams is discussed in Ernest Samuels, Henry Adams: the Middle Years (Cambridge: Belknap, 1958), pp. 358-359. "It is apparent from all the scientific allusions that pervade the History that he believed that there was one scientific hypothesis by which the data of history could be successfully organized, the evolutionary hypothesis of Herbert Spencer," Samuels points out. "John Fiske's popularization had made it one of the leading commonplaces of educated circles."

46. Ford, Letters of Henry Adams, II, 506. Adams to Margaret Chanler, September 4, 1908.

47. Frances Snow Compton [Henry Adams], Esther, A Novel (New York: Henry Holt, 1884),

p. 191; Henry Adams, The Education of Henry Adams.
An Autobiography (Boston: Houghton Mifflin, 19-
61), p. 451. (Hereinafter cited as Adams, Education.) Henry Wasser notes that Adams was impressed by a certain basic similarity in the science and religion of his day. They both assumed
an unknowable and proceeded accordingly. They
both strove for unity and apparently could attain
it only by relegating the supposedly insoluble
problems to the category of irrelevance in the
case of science or to the category of an infinite,
not comprehensible to mankind, whose finiteness
is all too evident, in the case of religion."
Scientific Thought, p. 51. Lyon finds that Adams
reserved his final belief for the aphorism, "Chaos
was the law of nature; Order was the dream of
man." Symbol and Idea, p. 158.

48. Adams, Education, p. 431.

49. Henry Adams, Mont-Saint-Michel and
Chartres. With an introduction by Ralph Adams
Cram (New York: Doubleday, 1959), p. 388. (Here-
inafter cited as Adams, Chartres.)

50. Ibid., pp. 413-418.

51. Lyon proposes "the dream, the machine,
and various water symbols" as the "most pervasive
and significant of Adams' symbols." Symbol and
Idea, p. 140.

52. Samuels, Adams: Major Phase, pp. 208-
221. Adams' response to medievalism is discussed
extensively in Robert Mane, Henry Adams on the
Road to Chartres (Cambridge: Belknap, 1971).
(Hereinafter cited as Mane, Road to Chartres.)
Lyon believes that Samuels exaggerates the extent
of the Pre-Raphaelite influence on Adams. He
points out that Adams "dissociates his concept
of the Virgin as a force from the conventional
nineteenth century sense of her as sentiment or
taste." Symbol and Idea, p. 277.

53. Adams, Chartres, p. 213. Some critics

have characterized Adams as primarily an artist. One of the most recent of these, Ernst Scheyer, suggests that "as a historian, Adams was primarily led by the esthetically felt necessity for sequences assuming relationships, and second, only by the truthfulness of such arrangements." The Circle of Henry Adams: Art and Artists (Detroit: Wayne State University Press, 1970), p. 258. Adams was undoubtedly an artist in his pursuit of truth, but I am not convinced that he ultimately put art ahead of truth.

54. Adams, Chartres, pp. 278-279, 284.

55. Ibid., pp. 290, 307. The Virgin "represents man at the zenith of his selfhood. The dynamo represents man at the nadir of that selfhood, his sense of unity almost gone, the reality of chaos on the point of breaking through his humanity. The absolute antithesis of the human Virgin is the nonhuman multiverse. The dynamo expresses the vestiges of unity that clung to twentieth century science and twentieth century man." Lyon, Symbol and Idea, p. 132. Wasser observes that "unity, to Adams, was an abstraction which encompassed order, harmony, causal relation, or anything which made for meaning in the universe. . . . Multiplicity. . .was an abstraction which encompassed chaos, disharmony, confusion or anything that made the world meaningless, or was a state in which the human mind found such a welter of different and conflicting meanings to the universe as to be unable to establish one unequivocal meaning for it." Scientific Thought, p. 15. Colacurcio emphasizes the element of antirationalism in Adams. It seems to him "only a slight exaggeration to say that fideism, the demand for faith without or even in spite of reason, is the American philosophy, so impressive is the list of its exponents. As Puritanism--America's one effective faith--declined, the voices urging the absolute primacy of faith became more and more urgent. Mont-Saint-Michel and Chartres is certainly an important moment in this phase of American intellectual history." "Dynamo and the Angelic Doc-

tor," 711.

56. Adams, <u>Chartres</u>, p. 289.

57. <u>Ibid</u>., pp. 196, 22. Cf. Philippe Ariès, on medieval as opposed to post-medieval life. "People lived in a state of contrast; high birth or great wealth rubbed shoulders with poverty, vice with virtue, scandal with devotion. Despite its shrill contrasts, this medley of colours caused no surprise. . . . But there came a time when the middle class could no longer bear the pressure of the multitude or the contact of the lower class. It seceded; it withdrew from the vast polymorphous society to organize itself separately, in a homogeneous environment. . . . The old society concentrated the maximum number of ways of life into the minimum of space and accepted, if it did not impose, the bizarre juxtaposition of the most widely different classes. The new society, on the contrary,provided each way of life with a confined space in which it was understood that the dominant features should be respected, and that each person had to resemble a conventional model, an ideal type, and never depart from it under pain of excommunication.

"The concept of the family, the concept of class, and perhaps elsewhere the concept of race, appear as manifestations of the same intolerance towards variety, the same insistence on uniformity." <u>Centuries of Childhood: a Social History of Family Life</u>. Translated from the French by Robert Baldick (New York: Alfred A. Knopf, 1962), pp. 414-415.

58. Adams, <u>Education</u>, pp. 287-288.

59. Adams, <u>Chartres</u>, p. 408.

60. Adams, <u>Education</u>, p. 380. Lyon points out that the significance of the Dynamo "changes radically" between "The Rule of Phase Applied to History" and "A Letter to American Teachers of History." In the first, "the symbol stands for

ultimate reality and suggests that the movement of man's thought is completely involuntary and mechanical." In the "Letter" "the dynamo has become a symbol for human reason considered to be a passive mechanism wholly moved by some other, greater force." *Symbol and Idea*, pp. 156-157.

61. Samuels, *Adams: Major Phase*, p. 378.

62. Adams, *Education*, p. 475.

63. *Ibid.*, p. 85.

64. *Ibid.*, pp. 8, 43-45, 268.

65. Henry Adams, *Tahiti: Memoirs of Arii Taimai e Marama of Eimeo, Teriirere of Tooarai, Terrinni of Tahiti, Tauraatua i Amo: Memoirs of Marau Taaroa, Last Queen of Tahiti*. Edited with an introduction by Robert E. Spiller (New York: Scholars' Facsimiles and Reprints, 1947), pp. 20, 35-38, 126, 137; Cater, *Adams and His Friends*, pp. 198, 210, 237. Adams to John Hay, October 16, 1890, January 4, 1891; Adams to Rebecca Gilman Rae, November 8, 1890; Robert A. Hume, *Runaway Star: an Appreciation of Henry Adams* (Ithaca: Cornell University Press, 1951), p. 125.

66. Adams, *Education*, pp. 406-407.

67. Jacob Claver Levenson, *The Mind and Art of Henry Adams* (Boston: Houghton Mifflin, 1957), p. 296; Adams, *Chartres*, p. 411.

68. Ford, *Letters of Henry Adams*, II, 291. Adams to John Hay, June 26, 1900.

69. Samuels, *Adams: Major Phase*, p. 212.

70. [Henry Adams], *The Life of George Cabot Lodge* (Boston: Houghton Mifflin, 1911), pp. 109-110.

71. Adams, *Education*, p. 408.

72. Ford, _Letters of Henry Adams_, II, 547.
Adams to Albert Stanburrough Cook, August 6, 1910.

73. Adams, _Education_, p. 385.

74. _Ibid._, p. 4.

75. _Ibid._, pp. 498, 53.

76. Adams, _Democratic Dogma_, pp. 305-308.
James Truslow Adams suggested in 1930 that the
prediction "has, in an utterly unforeseen way,
come about, and the physicists themselves have
been most unwillingly forced to admit that we _have_
reached a point beyond which our reason is now
powerless to proceed in our investigation of the
structure of the universe, a blank wall which
marks the end of knowledge and on the other side
of which the categories of human reason no longer
hold sway." _The Adams Family_ (Boston: Little,
Brown, 1930), p. 345. At any rate, the hypothesis
did represent certain realities in Henry Adams'
own milieu. If human thought was not reaching the
limits of its possibilities, scientific thought
within the Newtonian framework was, and the gradu-
ation to more "etherial" ways of conceiving of
the universe beyond the relatively clearcut nineteenth century categories of energy and matter,
was sufficiently revolutionary as almost to jus-
tify Adams' hyperbole.

77. Adams, _Education_, p. 472.

78. _Ibid._, p. 266.

79. Adams, _Democratic Dogma_, pp. 32, 83.
To Bancroft, of course, the same event was evidence of the working out of the providential plan
of history.

80. Ford, _Letters of Henry Adams_, II, 35.
Adams to Charles Milnes Gaskell, November 26,
1893. Adams' anti-Semitism was not systematic,
but involved a facile identification of Jews with
"gold-bugs" or capitalists. The subject is touch-

ed on in John Higham, "Anti-Semitism in the Gilded Age: a Reinterpretation ," Mississippi Valley Historical Review, XLIII (March, 1957), 572-573.

81. Gerrit H. Roelofs, "Henry Adams: Pessimism and the Intelligent Use of Doom," ELH, a Journal of English Literary History, XVII (September, 1950), p. 235.

82. Mark Antony DeWolfe Howe, ed., Holmes-Pollock Letters: the Correspondence of Mr. Justice Holmes and Sir Frederick Pollock, 1874-1932, 2 volumes (Cambridge: Harvard University Press, 1941), I, 64. Holmes to Pollock, October 21, 1895.

83. Adams, Civilization and Decay, pp. vii, ix.

84. Ibid., pp. x-xi, and passim.

85. Ibid., p. 37.

86. Mircea Eliade, The Sacred and the Profane: the Nature of Religion. Translated from the French by Willard R. Trask (New York: Harcourt, Brace, 1959), pp. 107, 113.

87. Mane, Road to Chartres, pp. 219-220. Mane quotes Adams, Chartres (p. 413): "The scheme seems to differ little, and unwillingly, from a system of dynamics as modern as the dynamo. Even in the prime motor, from the moment of action, freedom of will vanished."

88. "Underneath he still looked forward with fiendish satisfaction to the enslavement of everybody by the Jews and other capitalists; but on the surface he allowed his fancy a moment's lurid play as to the possibility of my heading some great outburst of the emotional classes which should at least temporarily crush the Economic Man." Elting Elmore Morison, et al., eds. The Letters of Theodore Roosevelt, 8 volumes (Cambridge: Harvard University Press, 1951-1954), II, 1021. Theodore

Roosevelt to John Hay, June 17, 1899.

89. Adams, <u>Education</u>, p. 505.

90. Vern Wagner has characterized Adams'
customary position as one of "suspension" between
opposing ideas, which parallels to some extent my
use of the Roycean concept of interpretation.
"Suspension" however emphasizes the Adams' incon-
clusiveness, whereas my use of "interpretation"
emphasizes Adams' active efforts to make sense of
the antinomies which assailed his instinct for
order, particularly those antinomies which ran
the scale of historical time. "All dilemmas Henry
Adams encountered left him inconclusive, irreso-
lute, uncertain, doubtful," according to Wagner.
"They left him in transition. He ended with tentative silence which is an image of non-commit-
ment, of balance between all positions, in suspension. Such a position was Adams' ideal, and
though he failed to realize it completely he did
come closer to it than most." <u>The Suspension of
Henry Adams: a Study of Manner and Matter</u> (Detroit: Wayne State University Press, 1969), p.
15.

EPILOGUE

The subjects of this study, so different in
some respects, are joined by their need to find a
proper field in the world for originally religious
ideas and values to become, if not Henry Adams'
dilute mixture of Lord Kelvin and St. Thomas Aquinas, at least an amalgam of John Calvin and Thomas
Jefferson, or of Charles Darwin and Jonathan Edwards, or another variation on the same pattern.
Considered from the religious side, our subjects
look quite different than they do from the secular, which has been the more usual vantage point.
Viewed as religious thinkers, they offer a remarkably rich and diverse expression of theological possibilities: the nature of God discovered
in progress and democracy; in evolution from in-
definite, incoherent homogeneity to definite, coherent heterogeneity, in universal community; in
real moral struggle in a pluralistic universe;
the divine qualities bifurcated, even, in the im-
ages of thirteenth century woman and twentieth
century machine. From an orthodox standpoint,
indeed, these were only attenuations of Christian
truths, tainted by the idolatries of secular philosophy, and fading from the still holistic and
providential sense of the universe of a Bancroft
to the chaos of agonized disbelief of an Adams.
Yet on their own terms, these thinkers sought to
give expression to facets of divinity that could
scarcely have been glimpsed other than in the

scientific and philosophical milieux of the nineteenth century, and whatever lasting worth lies
in their ideas is inseparable from their religious
impulse or, at least, residue.

At the same time, we are dealing with a phase
of American thought which cannot be thoroughly
considered apart from a context of the waning of
religious faith, at least among the highly educated, and as a component of formal thought. For
the generation which came to maturity about the
time of the Civil War, in particular, the apparent
encroachment of science on the realm of the sacred
was an emotional reality that perhaps no other
generation experienced in quite the same way. Oliver Wendell Holmes, Jr., spoke for many of his
contemporaries when he lamented in 1895 that science had

> pursued analysis until at last this
> thrilling world of colors and sounds
> and passions has seemed fatally to re-
> solve itself into one vast network of
> vibrations endlessly weaving an end-
> less web, and the rainbow flush of
> cathedral windows, which once to enrap-
> tured eyes appeared the very smile of
> God, fades slowly out into the pale
> irony of the void.[1]

Yet Holmes was also representative in his
retention of the sense of cosmic drama. He might
not "see why a man should despair because he does-
n't see a beard on his Cosmos"; it was, he
thought, enough that "consciousness, purpose,
significance and ideals are among its possibilities," even as "finite expressions of the unimag-
inable."[2] And Holmes accused his father's generation of trying to find room in the loose joints
of naturalistic explanation for the "interstitial
miracle." Yet Holmes's agnosticism had a positive
character which was by no means devoid of the
overtones of religious teleology. The "soldier's
creed" that he espoused as a philosophy of life
summoned the individual to perform his duty even

while not understanding the plan of the campaign. The obvious implication was that there was a strategy in the universe, if not indeed a strategist. And if doubtful that the cosmos was after all conterminous with significance, the Justice at least conserved the feeling, as he suggested in 1925, that "it has significance in its belly."[3]

This was a feeling with which it was difficult for even the most heterodox of Holmes's generation to break--this was, indeed, a prime source of their intellectual strength, and it helps to set them apart from their successors. There was much of the existentialist in William James, for example, but there is an emotional chasm between the Jamesian sense of the cosmos as a field of struggle for contending forces, in which the individual must choose his cause, and the bleaker Sartrean vision of "the void which encircles us," in which "freedom is the human being putting his past out of play by secreting his own nothingness."[4] Holmes's void, unlike Sartre's, was ironic not only because it mocked reliance on Providence, but because it withheld assurance of its own vacuity. Henry Adams might lose faith in his ancestors' cosmos of ordered liberty, but it would not have occurred to him to pursue even his gloomiest speculations except in the same dimensions; thus he constructed his anti-cosmos of determined chaos.

But Adams represented the declension of this style of thought. In others--in Fiske, Royce, James, and in a more old-fashioned way in George Bancroft--there is a certain attractive sense of balance. In the religious tradition which nurtured all of these men, man humbled himself before a God, conceived, it may be, as his own great apotheosis, but Whose infinite concern guaranteed a standing to the human soul that was itself limitless in the dimension of time. Modern secular man starts from the opposite pole of hubris, reaching out to conquer the world, and space beyond, only to arrive at the conviction of his own nothingness, an alien in a universe

311

in which he usurps a god-like role. Nineteenth
century minds were more capable of holding in the
same field of vision human endeavor and providential purpose, human creativity and creaturehood,
and consequently were better able to feel the
cosmos as man's proper home, possibly even as
Royce's universal community. Whether God was Absolute, or an autonomous power in a pluralistic
universe, was a matter of less importance than
the shared conviction of relatedness and significance on a cosmic scale.

The exact nature of the religious element
in the thought of these figures remains elusive,
and not susceptible to a facile reduction to
categories of faith and reason, temperament and
intellect, Puritan legacy and scientific doubt.
Plainly the sense of Providence--or the anxiety
of its loss-touched a range of rational and
emotional sensibilities. It provided meaning for
history and the moral struggle, unified force,
made possible a sense of order without determinism
and of freedom without chaos; it made a universal
community of mere multiplicity and diversity. In
the United States it was the Providential which
made plausible the entente of democracy with science in a scheme of progressive evolution. Without these divine traces, the world would look
quite different.

Religious sensibility appears from the
present cases, then, as a qualitatively irre-
placeable element of thought, however attenuated
or diffuse it may become, however confused with
other aspects of mind and personality. History,
the study of the temporal, and religion, the con-
templation of the eternal, never converge. But
for many in the nineteenth century, at least, time
and timeless continued to imply each other, and
the intellectual history of the period will retain
as one of its necessary concerns the prolific relation between the two.

Footnotes

1. Julius J. Marke, ed., The Holmes Reader
(New York: Oceana Publications, 1955), p. 149.
("The Soldier's Faith," address delivered May 30,
1895).

2. Mark Antony DeWolfe Howe, ed., Holmes-
Pollock Letters: the Correspondence of Mr. Justice Holmes and Sir Frederick Pollock, 1874-1932,
2 volumes (Cambridge: Harvard University Press,
1941), I, 161 (Holmes to Pollock, April 1, 1910).

3. Max Lerner, ed., The Mind and Faith of
Justice Holmes: His Speeches, Essays, Letters
and Judicial Opinions (Boston: Little, Brown and
Company, 1943), p. 427 (Holmes to John C. H. Wu,
March 26, 1925).

4. Jean-Paul Sartre, Being and Nothingness:
an Essay on Phenomenological Ontology. Translated and with an Introduction by Hazel E. Barnes
(New York: Philosophical Library, 1956), pp. 40,
28.

196

318

Pannill, H. Burnell, 72
Parker, Theodore, 71,
  116n.
Parkman, Francis, 265
Parrington, Vernon Lou-
  is, 70
Peirce, Charles Sanders,
  161, 169n., 194, 204,
  234n
Penn, William, 36-37
Perry, Ralph Barton,
  184, 194, 200, 203,
  223
Philip II (King of
  Spain), 102
Plato, 19-20, 75, 216,
  225
Protestantism, 3-5, 9,
  12, 14, 16, 23, 28, 37,
  53-54, 73-74, 76, 78,
  113, 122n., 141, 153,
  163, 166, 187, 213,243
  -244, 268, 283-284
Puritanism, 3, 9-12,23,
  37, 53-54, 73, 76-78,
  193, 208-209, 213, 252-
  253, 286, 312

Rathbun, John W., 22
Reid, Thomas, 19
Renouvier, Charles, 200-
  201, 204
Ricardo, David, 109
Roelof, Gerrit H., 289
Rothschild family, 290
Rousseau, Jean Jacques,
  19
Royce, Josiah, 1-2, 4,
  49, 226, 228, 241n.-
  242n., 293, 311-312;
  and German Idealism,
  127-130; and transcen-
  dentalism, 130-131,
  139-140, 170n.; re-
  lates ideal to con-

crete, 131-133; and
  pragmatism, 133-134,
  171n.-172n.; on the
  "Absolute,"135, 141-
  146, 153-154, 162,
  173n.; concept of com-
  munity, 135-141, 144,
  150-151, 161-167; con-
  cept of "interpreta-
  tion," 136, 148, 161-
  163, 178n.; on indi-
  viduality, 141-144,
  153-154, 157, 165-167;
  relates unity to mul-
  tiplicity, 144-147,
  166-167, 173n.-175n.;
  conservatism of, 148-
  151, 161, 176n.; his-
  tory of California,
  148, 161; and "Provin-
  cialism," 151-152; as-
  sociates individualism
  with collectivism,152-
  155; and Spencerian
  philosophy, 155-157;
  philosophy of Loyalty,
  157-160, 165-167; on
  Christianity, 163-167
Royce, Sarah, 128

Samuels, Ernest, 253,
  261, 278
Santayana, George, 22
Sartre, Jean-Paul, 311
Schleiermacher, Fried-
  rich, 17, 19-21, 66n.
Schopenhauer, Arthur,
  222, 282
Scotus, John Duns, 22
Smith, Adam, 42
Spencer, Herbert, 69-
  70, 72,81, 83, 89-91,
  95, 100, 103-104, 111,
  113, 117n., 118n.,119
  n.-120n., 121n., 125n.,

ABOUT THE AUTHOR

Michael Dorsey Clark was born in Baltimore, Maryland, November 5, 1937. He graduated from St. Paul's School in Brooklandville, Md., and, in 1959, from Yale University. Professor Clark obtained his M.A. and Ph.D. degrees from the University of North Carolina. Since 1964 he has been a member of the Department of History of the University of New Orleans, where he teaches American intellectual and religious history. He is married and has two children.